Logic and reality

By the Same author:
THE CONCEPT OF TRUTH
Van Gorcum, Assen, The Netherlands 1969.

LOGIC
AND
REALITY

An Investigation into
the Idea of a Dialectical System

by

Leslie Armour

Professor and Chairman, Department of Philosophy,
The Cleveland State University
Adjunct Professor of Philosophy, The University of Waterloo

ASSEN, 1972
VAN GORCUM & COMP. N.V. – DR. H. J. PRAKKE & H. M. G. PRAKKE

The publication of this book was made possible through a grant from the Humanities
Research Council of Canada
Une subvention du Conseil Canadien de Recherches sur les Humanités, a rendu possible
la publication de cet ouvrage

ISBN 90 232 0961 3

Printed in the Netherlands by Royal VanGorcum Ltd.

Preface

The expression "dialectical logic" at once suggests Hegel. Hegel, of course, has a place in a long tradition which began with Plato or before Plato, left its high water marks on Plotinus, Scotus Erigena, Nicholas of Cusa and Fichte, and continued through Lotze, Ferrier, Bradley, Green, Bosanquet, McTaggart, Royce and Collingwood. But Hegel's *Science of Logic* and the companion portion of the *Encyclopedia of the Philosophical Sciences* continue to stand out as the most systematic attempts to develop such a logic and to establish the relations between logic and reality.

This book is not, however, a commentary on Hegel's logic. It attempts the same task — at least in outline — and it attempts, further, to develop an account of the procedures and rules by which a dialectical system can be developed. It starts with a position very close to Hegel's and it finishes with a position which is, at least, within hailing distance of him. Between the two points, it diverges rather sharply. And there are differences even at the beginning and the end. Reasons are given for these divergences. If I am right, in other words, this book represents a development within the Hegelean tradition. If I am wrong, the fact that alternative systems are available for comparison may help in our understanding of Hegel and help, thereby, to make a genuine development possible.

Hegel saw his logic and his philosophy generally not as overthrowing the logics and systems of his predecessors but, more often, as showing the place those logics and systems should hold in a more embracing scheme of things. But there has been a tendency, since, to regard dialectical logics and other logics as incompatible or as two traditions with no meeting point, two activities with nothing in common. The view which I try to defend in this book is that traditional logic and its modern developments can be regarded as special cases which have a precise and clearly determinable place within a dialectical scheme. The reader will find Russell mentioned frequently and Quine mentioned nearly as often as Hegel. Though neither Quine nor Hegel is cited uncritically, the references are intended to be, as Collingwood used to say, *honoris causa*.

The focus of my interest, of course, is as much metaphysical as logical, but the point of it is to show that the two interests are not separable in the end and, though metaphysics predominates as a concern at the end and logic at the beginning, this is due to the structure of the argument and not to a change of interest.

The book is subtitled' "An Investigation into the *Idea* of a Dialectical System" and that should be explained. If, as the argument suggests, logic and the subject matter it presides over are not, ultimately, separable, then the concerns of the dialectical logician will be co-extensive with the limits of discourse and knowledge, though his system need not degenerate into a kind of ratio-mania which leads him to think that he can deduce all knowledge by some miraculous technique. Still, his methods and his system will have a central core of organising concepts which provide the skeletal structure around which the rest hangs. This book is concerned with just that skeletal structure of concepts and principles — the structure which may be regarded as the animating *idea* of a dialectical logic. If it is not so rich in detail as Hegel's system, it may profit from the fact that the skeleton stands out more starkly and is, therefore, more amenable to assessment and criticism.

It is part of the argument of the book that there are conditions which apply to *any* conceptual structure which can do the work required of such a skeleton and part of the business of the argument is to consider how it is related to the body of discourse and knowledge which must clothe it. It is not externally related to that body and so there are ways in which any piece of knowledge may influence it. In these respects any system such as the one discussed here must be provisional. But there are other respects in which the requirements of basic conceptual structure are independent and, in these respects, we may hope to find the right answers eventually even if they are not contained in this book.

It remains here to offer thanks to those who have played a part in making the book possible. I do so, as always, with some trepidation but, as usual, I offer the assurance that I alone am to blame for whatever blunders it contains.

An earlier draft of the book was written for a graduate seminar which Dean J. S. Minas and I offered during the spring term of 1967 at the University of Waterloo. The task was, indeed, undertaken at "J" 's suggestion and I am grateful to him for numerous suggestions and criticisms which developed during our weekly sessions. There is scarcely a single complete sentence of that version in this one, though many ideas have been carried over. This version is not merely twice as long. It is, I think, much clearer and it is certainly different. If more "orthodox" logicians would follow "J" 's example, dialecticians might, at any rate, become more readily comprehensible — to the equal profit, I think, of logic of all kinds.

A large number of my graduate students have also helped — knowingly and otherwise — through long discussions of these and closely related matters. In particular, Bryan Black, Michael Kubara, Nathan Brett, Lee Werth, Betty Trott, Jean Wallace, Peter Smale, Frank Jordak and Savario Pagliuso deserve special thanks, though there are many others as well.

The University of Waterloo granted me a sabbatical leave and the Canada Council provided the necessary funds to enable me to spend a year in England writing this book. Without them it would have taken much longer and it might not even have been possible. For the necessary sustained concentration requires freedom from other duties.

The staff of the British Museum were unwitting collaborators — kindly and helpful as always despite a growing body of work which seems to expand much faster than their resources.

The staff of the British Waterways Board provided a place for my "house" — the M.V. Marion II — to float in peaceful surroundings while I wrote, and Mr. Cyril Harfield, a mechanical genius, enabled me to go my way without nautical disaster.

Without editorial — and much other — help from my wife, Diana, the project would not have come to completion.

Finally, the financial assistance of the Humanities Research Council of Canada in making publication feasible is gratefully acknowledged.

Shakespeare, Ontario, Canada
August, 1971

Contents

Chapter 1

Logic, knowledge, and the case for a dialectical system

The justification of logical systems and of theories about such systems presents peculiarly intransigent problems. Indeed, the very idea of a "justification" or a "rationale" for a "logic" suggests an enterprise in which one is almost certain to trip over one's own feet.

For, though there seems to be no agreement even amongst those logicians whose work constitutes the main current of contemporary logical orthodoxy about just what "logic" is, it is surely agreed that it has much to do with the development and clarification of canons of inference and with the distinction between acceptable and unacceptable argument forms. Obviously, however, any attempt to show that a given "logic" is justifiable must involve inference and argument. How, then, is one to argue in favour of a given "logic" without employing it or some other "logic"? If one employs it, the argument is circular. If one employs another, one is surely in a curious position. For then one's arguments are, themselves, dependent upon a logic other than the one one wants to defend.

The alternatives to justification are, unfortunately, rather unpalatable. One way out is to hold that one simply starts with arbitrary postulates and another is to maintain that we have adequate logical "intuitions" and that these need merely to be clarified and formalized.

Both these alternatives have their partisans though professional logicians spend relatively little time arguing about them. The first or "postulationist" alternative has an unusually untoward consequence: it seems to render all knowledge arbitrary in a peculiar way. The reason is this: the choices that one makes about inference patterns influence the form in which all statements which purport to contain knowledge must be cast. For instance, if you want to use traditional Aristotelean syllogisms, you must first cast all your propositions in such forms as "All S is P," "Some S is P," "Some S is not P," and "No S is P." There are various ways of interpreting statements or propositions cast in these forms, but they all restrict, in one way or another, the domain of what can be said. For other kinds of inference patterns there are other ways of casting what one wants to say. They are all, however, restrictive in some way or another and they all restrict the kinds of pictures one can have of the world and the kinds of theories one can build. Hence the "postulationist" position about logic spreads and becomes, to a degree, a postulationist position about everything that we can say.

An extension of the same argument seems to tell equally against the "intuitionist" alternative. For it is one thing to hold that you know by intuition that the statement, "Either Socrates is mortal or Socrates is not mortal" is necessarily true and another thing to hold that your intuitions are so good that you can tell whether or not all statements about the world can be strait-jacketed into a standard logical mould. Who, indeed, has intuitions like that? And what do we do when it turns out that different philosophers — for instance Hegel and Lord Russell — have radically different logical intuitions? (Lord Russell's intuitions are so different from Hegel's that, by the time he has tried to interpret Hegel's utterances in terms of his own logical moulds, he can only, seemingly, conclude that Hegel is quite mad.)[1]

Surely, however, there are other alternatives. One of them is to take some branch of enquiry which one assumes to be adequately ordered and then to construct a logic which will explicate the inferences involved in *that*. The logic will then, in a sense, be justified at one remove. For it will be what secures *those* inferences and they, one has decided, are acceptable. Russell and Whitehead, indeed, adopted just this kind of procedure in *Principia Mathematica*.[2] Their aim was to find a logic which would be adequate for a certain restricted domain of mathematics. What they hoped to show, for the most part, was that the inferences involved in ordinary arithmetic are a special case of the inference patterns they developed. Such procedures, of course, have their own special justification and their own advantages but, if they are generalized, they become an indirect form of the "intuitionist" option. For it is only, then, by intuition that one knows that the subject matter chosen for analysis is itself well organized and that other inferences can be structured according to the same pattern.

All that these arguments show, of course, is that the options I have been suggesting have obvious disadvantages — that they involve kinds of commitments which it would be as well to avoid if one could. If, of course, there are no other alternatives we shall have to make what we can of them.

II

The remaining obvious alternative is to try to find some procedure which will avoid the circularity which is involved in trying to justify one's logic

---

[1] *A History of Western Philosophy* (London: George Allen and Unwin, 1946), Chapter *XXII*.
[2] Second edition (Cambridge: Cambridge University Press, 1925).

by arguments which, themselves, presuppose the logic in question or some other and, at the same time, to avoid being forced back on arbitrary postulates, logical intuitions, or some assumedly well-ordered subject matter.

The difficulty could be avoided if it were possible to develop one's inference rules and arguments together with one's subject matter. If the two are related in such a way that neither presupposes the other but both are generated from the same source, no circularity, of course, results.

One way to do this would be to start with a basic concept, idea, or proposition which was so general that it could be seen, by an analysis of its own internal structure, to be entailed by and involved with every possible system of rational discourse. If there were such a concept it would, of course, have necessary connections with every other possible concept. The development of these links would provide an account of the required inference rules and argument forms and the development of the concepts so linked would provide an outline of the domain of possible subjects of discourse.

Now any concept which had the required properties would, by reason of its essential links with all other concepts, include those other concepts, and, by reason of its separate identity, exclude them. There is nothing particularly mysterious about this: every concept insofar as it serves to mark out, identify or "come to grips" with anything refers indirectly to everything by reason of the fact that it separates the thing it seeks to identify from everything else. It must specify, by implication, what it is not in order to specify what it is. (It is for this reason, presumably, that Hegel wrote, rather darkly, in the introduction to his *Science of Logic*, "The one and only thing for securing scientific progress is knowledge of the logical precept that Negation is just as much Affirmation as Negation.")[1]

What *is* rather more mysterious and difficult is the determination of an appropriate concept with which to begin and the development of a procedure for tracing out the required connections. The second problem ought not, if the required initial concept were forthcoming, to be so fantastic a task as it might seem — for the nature of the concept ought, itself, to suggest the nature of the next required concept in much the way, perhaps, that one piece of a jig-saw puzzle suggests something about its intended neighbours (though it will prove rather harder than that). The problem of finding an initial concept is obviously, however, very troublesome.

[1] Translated by W. H. Johnston and L. G. Struthers (London: George Allen and Unwin, 1929), Vol. 1, p. 64. (In the translation by A. V. Miller [London: George Allen and Unwin, 1969], p. 54. In the Felix Meiner German edition [Hamburg, 1967], Vol. I, p. 35.) The occasional quotations in this book are all from the Johnston and Struthers translation which, for the present anyway, is likely to be more readily available. References are given, however, to Miller and to the easily available German edition published by Felix Meiner. Subsequent references are abbreviated to "Johnston and Struthers," "Miller," and "Felix Meiner." Isolated passages should probably not be subjected to judgement with respect to the rival translations since consistency of meaning throughout the whole text is vital.

Even if it is true that every concept must have some connection with the other concepts which form parts of the domain in which it marks out a place (just as the concept "six" must have links with the concepts of the other numbers), an ill-chosen concept will have links with other unsatisfactory concepts and may link parts of a fantasy world with a system of fantasy inferences.

There are, however, ways of tackling this problem. It may seem that, at this point, one will surely be thrown back, in any case, on intuition, postulate, or reference to established subject matter. But it may turn out that there are concepts which would be required whatever kind of conceptual system one chose, however arbitrarily, and that these have, therefore, a special kind of objectivity.

Still, such a possibility must seem rather remote and the effort required out of proportion to the chances of success. The thing has, after all, been attempted before.

III

Hegel's *Science of Logic* is the obvious example though there are strains of the same thought in Plotinus, in Scotus Erigena's *On the Division of Nature*, and elsewhere. (All these enterprises are sufficiently obscure for there to be ample room for argument about just what is going on in them. It seems to me fair enough, however, to regard Hegel as doing the kind of thing I have been suggesting.)

Hegel did have followers, but most of them were rather skeptical about his central logical endeavours. The testimony of some of his English-speaking heirs ought to give us pause for thought.

Edward Caird quoted T. H. Green as saying, "It must be done all over again."[1] Bradley spoke rather sharply of Hegel's dialectic. Bradley did have his own "dialectic" though he usually let his arguments speak for themselves and his own *Principles of Logic*[2] is a rather cautious piecemeal review of traditional logical problems from the vantage point of his general philosophical position. Bosanquet, too, had his doubts though, on the whole, he was more hopeful about the "dialectic" than Bradley and he tried to lead it in his own more down-to-earth direction.

"If ideas do not pass into each other, each in virtue of its own nature being the ground of certain others," he wrote, "it is hard to see how a system of ideas is possible, or how any synthetic judgement can be true."[3] Yet his own logic is not the "doing all over again" which Green had demanded but had not lived to do but a much more limited review of traditional

---

[1] In *Essays in Philosophical Criticism*, edited by Andrew Seth and R. B. Haldane (London: Longmans Green, 1883).

[2] Second edition (London: Oxford University Press, 1922).

[3] In *Essays in Philosophical Criticism* (see footnote above), p. 79.

4

topics in logic and epistemology making such revisions as Bosanquet had found necessary in the light of his own investigations.[1] He was inclined, in the end, to hold that the pattern of logic was to be found in the current of human experience. "Experience, in short," he said, "forces thought along certain lines from partial to more complete notions."[2] Just how this happened or why we should trust experience in such a matter was something that Bosanquet seems to me less enlightening about.

I doubt whether, like the sympathetic but highly critical L. T. Hobhouse, he would wholly have accepted the proposition that "the [dialectical] process must be thrown back into the mind of the dialectician."[3] McTaggart, however, did admit that the dialectic of Hegel is not "objective in the sense that it takes place otherwise than in thought" though that had to do with his conviction that both he and Hegel were committed to believing that reality, ultimately, was a timeless state.[4] And even he did, finally, abandon the dialectical method though he was not, absolutely, convinced that it was impossible in principle.

All these doubts do lead one to be pessimistic about the attempt to construct a dialectical system. Reading Hegel may not dispel this pessimism. It may be that the reason is that Hegel is at once over-generous and rather parsimonious. *The Science of Logic* is full of long and often interesting digressions and detailed discussions of matters which may well be beside the immediate point. But it is, on principle, rather short on detailed explications of the principles of inference involved and rather full of what seem, to me and to many other readers, to be intuitionistic leaps. Hegel, of course, thought that logic and its subject matter must be inseparable if either were to form part of a justified "system." Hence he thought that the inference rules, on the whole, should be apparent from the inferences themselves and could not be in any way separated from them. Many have thought this to be a mistake and various attempts have been made to detail Hegel's inference procedures more sharply than he himself thought appropriate.[5]

[1] *Logic or the Morphology of Knowledge* (2nd ed., London: Oxford University Press, 1911).
[2] *Essays in Philosophical Criticism*, p. 80.
[3] *The Theory of Knowledge* (London: Methuen and Co., 1896), p. 200.
[4] *Studies in the Nature of the Dialectic* (Cambridge: Cambridge University Press, 1896; and New York: Russell & Russell, 1964), p. 7. McTaggart, indeed, goes on to say in the same passage that "reality is a stable and timeless state." If that were true, reality could not be represented accurately as a dialectical process. But such a break between thought and reality would seem to vitiate the whole enterprise.
[5] Indeed, there have been a variety of attempts to formalize Hegel's logic. An account of the recent literature is to be found in Yvon Gauthier's "Logique Hégélienne et Formalisation," *Dialogue*, Vol. VI, No. 2, September, 1967, pp. 151-165. An example of such attempts is Michael Kosok's "The Formalization of Hegel's Dialectical Logic," *International Philosophical Quarterly*, Vol. VI, No. 4, December, 1966, pp. 596-631. Gauthier makes cogent observations about the problem. I shall pursue the matter in my own way but, obviously, "formalization" is apt to be beside the point since, once the form and

Most people are not at once convinced by reading Hegel and one may easily wonder whether, in setting up the problem as I have and in suggesting that the only solution to it is to try, once again, to fight one's way through the darkness of the dialectical tunnel, I have not missed some very obvious point.

In particular, it may be wondered whether logic is not an altogether simpler business than I have been making out. Professor Kneale, after all, called it "this relatively simple study."[1] And we all know that most professional philosophers, nearly all professional logicians, and some undergraduates act as if they know what logic is and can tell good from bad logical systems. Indeed, we all do know what goes into logic courses and how to pick a logic text for an introductory course.

If I have been making too much of it, it ought to show itself in the way in which reasonably orthodox and competent logicians attempt to define their subject matter. Perhaps, then, in the hope that we can at least clarify our problem a little before setting out on our protracted and intellectually perilous journey, we ought to look at some attempts at definition.

Tarski has defined logic as "a discipline which analyzes the meaning of concepts common to all the sciences and establishes general laws governing all the sciences."[2] But that seems even more demanding than the kind of thing I have been suggesting. Surely, if that is our task, we can have no intuitions adequate to it and we shall scarely dare risk proceeding under the shaky power of the arbitrary postulate.

Perhaps, though, Tarski was staking a claim rather than trying to offer enlightenment. Professor Kneale has offered a seemingly less demanding account of the matter. He suggests that the "logic of tradition" has been "concerned primarily with principles of inference valid for all possible subject matters."[3] But this comes pretty much to the view I took earlier in this chapter.

The clue, however, *may* be found in the fact that one can imagine the principles of inference to be so simple that they can be seen to be valid immediately and unquestionably, and can be imagined to be quite separate from "all possible subject matters" so that the justification problem will not really arise. (After all, Professor Kneale does not review all possible subject matters in his history of logic.)

Thus one may find comfort in reading Professor Quine. He dismisses at once such definitions as "the science of forms" and "the science of necessary

content are separated, the relation between logic and its subject matter will become problematic in just the way that is at issue.

[1] *The Development of Logic* (London: Oxford University Press, 1962), p. 742.

[2] *Introduction to Logic* (New York: Oxford University Press, 1947), p. xiii.

[3] *Op. cit.*, p. 741.

inferences" on the ground that they are vague and unhelpful. Instead, he suggests that one can, quite easily though superficially, locate that domain of statements which is the proper concern of logicians. "Basic particles such as 'not,' 'and,' 'or,' 'unless,' 'if,' 'then,' 'neither,' 'nor,' 'some,' 'all,' etc. occur in them in such a way that the statement is true independently of its other ingredients."[1] Thus, he says, the statement, "Socrates is mortal or Socrates is not mortal" is true independently of components like"Socrates" and "mortal." He hastens to assure us that there is no special problem about "truth" since to say that something is the case and to say that the statement asserting it is true is to say the same thing.

It is not obvious, however, that this achieves the narrowing required if we are not to worry about the justification problem. How obvious is the "law of excluded middle"? And why? How does one find these "basic particles"? What if one is challenged?

Most noticeably, Professor Quine's proposal suggests that one starts one's logic on the level of statements or propositions. But one of the great problems is just that there is a certain form or structure which anything must have in order to be a statement or proposition which will fit into the required form to permit the kinds of inferences which Professor Quine finds to pivot on his "basic particles." One thing which we need to know is whether or not everything we want to say and need to say in order to talk sensibly about the world can be fitted into this form. That, somehow or other, much that Professor Quine wants to say about logic is sound is fairly obvious. What is to be doubted is whether or not it is the whole picture. We still need some technique for finding out.

That one's logic is not something which one thinks about independently of the way in which one wants to portray the world is, of course, something that Professor Quine wants very much to assert and, elsewhere in his writings, he has devoted perhaps more serious effort to delineating the relations between logic and ontology than any other professional logician.[2] Whatever the merits of his proposed definition, they do not include, apparently, absolution from the problems which seem to me face anyone who takes logic seriously. And, in any case, to raise the concept of "truth" will not, as I have argued elsewhere,[3] simplify the problem at all.

In fact, whatever impression may sometimes be conveyed by elementary text-books, there do not seem to be many logicians about who actually

[1] *Mathematical Logic* (Second edition, Cambridge, Mass.: Harvard University Press, 1951), p. 1. Quine did note that this is a "superficial" way of making the distinction but he appeared to think (when he wrote the passage quoted at any rate) that it did useful work and he did not offer an alternative. It represents a clear statement of a position which has been, I think, held quite seriously and there are similar remarks in *Principia Mathematica* (Vol. I, p. 93) though they are not offered there as a theory.

[2] See — of course — *From a Logical Point of View* (New York: Harper & Row, 1963); and *Word and Object* (Cambridge, Mass.: M.I.T. Press, 1960).

[3] *The Concept of Truth*, Van Gorcum, Assen, 1969.

believe that there is some simple solution to the problem of identifying a justifiable logic or who actually believe that the problems can be easily separated from surrounding issues of an epistemological and ontological kind. Professors Cohen and Nagel, who have a reputation for hard-headedness, remark that logic is evidently "concerned with ontological traits of the utmost generality" though they add, in case anyone is inclined to be led down the most slippery paths to logical perdition, that there is "no non-Aristotelean logic in the sense that there is a non-Euclidean geometry."[1]

All these remarks should probably be taken much as lawyers take the *obiter dicta* of English judges — as guidance but hardly as binding on their authors or anyone else. For professional logicians, for the most part, are concerned with rather more mundane and technical matters which arise within the context of systems whose outlines are pretty much accepted.

The point is that no one seems to have a simple and ready solution to the problems which I raised at the beginning of the discussion. It does seem worthwhile, however, to explore, at somewhat greater depth, the possibility of "defusing" logic — of rendering substantial parts of it neutral and harmless.

v

One such proposal would be to try to make a sharp distinction between logic and other kinds of subject matter by construing logic as a straightforward *deductive* enterprise conceived in the simplest possible way.

The barest skeleton of such a plan might be illustrated thus: if you want to test the soundness of a very simple logical endeavour, the construction of a syllogism, you can make an illustrative diagram such as a series of Euler circles. If your syllogism reads "All *S* is *P* and all *P* is *Q*, therefore all *S* is *Q*," you can diagram the two premises with circles which you can take to represent the inclusion relations which hold between the entities, classes, or properties indicated by the letters "*S*," "*P*," and "*Q*." The circle representing "*S*"s will be shown inside the circle representing "*P*"s and the one representing "*P*"s will, in turn, be shown inside the one representing "*Q*"s. If you take it that the premises are intended to assert that just these inclusion relations hold, you will have no difficulty in "reading off" the conclusion from the premises. In an obvious way, therefore, the conclusion has been "shown" to be "contained" in the premises and the "validity" of the argument may be taken to derive from that fact. If "deduction" is literally as the word suggests a "drawing out," this account of the matter seems sound enough.

There are various constructions you could put upon this situation. You

[1] *An Introduction to Logic and Scientific Method* (London: Routledge & Kegan Paul, 1934), p. viii.

might, like George Boole, actually hold that the validity of all inferences is, finally, grounded in experience or even observation[1] and you might hold that looking at Euler circles is such an observation. Boole thought that one appropriate experience was enough to justify a genuine logical principle and he thought that rather a lot of complex logical machinery could be justified in this way for "the general truths of logic are of such a nature that, when presented to the mind, they at once command assent."

The trouble with this view, of course, is that it becomes a good deal less convincing when someone starts to question the meaning of such expressions as "inclusion," "all," "some," "any," and so on and to demand to know what "classes," "properties" and so on are. Furthermore, there are logicians who have had, say, the law of excluded middle presented to their minds, and found themselves very doubtful about it. It would be open to Boole or anyone to hold that one is simply not in the presence of a genuine logical truth if one is presented with a proposition which does not "at once command assent," but this would seem likely to reduce dramatically the range of genuine logical truths.

Alternatively, however, one could hold that the "defusing" actually does take place and by a much simpler process. For one might hold that what is important is not the fact that the inferences are obvious (it is only an accidental feature, perhaps, of my skeleton illustration, that it seems obvious) but rather the fact that the process is deductive in the simple-minded sense that I suggested. Surely, if one restricts one's logical rules so that they do not permit one to go beyond one's premises, the whole enterprise is, indeed, harmless.

A more sophisticated view of the same point may actually be the one implied by Professor Quine's remarks and by the passage on page 93 of *Principia Mathematica* from which Quine's doctrine is very likely derived. If it is the case that Quine's "basic particles" are such that they guarantee the soundness of an inference independently of the other expressions in any statement, then they are effectively insulated from the rest of discourse in some rather important way. They cannot lead us astray, after all, for they have no logical intercourse with other expressions. The complexity of their work will not matter, nor will the relative obviousness or otherwise of the result. So long as they can be held to their neutrality, we can do as we please with them.

One feature of such a procedure, inevitably, is that the more we secure their neutrality and insist upon their total insulation from the rest of discourse, the less use they will be for expanding, codifying, or even organizing knowledge. But, perhaps, that is a feature of logic.

This kind of view is part of what lies behind the empiricist doctrine that

[1] Collected Logical Works, Vol. II, *The Laws of Thought* (Chicago and London: Open Court, 1916), p. 3.

actual knowledge is, in some way, independent of reason. On this view, reason is pretty much confined to the manipulation of logical symbols with which, in view of their neutrality, one may do as one pleases. If our logical devices distort, we can abandon them where we find them pinching and invent others which will do the job with less commitment.

It seems to me that this position, however skilfully one might elaborate on my crude sketch of it, simply will not do.

To start with, there appears to be no way of getting general agreement on the nature and functions of even a limited list of the "basic particles" Quine offers. And his list, or some equivalent of it, is a crucial part of the enterprise.

When he says "Either Socrates is mortal or Socrates is not mortal," it seems obvious that the statement is true and that is does depend for its truth simply on the "logical ingredients" of it. When one comes to specify the precise functions of the expressions involved, however, one's doubts begin to grow. Is it really true that there is an assignable set of operations governing and limiting "either," "or," "is" and "not" such that it will not matter at all *what* subject matter one interposes between them?

For instance, earlier in this chapter I suggested that, if there are concepts which really do succeed in identifying, classifying, locating and so on, then they must both refer to the things they so identify and also, in a different way, to everything. If this is true, there is some difficulty over the expression "Either P refers to Q or P does not refer to Q." It may be urged that this problem can be settled by distinguishing between two different functions of the concept. But then you seem to have two concepts, and the function of uniting the appropriate domain of discourse while sustaining the distinctions within it is lost. This, of course, is a facet of the "identity in difference" problem which may well be the heartland of a dialectical logic. For all statements of the form "P is Q" seem, as Bradley was fond of noting, to involve the difficulty that they assert both an identity and a difference. We shall eventually come to try to assess these difficulties. The point here is simply that there does seem to be some difficulty in substituting some subject matters in "either, or" assertions, and it does not seem to have been obvious to everyone that there is a simple answer to it.

If one is going to make one's objections stick, however, it may be as well to proceed to more neutral ground. It is not only idealist logicians who have had some difficulty in maintaining that propositions of the form in question are necessarily true independently of their subject matter.

From Aristotle to Lukasiewitz, logicians have worried about such expressions as "Either the sea-battle will take place to-morrow or the sea-battle will not take place to-morrow," on the general ground that the subject matter, to-morrow, does not, yet, exist. Can there be true or false propositions about it?

Again, there are problems which confront those who want to talk about

10

God whether they are theologians who want to traffic in actual assertions about him or philosophers who want to know what they are talking about so that they can try to marshal the arguments which suggest that there is or isn't a God. For God, on the traditional view, being omnipotent and so on, seems to have the largest set of compossible properties. There are certain "powers," obviously, associated with the possession of every possible property. Even something very simple, like being red, is a property seemingly necessary to an "omnipotent" being. For only things which are red have the power to appear red to someone who cannot be deceived about colours. Now this kind of thing has made it hard to talk about God, for everything which one can mention as a property of anything in the ordinary world will also be (in some, perhaps, "transmuted" sense) a property of God. If this is so, then assertions of the form "Either what I am talking about is a part of God or what I am talking about is not a part of God" will be difficult to handle. The answer could be that all talk about this kind of God is nonsense, but this seems to be a question which needs investigation and that is what I am trying to assert.[1]

It may well seem that all the things I have been saying in the last paragraph involve problems which verge upon the fantastic and that, indeed, they verge on the fantastic just because they do involve us in tripping over our logical feet. There are, however, more homely examples.

Consider the statement "Either this is a butterfly or this is not a butterfly." It seems about as obvious as Quine's example about Socrates. Yet it also seems to imply that, as the creature develops from egg to butterfly, there are sharp breaks in the process so that one can say "Now it is an egg," "Now it is a chrysalis," "Now it is a butterfly." Perhaps this *is* so, though I do not think so. In any case there ought to be some way of talking about the possibility that there are processes which cannot be subdivided in this way just so that one can think about the counter hypothesis.

Finally, what about the very example — the "mortality" or "immortality" of Socrates? What is "Socrates" the name of, anyway? It seems to refer, rather tenuously, to a wide array of features — to the body of Socrates, to a continuing subject of moral discourse (which is clearly not his body), to his mind, and so on. Now the "mortality" of Socrates does not apply to these features equally or in the same way. We should have to make ourselves clearer and say "Either the body of Socrates is mortal or the body of Socrates is not mortal." But, then, the same problem faces us again. The body of Socrates can be viewed either as a pattern continuing in space and time or as a series of particles themselves continuing in space and time. No doubt we should make ourselves clearer.

But can't we go on forever? The fascinating presumption behind the exam-

[1] I have tried to investigate just this issue. See *Logic and the Concept of God*, Proceedings of the Seventh Inter-American Congress of Philosophy, 1967, Vol. II.

ple is that, eventually, you will get down to rather basic components which can be dealt with neatly in the required "Either it is or else it is not" kind of way. What would they be like, these logical atoms which are the subject matter which *really* can be linked by those "basic particles" which are supposed to be the subject matter of logic?

This is a facet of a question which I shall look at later in this investigation. But I have doubts about the scope of discourse conceived of in this way. Nor am I alone in wondering about this. Constance Jones (an eminent logician of not so long ago whose name seems to have faded from the minds of her successors) wrote a small book called *A New Law of Thought* which was devoted to sustaining the proposition that "Every subject of predication is an identity of denotation in diversity of intension."[1] But if this is so it would seem that the subjects of predication are always collections at once unified and diverse and that one never does quite get to the point at which one can deploy the "Either it is or else it is not" technique except as an approximation. I do not want to try to settle this question now. The only point of this argument is to show that there are problems in a certain way of looking at logic and that they do seem to be the kinds of problems which might give the dialectician cause to get on with his work.

VI

The reasonable doubt produced by the preceding argument seems to me to grow much stronger if one goes on to consider the results of taking seriously the kind of "logical atomism" which would result from sustaining the distinction between logic, considered as some fairly simple kind of "deductive" process, and the kinds of knowledge which would give us information about the "atoms" on which such a logic could work.

One of the implications of this view of logic is that logic, as such, is impotent to create knowledge. Logic, on such a view, is simply used to manipulate what we have already got. In effect, all kinds of reasoning and inference become separated from the basic business of getting knowledge.

It is difficult, however, to maintain seriously that our concepts arise directly out of our experience and require only to be related to each other in this "neutral" way.

One might, as perhaps Hume did, maintain that there are bits of empirical intake, which he named "impressions," and that these are linked by some natural associative process and sustained by some body of natural beliefs. Apart from the technical difficulties involved in these notions, there is the further difficulty that such a doctrine must lead to a kind of skepticism. Perhaps we are all dupes of our mental gymnastics, but it seems unfortunate to be forced to this view by a rather arbitrary choice of views about logic.

[1] Girton Studies, No. 4, Cambridge, 1911.

More seriously, the facts of quite ordinary life suggest a different view — the view that our experience and our conceptual apparatus are linked. What we experience is very heavily dependent upon the conceptual apparatus we have available. The study of music makes us aware of new sounds, the man who reads bird books sees more kinds of birds than he used to. Furthermore, experience is often constricted by a hardening of our conceptual moulds. It is doubtful that middle-aged fathers hear what their teen-aged daughters hear when the record player is on, and the thoughts and feelings of constituents do not come through to old and hide-bound politicians. On a more sophisticated level, you cannot really see what the microbiologist sees in his microscope or pick out what is blindingly obvious to the astronomer in a photograph unless you have developed the ranges of concepts which make the disciplines intelligible.

The formation and ordering of this conceptual machinery is a task which involves inference and experience. There seem to be no suitable logical atoms to be linked by basic particles. Indeed, if there were, it is difficult to see how the requisite links could be formed.

If one makes the separation absolute, Bosanquet's complaint is sustained. How, under these conditions, can any synthetic proposition be valid? If part of the process of making logic harmless and immune from the need for justification consists in making it strictly "deductive" then propositions sustained by *it* will be those which Bosanquet called "analytic." (The meaning of "analytic" is by no means clear, but I suppose what Bosanquet meant, in a general way, is that such propositions are those which can be sustained by the *analysis* of other propositions. This suggests the "drawing out" and "containment" views of deduction. Such views are metaphorical and imprecise, but they suggest what is at issue.)

The point is that the other propositions, those referred to as "synthetic," will be wholly isolated from the logical ones by a basic difference in kind. They will all have, as their components, logical "atoms" which simply have no links to each other. Hence any assertion of a link, a synthesis, between them, will have no ground of formal validity.

The combination of these conclusions seems to suggest a situation in which logical commerce is mere game playing and knowledge is finally impossible.

There may, however, be ways around this impasse. If the "analytic, synthetic" distinction is bothersome, we can regard it, after all, as rather arbitrary and we can widen or contract the domain of logic as we please and throw the burden of "testing" on to experience in a rather different way.

Let me explain. It may be that the only sustainable statements, on the view I have been discussing, will turn out to be "analytic" ones if we simply look on them as ways of "linking" ideas so as to form descriptions of the world. But, first of all, we can expand the domain of the "analytic" as much as we please. We would ordinarily regard the statement "All men are mortal" as being "synthetic," as showing a link, somehow discovered, between the notions "man" and "mortal" in such a way that a mere analysis of the meaning of "man" would not reveal the required link with "mortality." Hence, "This is mortal" is not a statement which we would usually think of as "deducible" from "This is a man."

Suppose, however, you came to the conclusion that you would want to call anything which turned out to be immortal something other than a man — an angel or a machine, perhaps. You might well do so on pragmatic grounds, on the grounds that it would make for a more convenient arrangement of all your imaginable experiences to be able, always, to make that distinction.

Thus we would say that there is no final distinction between the analytic and the synthetic or between the domain of "logic" and other domains. There are only decisions of convenience which we can test, perhaps, by their relations to the ebb and flow of our experience.

Like Dewey, we might hold that all assertions are instruments of one kind or another and what they are used for is to enrich and stabilize the flow of experience. Thus, if we regard "All men are mortal" as an analytic statement, we may be forced to make a distinction between men and certain other things which we could avoid if we decided it was synthetic. Either route will suggest some investigations and tend to close off others and their outcomes will have various effects on our experiences.

Professor Quine has suggested variations of these very points. He wrote (later than the remarks I quoted previously) "For all its a priori reasonableness, a boundary between analytic and synthetic has not been drawn. That there is such a distinction to be drawn at all is an unempirical dogma of empiricists, a metaphysical article of faith."[1] In the same essay he added "Each man is given a scientific heritage plus a continuing barrage of sensory stimulation; and the considerations which guide him in warping his scientific heritage to fit his continuing promptings are, where rational, pragmatic." That his pragmatism extends or extended generally over much of his "logic" may be inferred from the additional sentence "Carnap, Lewis and others take a pragmatic stand on the question of choosing between language forms, scientific frameworks; but their pragmatism leaves off at the imagined boundary between the analytic and the synthetic. In repudiating such a boundary, I espouse a more thorough pragmatism."

Alas, though this *does* throw the burden back on experience in a new way, it does not seem to help us to believe that experience can carry that burden. For the trouble is that we must believe (if we are to shuffle our "analytic" statements, our tools of inference, and consequently our lan-

---

[1] *From a Logical Point of View* (New York: Harper and Row, 1963), Chapter III. The quotation is from "Two Dogmas of Empiricism," the first version of which was written in 1950 — later than the first edition of *Mathematical Logic* though before the publication of the second edition in which the remarks I quoted earlier remained unchanged.

guage itself on the basis of our beliefs in the good or bad outcomes for the ordering of our experience) that there is some standard or some pattern to which the result ought to conform.

The problem is to get information about this standard without developing, with independent justification, the necessary logical tools. One can, of course, simply say that we shall make up our minds about logical "laws," patterns of inference, claims to validity and so on when we see how, given these, we can actually organize our experience. If we like the result, we will accept the implied systems and, if we don't, we shall chop and change as much as we please, relying on experience, on the whole, to put us right in the long run.

If we didn't mind being simply wrong about the result there would be no harm in this. But the belief that experience will "put us right" supposes a separation between thought and experience such that experience will, in the end, have its way with us whether our conceptual systems are any good or not. There seems, however, every reason to believe the contrary, the proposition that experience can be moulded by the concepts we bring to it and will not shine through our conceptual blunders to anything like the extent which would be required to ensure automatic correction.

Even if it did, what reason would there be to believe that it was not, itself, thoroughly misleading? There may be such reasons, but the trouble with them, from this point of view, is that they are *reasons*. If you have a reason to trust experience, you must be able to sustain that reason independently of the experience. Then the burden has been shifted back to reason again.

The upshot of it all is just this: if we are not to suffer a breakdown in knowledge itself, we must find some way of making reason bear the necessary burdens. And that means both justifying our logic and relating it adequately to its subject matter.

But does this demand what the "absolute" idealist and the "dialectical" logician seem bent on maintaining: that there must be a single unified system of ideas or else there is no effective knowledge at all? This view is not, still, very easy to swallow. And there are other issues yet to be considered before it can even be made to seem reasonable.

VII

It might be imagined — indeed, it seems to have been imagined — that there is some relatively uncommitting middle ground between the atomistic view and the "absolutist" view. C. R. Morris, in fact, suggested that the British post-Hegelean idealists were seeking such a position and that a chief merit in their doctrine was its rejection of any form of "*a priorism*" and its insistence on the relation between logic and particular subject matters — the sort of connection, he thought, which was evident in ordinary scientific practice.[1]

[1] *Idealistic Logic* (London: Macmillan, 1933).

There seems to be no such middle ground though there may well be a justification for the kind of cautious approach characteristic of Bosanquet. The reason that there is no viable middle ground is this:

Logic has to be, in some way, perfectly general to provide what Kneale called "principles of inference valid for all possible subject matters." A logic which is more limited in scope invariably shows some unexplicated presumption. When I complained that Quine's paradigmatic "Either it is or else it is not" form would not, apparently, do its work because there were subject matters which seemed unlikely to fit it without distortion, I was suggesting that the form of the argument did not, in fact, reveal, exactly, the conditions of its validity and invalidity. It may work within some limited domain — indeed I shall argue that the kind of logic suggested by forms like this *does* work within a specifiable domain — but, to know what that domain is we must know, as well, what is excluded by it. To know *that* we must know what the bordering domains are and so on until we reach what Hegel called "the Absolute" or, less picturesquely, that domain which is not, itself, limited by still others.

The difficulty, then, with any attempt to place limits or borders around some region or branch of our logics is just that, if we do, we then have left unexplored some of the features of its intelligibility.

VIII

Suppose, however, that there simply is no unified system of ideas. Suppose, more drastically, that the very notion of a "unified system of ideas" is not intelligible.

The arguments I have been using have not been based explicitly on the premise that there is such a system, but they have been intended to suggest that short of a very general skepticism, there seems no alternative to the attempt to show that there is such a system and to explore its relevance for knowledge in general and for logic in particular. What I have been suggesting is simply that there is no easy way to sustain one's logic and no effective way of insulating it from encroachment from the surrounding areas of knowledge.

One is forced to ask, though, whether or not there is some preliminary set of assumptions one must make in order to get started with the exploration I have been suggesting. The exploration is, indeed, going to depend upon showing that ideas, in some way or other, hang together and that, within the confines which I shall be exploring, the "hanging together" is what gives them validity.

I shall eventually try to fit this issue into the general context of what is properly "the problem of truth" though the problem of a "justifiable logic" is, in ways which I shall try to explain, not merely the problem of truth. In other ways, it is not quite so general as that. Hence I am not arguing for a "coherence theory of truth," but I shall be arguing for a position which is, in important ways, a "coherence theory of logic."[1]

IX

This suggests, of course, at least the following problems about which something should be said before the discussion gets going in earnest: One of them is the problem posed by the notion of "a system": who is to say that all ideas must have connections with each other and that it must always be possible to work one's way from one of them to another? The other is the problem of a multiplicity of systems which may well meet all the requirements: why should there not be several systems which each meet all the requirements we can reasonably lay down — which are all perfectly general, have components which are all inter-linked in just the right way, and so on?

One might well argue that such questions ought not to be asked in advance, that the properties of the system under development will exhibit themselves as the system develops and the guarantees demanded can be given when their appropriateness has been investigated. In the face of most questions which might be asked, this would be a sound defence but not, I think, against anyone who asks these particular questions.

For, as one attempts to put together a dialectical system, one must sift and sort ideas on some principle or other. It will turn out, on my view, that there are rules for doing this but, though they enable one to pick and choose on the basis of reasons, they do not actually "produce" the ideas. They are somewhat like the rules for a valid syllogism which scarcely suggest what the "conclusions" might be which can validly be inferred from two premises. They do, combined with the available information, form parts of the conclusion, but the sorting process must be carried out somehow. However it is carried out, some ideas will be rejected precisely on the ground that they do not lead anywhere. More importantly, if there are ideas which lack the required links and which lie within the appropriate domain, they will fail to appear in any scheme of this kind just because no ideas lead to them. Hence a dialectical logic might disguise just the viable ideas which opponents of the whole scheme might be supposed to rely on.

Similarly, if there are complete systems which meet all the requirements but which are different, only one of them, presumably, will appear in any such scheme. In case they were incompatible with each other, this would be a disaster.

The difficulty in dealing with these questions is that it is not very easy to say just what they mean. Russell did think that the "multiplicity of systems"

[1] The kind of logic I am developing here seems to me to provide part of a background of ultimate presuppositions against which truth becomes possible and intelligible. For my detailed view about this see *The Concept of Truth*, Van Gorcum, Assen, 1969. Some discussion of this issue can be found in Chapter 6 of the present book.

problem was important and serious enough — seeing that there was, in his view, no answer to it — to discredit coherence theories generally.[1] But he did not elaborate at any length. The problem about the "unity" of the totality of ideas is not generally urged in just the way I have suggested, but it surely represents some part of what is in the minds of those who object to philosophical "systems" in general and to the kind of system which I propose to entertain in particular.

One answer to the "unity of ideas" problem is the one which I have, already, briefly entertained: If by "ideas" one means "concepts" and by "concepts" one means whatever it is by way of logical machinery which serves to mark out, identify, classify and so on whatever there is to be marked out, identified, and so on, then the answer is quite simple. For such activities presuppose that one has, if successful, found a way to separate the things, groups of things, classes of things (or whatever) from everything else. Otherwise, one does not have, in this sense, a proper concept, but only an ambiguous approximation. Thus, all proper concepts — of this kind — are related to each other in some obvious way.

This "answer" is, however, open to objections: One of them is that some of our ideas are simply atomic, they derive not from a system in which things are placed and classified but directly from unique experiences. Another is that whatever there is to be classified may simply not fit the pattern. The world may be pluralistic in a way which prevents there being the required links between things.

We can make some progress, however, if we notice that the two objections are linked. The "unity of ideas" problem will be disturbing only if there are things to be experienced which exhibit the pluralism suggested by the "multiplicity of systems" problem. For if there are not, then the concepts in question will turn out to be linked in the way which is denied. If, that is, the entities to be classified have links to each other, the concepts marking out those entities will have similar links. If not, not.

The first objection would, indeed, be more plausible if there were a gap between experience and our conceptual apparatus. I have already argued here and elsewhere that there is not a gap, that what we experience is linked to the concepts we have available. I have not argued here that it is literally inconceivable that there could be such a gap, but it is easy to do so — for what is it to be aware of something for which there is no concept? Can you be "aware" of "red" while having no notion of "red" and no

---

[1] *The Problems of Philosophy* (New York: Oxford University Press, 1959 [first edition, 1912]), p. 122. Actually, Russell gives two reasons for rejecting coherence theories. The other is that "Coherence presupposes the truth of the laws of logic" and is, therefore, not an ultimate notion. But it is debatable whether coherence is a basic notion upon which "the laws of logic" depend or vice-versa. There does, however, seem no doubt that he would, if persuaded of *that*, have wanted to rest his case on the point mentioned in the text above.

notion of "colour"? What would that amount to? If a man were asked what he was aware of in conditions under which his concepts were separated from his "sensory input" or whatever in such a way as to involve such a gap, he would, of course, have to give one of two answers: "Nothing!" or "I don't know what it is, but I am aware of something which is unlike anything I know about." If he gives the first answer, "awareness" is surely being misused. It is being used in a way which confuses it with something else, the mechanical receipt of stimuli — the kind of process which may well be characteristic of dials and gauges on ordinary machines and of the workings of computers. If he gives the second answer, he has, obviously, already closed part of the gap between his experience and his concepts. He has identified the thing to the extent that he knows it to be unlike other things. But he cannot know that without *some* concept of the thing in question.

The road from knowing what it is not to knowing what it is may, of course, be long and difficult — beyond, perhaps, the powers of the observer in question and even beyond the capacities of any existing human being. But, in principle, there is no reason to suppose that it cannot be travelled. A complete "conceptual map" is, in principle, possible given only that there are no gaps which could never be filled by any kind of construction.

But this brings us to the second and more dramatic objection. What if the world is, essentially, pluralistic? What if, that is, it consists of a number of disparate things which literally have no relation to each other? The dispute between monists of one kind and another and pluralists of one kind and another is both old and confused. It seems to be confused, in part, because neither side has usually wanted to adopt an extreme form of its doctrines. Monists, in general, do not really want to hold that the world is a unity of such a kind that it contains only one entity which, in turn, has only one property. Pluralists, on the other hand, have not usually wanted to hold that the world is such a disunity that some components of it stand in no relation to one another.

All that is required for the argument here is that it should be possible to show this extreme form of pluralism does not hold and that the truth of the counter position is not trivial. It would not do, for instance, merely to "show" that the world is a unity in the sense that every part of it stands in some relation to every other part of it if that relation turns out merely to be the relation of being "part of the same world." (This argument would do if we were able to restrict the concept of "world" in some special way, but that is a different question.) If, however, some relation can be held to exist and it is non-trivial, then this objection will have been overcome. Given this, it will follow that every concept which actually marks something out in such a world will perform the function it does in such a world precisely because it is different from every other concept which marks something out. It will, therefore, be related to all other concepts in a way which should not defy *every* kind of inference since such relations constitute the very nature of the concept.

Such a system of concepts, of course, can contain only the sum total of the possibilities latent in any world and the actual world of any observer will, of necessity, fall short of its actualization. To an observer, the world will seem to be a special kind of temporal process for various reasons which will, I hope, emerge in due course, but which include, at least, its apparent incompleteness. Such a system of concepts will, therefore, be the logical background of the world and not the whole truth about it. But this is not an objection to the notion that there is such a system of concepts and that it has its own kind of validity.

But what kind of relation is it which necessarily links all the concepts in any possible world and why should this extreme kind of pluralism be known be known to be false *a priori*?

To begin with, if two things are not related to each other at all, then they are neither the same nor different. It may be (I think it is) the case that identity and difference are not, in any ordinary sense, relations at all. They both seem to be cases of an absence of relation. If two things are identical, they are not related because they are not independent of each other in a way which would make any relation possible and, if they are different, then, in the *respect* in which they are different, they are *not* related. Despite this, to be either identical or different does imply the presence of relations. The difference case is, I think, the crucial one. For A and B to be different, they must stand in some linking relation to each other. To say that A is not like B is to say that they are both parts of the same system but that they occupy separable positions in it. If they are parts of wholly unrelated systems then we can specify the difference between them only by indicating how the different systems are related. For the notion of difference implies the possibility of comparison.[1] And to compare any two things they must be brought into juxtaposition with each other. If this account of difference will do, identity can be defined as the state of affairs which results when two entities are brought into juxtaposition and found to occupy the same position in the same system. It will therefore follow that two unrelated entities cannot be either the same or different. But the notion of separateness clearly implies either identity of difference. (One might argue that separate-

---

[1] It may seem that this argument slides from the notion of difference *per se* to the notion of specifiable difference. Thus one might want to say "*A* and *B* are different but the difference cannot be specified because they cannot be linked for purposes of comparison as joint members of any system." But this is to say that the difference, though real, can never be known. That, in turn, is to say that no justification of whatever kind can be given for the assertion "*A* and *B* are different." In turn, that renders the original statement meaningless on the grounds that there is no possible *point* in uttering it or denying it. Thus, for meaningful discourse, difference *per se* and specifiable difference are, necessarily, the same.

ness implies difference, but this is a stronger principle, more difficult to justify and obviously not required here.)

The upshot of this seems to be twofold: the notion of the kind of separateness our hypothetical objector has in mind is not intelligible and the relation which links all proper concepts into a unified system is the notion of intelligible system — the kind of system necessary to sustain the notions of identity and difference themselves.

This leaves us with the second — Russellian — question: Why should there not be several complete systems each of which meets every possible criterion? It seems to me, however, that the answer to this question follows from the answer to the last question. For these complete systems will have, themselves, to be unrelated to each other. In that case, again, they are not intelligible — they are neither the same nor different.

Such an answer may well sound like a debater's trick. And it is true that something more is needed just because the answer only holds if the question is taken literally and the questioner is held to the letter of an utterance which, after all, I have cast in my own words.

Russell, actually, is little help in elucidating a form of the question which will cut deeper, but it is easy to see what might well be in the mind of someone who asked the question. Suppose that what happens is simply that, given the criteria we are able to develop, it turns out that many alternative systems, or at least two, will meet them. What guarantee have we that the capacities of the human mind are not, in fact, so limited that we shall never be able to tell whether one system will do, or two, or several?

Hegel, indeed, seems to have worried somewhat about a question which is not too distant from this one. For he says, in the introduction to the *Science of Logic* that he assumes, there, "the concept of science."[1] He says that it has already been demonstrated in the *Phenomenology* and that he is, therefore, entitled to assume it. The concept he is talking about is, as it is described in the *Logic*, apparently, the concept of the systematic unity of knowledge in its presentation to consciousness. "To consciousness, all its forms are resolved into this concept, as into truth."

In the kind of systematic unity which Hegel has in mind, the distinction between, as he puts it, "thought and thing" disappears and, indeed, the whole distinction between mind and its objects becomes, for certain purposes, insignificant.

If that kind of position could be sustained, the question, in part, would not seriously arise. For what the mind is capable of, the world is capable of, and vice-versa if these distinctions really disappear.

I do not think, however, that so drastic a notion need, really, be argued for before one can go on to the main task of actually developing an equivalent of Hegel's *Logic*. Part of the job Hegel has in mind has already been

[1] Johnston and Struthers, Vol. I, p. 59; Miller, p. 49; Felix Meiner, Vol. I, p. 29.

done if my arguments to show the *possibility* of a unified system of ideas carry weight. The other part, the part which is dependent upon showing that the criteria that we can think up actually do serve to identify a *unique* system, can be done as we come to specify and develop the criteria themselves.

The latent suggestion in the objection, the suggestion that we may only, after all, succeed in identifying a system of ideas which is of our own fabrication and of no relevance to the outside world, must also depend upon just how such distinctions develop within the system. If we cannot sustain the necessary links, the system will break down and will surely be seen to break down.

X

The preliminaries, then, seem, at somewhat tedious length, to have been completed. The problem now is to try to find a starting point and the beginning of a pattern of inference.

Here, it is appropriate to sketch briefly the course which the investigation will follow. In the next chapter I shall try, first, to find a starting point for the development of the kind of system in which form and content can be developed together — a concept which will be so general as to be a necessary part of *any* system of discourse and yet fruitful enough in its logical structure to provide a basis on which to build. I shall then, by searching for accounts of other concepts which must have a place in any system in which the first concept is built, try to assemble the beginnings of the kind of system of ideas for which we are looking. Throughout the next chapter, however, I let the arguments develop in just the ways that the structures of the concepts seem to dictate. I shall try to exhibit the beginnings of the system through four "categories."

In Chapter 3, I shall try to locate the various levels which are characteristic of such systems of ideas — to distinguish between the concepts which form the "core" of such a system of ideas and the concepts which provide the inferential links between them. I shall also try to distinguish the concepts which are, in turn, organized by the "core" concepts. On one of these "levels" will be found "categories" or general ways of focussing the universe of discourse and of things considered as a totality. On another will be found inference rules and patterns. Concepts which form the "domains" which the "categories" govern will form a third level. Thus the four "categories" developed in Chapter 2 will, I hope, be rendered intelligible by reference to the appropriate detailed concepts and inference patterns discussed in Chapter 3.

In the succeeding three chapters, I shall try to exhibit the development of the system through five additional categories. At each stage, I shall try to show how the rules developed in Chapter 3 carry through the development of the categories and also how, gradually, the levels of the system coalesce

22

so as to provide a gradually increasing unity. The last category is intended to reflect back on the whole of the system in such a way as to show the necessity of its overall structure and to provide for a notion of "completion" as a system of ideas which is, still, compatible with the kinds of openness and freedom which the structure logically requires.

At every stage, hopefully, it will be possible to show how the materials for the required development are to be found in the development of the initial concept and the concept of the system itself, though, of course, examples to render it intelligible will have to be drawn, continuously, from a wide range of thought and experience.

The reader, thus, is asked to be patient — especially perhaps in the next chapter where I have to face the problem of developing a structure of thought before I can undertake to reflect upon it and draw out the rules and procedures by which it is developed.

I have tried to use as little strange language as possible though, some of it, like the names of categories and the names of specialized components of inference structures is, I fear, inevitable. Even there, I have tried to use names for categories — such as "systematic unity" and "determinate process" — which suggest the dominating ideas, and names for components of inference — such as "specific exclusion reference" — which mean what they say. The detailed meanings of such expressions, however, are to be had only by examining the contexts in which they are used, and too much weight should not be put on these shorthand attempts at intelligibility.

Where feasible, I have provided comparisons of my approach and those of Hegel and other philosophers in the hope that they will add to the intelligibility of the discussion. There are only a limited number of places in which I come close enough in detail to Hegel to make this possible and, as I have explained in the preface, this is not meant to be a commentary on Hegel's logic. In general, indeed, all references to other works are intended to help with the job of making this book intelligible and they should be read with that in mind and not as capsule commentaries.

Chapter 2

The beginnings of a system — the problem of a first concept — the initial categories: pure being, pure disjunction, determinate being and systematic unity

I

If one is to find a starting point for a dialectical system, one must, somehow, face simultaneously the traditional issues about form and content. The case for a dialectical system depends heavily on the contention that form and content must be developed together but, to show the interrelation and interdependence of any two subject matters, one must be able to consider them separately and then to show the deficiencies which result from their separation.[1] The difficulty about this, of course, is that they depend upon each other in a way which makes one's views about the initial delineation of each prejudice what one can say about the other.

If one were to start with a proposition — however certain and general — then the content expressible within the confines of that proposition would necessarily be limited by the propositional form. If one were to start, as Hegel at first glance seems to, with content or subject matter ("pure being" in his case) then the form of the assertions one could make would be equally restricted. (Pure being, since it is undifferentiable, presumably cannot be encompassed within an assertion of propositional form or within any other form involving a distinction amongst components.)

The problem is compounded by the fact that one must, apparently, discuss the issues in an ordinary language which carries with it its own commitments and evident restrictions. Some way has to be found to avoid the original dilemma and to make ordinary language the neutral bearer of whatever discussion is under way.

---

[1] If, as will be argued here, the distinction is ultimately untenable, any proposed separation of form and content will turn out to be arbitrary. Indeed, a strong case can be made for the proposition that, in most "logics," the distinction *is* arbitrary. Still, the kind of unity which is required if a dialectical system is to be sustained will itself be dialectical and thus will not wholly obliterate the concepts which it transcends.

24

It would be instructive to follow Hegel's procedure with an eye to just these difficulties and to see whether or not one could catch the issues in action and devise strategies which would overcome the objections as they became apparent. I propose to do this as best I can, although I must admit that I do not find it possible to be sure about Hegel's intentions. The interpretation I shall offer is presented because it does seem a reasonable interpretation of what Hegel says and because it does seem to open up the issues in a way which makes them tractable. I shall first state what seems to be the Hegelean case and then proceed to my own critical analysis.

Hegel starts with "pure being." What he tells us about it is this:[1] It is without "any further determination"; it is "similar to itself alone" but "not dissimilar from anything else"; "it is pure indeterminateness and vacuity"; "it is not a subject matter of and for intuition"; "or again it is merely this pure and empty intuition itself"; and, finally, "there is in it no object for thought, or again it is just this empty thought."

These remarks are reinforced in the paragraph from which I have been quoting by others which make the same points. Approximately the same thing has been said in the preceding paragraph which introduces the category of "determinateness" and in the remarks about the "general classification of being." The paragraph concerned ends with the remark that "being, in-determinate immediacy, is Nothing, neither more nor less" — but that, presumably, is the beginning of the dialectical argument and must await further consideration. (It can be argued that Hegel starts with the concept of "nothing" and it is *that* which he is describing in the paragraph headed "being" since that is the "conclusion" which follows the description. On this view, the next paragraph, headed "nothing" really describes "being" and the dialectic runs, therefore, "nothing, being, becoming" and not "being, nothing, becoming.")

The important question, however, is about what is going on here in a logical way. It is true that the whole of Hegel's dialectic can be read as a series of assertions, each of which has the form "Reality is so and so" — e.g., "Reality is pure being," "Reality is nothing" ... "Reality is determinate being" ... "Reality is the Absolute."[2] On such a view, each proposition

[1] Johnston and Struthers, Vol. I, p. 94; Miller, p. 82; Felix Meiner edition, Vol. I, p. 66.
[2] A basis for this, of course, is the passage from the "Shorter Logic" in which Hegel says "Being itself and the special types which follow, as well as those of logic in general, may be looked upon as definitions of the Absolute or metaphysical definitions of God: at least the first and third forms in every typical triad may..." In an important way this is true throughout Hegel's system for every concept may be taken as a way of focussing the whole so as to bring out one of its crucial aspects. (The second "form" in a "typical triad" is rather different.) But these "definitions" seem not to be *propositions* and Hegel's language as he develops the early parts of the scheme suggest this strongly. I am only concerned here to cast doubts on the implication that Hegel has precommitments. The

leads to the next by reason of its inability correctly to characterize the whole of the "real," and the series is peculiar mainly in that each has the same subject but every predicate is different and linked to the preceding predicates by some established dialectical procedure. This analysis must be treated with caution since there is a danger of starting with a built-in bias toward a certain propositional form. But Hegel is careful in the paragraphs under immediate scrutiny.

In those paragraphs, two things are fairly clear: "Being" is regarded as a subject matter about which various assertions are being made rather indirectly and the transitions are not from proposition to proposition but from subject matter to subject matter. For one finds remarks such as "Being ... has passed over into nothing" and "[It is] a distinction which has equally immediately dissolved itself." Something is happening to the subject matters, not the assertions. Furthermore, language is used here in such a way as to point out its own inadequacy. Since pure being has no internal structure, its nature cannot be expressed in a proposition and Hegel does not, here at any rate, try.

The clue to what Hegel thinks he is doing may well be found in his remarks about the "empty intuitions" and "thoughts" of "being" and "nothing." He has doubts about the appropriateness of the expressions "intuition" and "thought" and prefaces his remarks about them with the words "in so far as mention can here be made." For they are parts, alike, of the world and of the rational structure of the "logic" which must be explored as he goes along. But what I think he wants to do is to get down to the most general form of thought and the most general form of anything which could exist. The "pure and empty intuition" and the "empty thought" which are, in a way, pure being, are also the simplest structure which anything could have. Whatever we want to say, it must include at least the form of intuition and thought itself if, indeed, the structures of intuition and thought have a common property. Similarly, whatever could be real must, presumably, have that much structure. For, if it did not, it could not be *said* to be real and the expression "real" could be given no function in our discourse. To posit a "reality" which failed in that requirement would be to utter a disastrous contradiction — to say both that something was and that one could not say that it was. (Alternatively, the statement could be regarded as meaningless.) Additionally, since this is apparently the minimum *form* describable, to say that something was real and did not have at least this would be to say that the real was formless. A formless real would not only be indescribable but also perfectly non-efficacious.

reference to "God" in the quotation is rather puzzling in terms of Hegel's final view but the "Absolute" here only means the "finally real." (The passage quoted is from *The Encyclopedia of the Philosophical Sciences*, Section 85. The translation is from Wallace's *Logic of Hegel* [Oxford at the Clarendon Press, 1874], p. 133. In the Felix Meiner German edition [Hamburg, 1959], p. 105.)

The advantages of this position are considerable. Hegel, if he is right, has linked thought and reality and he has been careful to use language first of all merely as a framework on which to focus attention on a subject which, if his choice of words is a guide, we can watch at work. It is not that we can see or feel or intuit "being" passing into "nothing" and both into "becoming" and "determinate being." But we can see the effects on the language which has been used to focus the subject. It is because of its effect on language that we notice "being" passing into "nothing."

Thus we see that we cannot grip "pure being" as such in our linguistic net and that it reacts exactly as if we had gripped "nothing." In ordinary language, therefore, it is nothing — for nothing can be said about it, it has neither qualities nor relations. But nothing, in its turn, reacts the same way — as if we had gripped "pure being" in our net. (Nothing, quite ordinarily conceived, has the absence of properties ascribed by Hegel to "being.") Our language, therefore, shows a logical tension building up and we can neither write it off as mere gibberish (for the subject matter concerned lies, somehow, at the root of everything and of all discourse) nor pin it down.

What Hegel thinks we can do is to see *that* this passage takes place — and thus glean the notion of "becoming" as the first "synthesis" of the system — and also *why* it takes place, namely because neither "being" nor "nothing" is a concept which includes the notion of "determinateness."

In this way, he builds the beginnings of the picture of a dialectical method. Seemingly, one finds a concept which is so general that it must have a place in the scheme of things; one finds that it collapses into the concept of whatever it excludes. (In this case the inference, though slippery, is apparently simple enough, what "being" excludes is "nothing." This process can be seen in the desperate attempts of language to express the result.) One sees the reverse collapse and then one sees what would be required to prevent that collapse. That the collapse needs to be prevented is apparently shown by the fact that the subject matter in question is both necessary for thought and the world and yet impossible as a characterization of thought and the world.

It should be obvious that this procedure would not work identically for any further move in the dialectic since the balance between "inclusion" and "exclusion" is only perfect for the most general concept. Any more specific concept will exclude more than it includes, but the principle may well carry over in recognizable though subtly developing form. (It is for this reason if for no other that any attempt to "formalize" a logic of this sort around a single principle which remains stable throughout the system is doomed to failure.)

Hegel's procedure, then, may be imagined as a search for the most general subject matter which can be talked about, a search for the point of necessary intersection between thought and reality, a search for an example of actual dialectical advance, and an attempt to avoid the form-content dichotomy and the paradoxes which issue from having to use language without yet having justified it.

Hegel offers here little commentary on his procedure. (Four rather long "observations" follow the main argument, but they are largely concerned with conceptual clarification and with historical matters.)

But it is reasonable to think that he has in mind what seem to be the obvious difficulties and objections. Whatever the truth of that, the reader can take what I have added to the discussion simply as an attempt to see how Hegel could be made to face up to these issues.

Even construed this way, however, there are a number of difficulties facing anyone who wants to follow Hegel to the letter. The scheme is hardly bare of presumptions of one kind and another. (For instance, at one point in my exposition, I was forced to seek recourse to a principle of non-contradiction or, alternatively, to an implied theory of meaning. Both of these are rich fare for the beginning of a dialectical logic.)

There are also expressions like "pure and empty intuition" and "empty thought" which are difficult to construe unless we are, in fact, being invited to think about what our intuitions are like apart from their contents or what our thoughts are like if they are considered just as thoughts rather than as thoughts about something. It might be urged that such notions are the names of important mistakes rather than of profound insights. Even if such contentions could be rebutted (and I think they might be), the appeal would seem to lead us back to some kind of intuition.

True, it would be possible for Hegel, as I suggested, to hold that it is not some experience or intuition to which he is appealing but rather to the results, evident in our language, of our attempts to say certain things. It does seem to be this to which he appeals, although he never says so. Valuable and important as this technique may be, it is obviously a difficult one to apply and one whose results are by no means easy to assess.

Finally, it may well be that the dialectic is set in motion by what *could* be construed as a rather unfortunate piece of verbal juggling. For the transition from being to nothing, on this view, does not amount to very much. It is done by making "pure being" so very thin that it is quite easily seen to be nothing. The reverse collapse — from nothing to being again — is made plausible by giving just enough ambivalent content to such illustrative expressions as "empty intuition" and "empty thought." When they are imagined as illustrative of being, they are presumably taken as important and significant but when they are taken as illustrative of nothing, they are taken in the way that someone who objected to such expressions might take them. In the transition from nothing back to being, Hegel says, "In so far as mention can here be made of intuition or thought, it is considered a distinction whether we intuit or think something or nothing. In that case, to intuit or think nothing has a meaning: so if intuition or thought of Being and of Nothing are distinguished, then Nothing *is* (or does exist)." He then goes on to tell us that, in that case, since nothing has "the same determination (or rather lack of it)" as pure being, it is "thus altogether the same thing." But, in the paragraph above, when he is leading from being to nothing, he is rather inclined to denigrate the empty thoughts and intuitions involved with the words "merely this pure and empty intuition itself."

The principle of a dialectical system may be well illustrated by what is usually called the "first triad" but it is not, it seems, equally well sustained.

Yet it seems obvious that Hegel is on to something and that it very nearly comes off. The problem is to see what modifications will make the underlying principles and issues clearer and whether it is possible to get the scheme moving on the basis of, at least, a set of presumptions which can be shown to be intrinsically reasonable.

III

It will be useful, I think, to back off a little and to consider the notion of "being" and the question of possible alternatives to it.

Unless it is given rather precise specification, the notion is apt to lead to a good deal of confusion. Since it is usually taken to be the central concept around which ontological enquiries pivot, to start by positing it is to start, apparently, by making a general declaration about the relations between ontological and logical concepts. In addition, it is apt to be vacuous and to convey little more than a sense of one's intentions. The word "being" can, after all, be construed as the name of *whatever* is investigated in ontological enquiries. By itself, it functions much the way that the word "science" does in the philosophy of science.

There is, however, a need for a fairly precise concept which might be given the name "being." The need arises in the following way. When we use concepts to identify and classify things, we are behaving as though we were marking something out on a map — we imply that there is a background system within which the discriminations we want to make have their place.

Usually, these background systems are rather limited in nature and structure. Number concepts work in the context of the number system and have intelligible functions because there is a body of theory describing that system. The concepts which figure in biological classifications function in the context of a rather general map which divides living things into kingdoms, species, and so on. Such concepts are also rendered intelligible by background theories concerning evolution, biochemistry, etc. Political concepts are rendered usable by reference to bodies of constitutional and legal theory. Concepts like "president," "senator," and "chief justice of the supreme court" form parts of intelligible American political life because their places are mapped in a constitution about which there is at least minimal agreement in interpretation and theoretical construction. But all these "reference systems" have to interlock at key points. If they do not, some of them become unusable and gradually atrophy. (We can see this happening with a broad range of theological concepts. Whatever may be said by pious chaplains, the relations between God and the President of the United States are no longer clearly specifiable according to any theory which would meet with general acceptance by those who use the political concept in question and anyone who tried to co-relate the activities of God with the discoveries of atomic theory would be generally regarded as having undertaken an unsound enterprise. And yet if there is a God of the traditional kind, his authority must stand in some relation to that of the President of the United States and his activities must bear upon every happening including those reported by atomic physicists.)

All such systems purport, after all, to specify some distinction which actually can be made in the world — to establish some reference point for a kind of discourse which can be carried on. They all, therefore, tread on two common grounds — the domain which consists of all the distinctions which are actually there to be made in the world and the domain of all possible intelligible discourse. These domains are not, finally, identical for one contains room for reflection on the other and has an aspect, therefore, within which a conceptual distinction can be made. At the same time, however, intelligible discourse is, itself, part of the world of possibilities which is the domain of the distinctions which are there to be made.

The area of significant intersection of these domains is, however, the most general subject matter imaginable. Whatever one's theory about anything, one has traffic of some kind with this intersection. We might, then, call this "being," and call those aspects of it which are its properties apart from the distinctions which are made within it "pure being."

The significance of this concept is that it is a point of intersection between thought and reality; it is the most general of the concepts one can imagine, and it does seem to function as a latent reference point in all our discourse so that, although, like Hegel's pure being, it cannot, as such, be described or experienced (the equivalent of Hegel's "intuited") or set up literally as an *object* of thought, it can be seen, by seeing how all our discourse works, to be at work. It is thus too general for the distinction between form and content and suffices both to take us back behind that distinction and to take us beyond what is marked out in ordinary discourse to what is only presupposed in that discourse.

Before proceeding to see how such a concept might, in fact, function, and whether it would actually serve to set the dialectic in train, it is important to consider what alternatives there might be. One alternative would be to start simply with the modern concept of a "universe of discourse" — conceived simply as the domain within which whatever we can say has its place. But this is, at once, to leave us in the position of trying to find a link between word and object, thought and reality, reason and experience and so on. Once one starts on a level at which these distinctions can be forced, there is no effective way of getting the components back together again. It would also force us to create appropriate rules governing discourse, inference, and thought before we could begin to give shape to the concept itself. This, in turn, would seem to throw us back amongst all the problems of the last chapter.

Another alternative would be to start with a purely ontological concept as, indeed, Hegel seems to. But this would seem to have a set of disadvantages corresponding exactly to those which would accrue to us if we started with a purely logical concept.

The remaining alternative would seem to be to start not with some part of the subject matter of the dialectic but with the dialectical process itself. The objection to this is that, unless we had shown, by some prior process, that a specific and intelligible kind of dialectical system was necessary, we should not, in fact, know where or how to begin. It is not just that the demonstration in the last chapter fell short of what would be required to show such a necessity. The detailed structure of a dialectical process is so complex and so closely related to the subject matter on which it works that such an enterprise would seem doomed to failure.

This brief survey of alternatives does not, by itself, constitute a strong argument for beginning with the concept I suggested. The special deficiencies, however, of each of the alternatives do suggest that some concept very like that one must be the only one available. As soon as one departs any distance from it, conundrums very quickly begin to appear. Furthermore, these considerations show that reasons can be given and assessed in the debate about an acceptable starting point — that we are not forced back upon a purely arbitrary postulate or fated to be governed merely by our intuitions. As the discussion develops, the initial concept will no longer float free and, given that it is not wholly misguided, it should be possible to clarify its functions and nature.

IV

Still, the question is: does it lead anywhere? And, in exploring the directions in which it may seem to point, can we avoid verbal jugglery and the importation of principles and premises which it does not justify? The production of a first concept necessarily involves a special kind of argument. Thereafter, in a dialectical system, restrictions immediately become more pressing.

Pure being, as I have described it, does have some of the properties which Hegel found in his analagous concept. Everything imaginable exhibits it and it, therefore, distinguishes nothing. It stands beyond the most basic distinctions which can be made — even beyond form and content.

It can be seen, therefore, at once to be presupposed in all discourse and yet to be capable of distinguishing nothing. It at once unites everything (by reason of being their common property) and excludes everything (by reason of being incapable of being anything in itself). This, in itself, suggests strongly that it is the most general concept possible, the one required for a starting point. For, if concepts, in general, mark something out and exclude everything else, then the most general of all concepts will be one which marks everything out and excludes everything.

v

Such assertions, naturally enough, are apt to bring out just that feeling of exasperation which Hegel has always aroused in many philosophers. For there are two genuinely exasperating suggestions latent in them. One is that the proposal cheats by seeming to get out of the original difficulties by producing a concept which, though it can be talked about for a while as if it *were* a concept, in fact escapes the limitations which attach to other concepts by actually doing none of the work of a concept. It neither marks anything out nor excludes anything. It does no logical work and is merely a form of words pretending to delineate a concept. The other, which is bound to be raised, if the first should be overcome, is that the description of the functions of this alleged concept is itself contradictory, or contains a contradiction, or implies one.

The conclusion which seems natural, therefore, is that this starting point should be abandoned on the grounds that at the very beginning of the first move, it breaks down and can be shown to be merely self-destructive. I shall try to deal with these sources of exasperation immediately. In dealing with them, I think I can actually advance the argument.

Two points have to be admitted at once. The first is that concepts do function by making distinctions: indeed, the very possibility of a dialectical system is founded upon that fact. The second is that, generally, any concept which has its scope expanded to the point at which it covers everything ceases to perform any function. As Ryle once suggested, to say that everything is an illusion, for instance, is to defeat one's purpose.[1] For the function of the concept of illusion is to make a distinction. If that distinction cannot be sustained, it has no work to do. The principle holds less obviously for some concepts than for others. It is quite possible, for instance, that everything should be red. In that case, however, given certain other conditions, being red and being coloured would be the same thing and we should have no need for specific colour concepts. (The proposition would hold only in case everything should always have been red, was now red, and would always be red. It would be different if some absurd god should

[1] *Dilemmas* (Cambridge: Cambridge University Press, 1954), p. 94ff.

merely happen to paint everything red for the time being. For then we should need other colour concepts to deal with what had been and with what might be the case in the future.) On the whole, though, something happens to concepts whose scope is widened in this way and they are, in general, never quite the same concepts after the operation.

The concept which I decided to call "pure being" is, however, immune from these particular criticisms. For it includes everything, considered as a totality, and excludes everything considered as a collection of individual things. It does, thus, serve to make *some* distinction. It contains within it the notions of unity and diversity and the notions of identity and difference. The possibilities of affirmation and negation are, thus, latent within it.

What is more — and more important — such notions would be incapable of functioning without *some* such concept. For to make an affirmation is to say that something is the case and all the subject matters of affirmation must have *something* in common, namely that they are what is thought to be the case. Whatever is the case must be the possible subject of some affirmation (i.e., it would never be false to make some affirmation with respect to it). So that, whatever there is, it must be true of it that all its components have something in common. Similarly, however, since every affirmation must suggest that something else is not the case, everything there is must be different from everything else in some way. So some concept must both unite and disjoin in some effective way.

In fact, by this route, it is possible to show, from the fact that we are engaged in intelligible discourse, that there must be some very basic concept which will work in the way that the concept I suggested does work. Once again, we can sustain the concept by watching the ways in which it turns up in and has effects upon the whole pattern of possible discourse. The one thing, surely, that we are entitled to assume is that we *are* talking about the problem.

This discussion, to a large extent, seems to me to obviate the second source of exasperation. There is no contradiction in the "everything"and "nothing" assertion. It is, of course, the case that we have not yet reached the point at which it is feasible or sensible to talk about the "principle of non-contradiction" as such. The arguments I have been mustering merely refer, in a general way, to the maintenance or destruction of the conditions for intelligible discourse. What a principle of non-contradiction is or how it might be sustained is something which must appear in a succession of subsequent discussions.

What there is, at the point of the argument which we have reached, is a problem of conceptual clash. The concept of "pure being" both seems to do work of an important kind and to require some other concept or set of concepts in order to do that work. It can be seen to be both efficacious and deficient, complete and self contained in one sense, and wholly incomplete in another.

The position is this: we start out by positing a concept which we have chosen because it seems to be the ultimate, basic link between all departments of rational discourse and all possible worlds within which and about which such discourse might function. What we then want to find out is what other concepts are required by it in order for it to be able to do its logical work. So far all that we know is (1) intelligible discourse is, somehow, possible, (2) one concept at least is required to sustain this possibility. We are, presumably, entitled to hold that (3) every additional concept which is required for the functioning of the original concept will be equally necessary. What is being imported into our basic system of beliefs about the principles of intelligible discourse at this point is the principle that, if any concept can be shown to be necessary for the functioning of the original concept, then both the additional concept and the principle of inference which leads to it will be equally necessary. The meaning of "necessary," in its interim function, is given by the original relation between the concept in question and the possibility of intelligible discourse and cannot be specified further except by developing the inference rules which will develop, if at all, from the relations between the original concept and the other concepts which are required by it.

It should, therefore, be clear that the procedure does not start, literally, in a vacuum. It starts against the background of the possibility of intelligible discourse. (Even Hegel is busy using words from the beginning.) But this initial possibility is not a kind of language prison of the sort which seems sometimes to have been envisaged by some of the followers of Wittgenstein and perhaps by Wittgenstein himself in the *Philosophical Investigations*.[1] For the possibility of intelligible discourse covers all sorts of discourse, both logically justifiable and otherwise so long as it remains within the domain of the intelligible. And that domain contains error as well as truth. The inference rules and regions of subject matter developed, however, will, if they are sound, consist only of the justifiable parts of intelligible discourse. Furthermore, the properties of intelligible discourse as it is assumed to be possible at the beginning of the investigation are extremely general while the properties of the dialectical system as it develops should become increasingly specific. We thus do not necessarily come out where we went in and the process is not necessarily circular — though mistakes in reasoning could lead to either result.

More needs to be said, however, about the way in which progress in the system, if it is possible at all, can take place. Hegel speaks at the beginning of the *Logic* as though the concept he had chosen for a starting point was simple in the sense of being without any internal structure. Such expressions

---

[1] (Oxford: Blackwell, 1953, [second edition with minor revisions, 1958.])

as "without any further determination" — used of "pure being" — and "simple equality with itself" along with "complete emptiness" — used of "nothing" — certainly suggest this. It is almost as if he were committed to Leibniz's occasional dream of finding the "great alphabet," the original list of simple concepts out of which everything else is compounded.

It should be clear, however, that a perfectly simple concept in this sense of simple could have no links with any other concept and could function in only one way for, by definition, it would lack the capacity for diversity of function. Its function, indeed, would be like that of a proper name, a mere tag arbitrarily associated with its subject matter. Though there are, of course, proper names, it seems doubtful that they can function at all as concepts and equally doubtful that there are any simple concepts in the required sense. For the least that a concept must do is to identify something and exclude something else. And, as I argued earlier, a concept, to function, must have a place in some system and, therefore, the kind of complexity of relations which does imply an internal structure of some kind.

Some internal structure — the kind that I was referring to when I suggested that the concept of pure being which I proposed to develop included the notions of unity and diversity and the notions of identity and difference, and contained, latent in it, the possibility of affirmation and negation — is not incompatible with simplicity in another sense. It is not, for instance, incompatible with the degree of generality of application which transcends the distinction between form and content. We cannot distinguish, by reference to the subject matter which this concept marks out, between the way in which the concept is structured and the way in which it refers to the world. For they are, in this case, one and the same. (There is nothing very novel about this considered simply as a doctrine about the nature of basic propositions about logic except perhaps the way of putting it. Logical "realists" [including, I suppose, Aristotle] have always held that the basic principles of logic are, somehow, part of the world. And this must mean that the structure of logic and the structure of the world are identical in some way. If this is so, certain basic logical forms, at least, are the subject matter of their own references and this is a way of saying that they transcend the distinction between form and content. Some such unity is required if thought and reality are to be kept together, but how such an assumption is to be justified has not usually been made clear. If I am right about my choice of initial concepts then such a unity is, indeed, necessary.)

VII

We ought, now, to be able to proceed from the initial concept to the development of its implications. It will not be true, given *this* initial concept, that it collapses into "nothing." It is true that "pure being," in this sense, is also the concept of what it is not to be a "thing" or a "property" of a thing. It is the concept of a subject matter which excludes both these ways of being determinate.

What is required, if the dialectical process is to get started, is that it should be possible to show that what each concept excludes is as essential for intelligible discourse as is what it includes. Our line of thought should be forced, in each instance, from one to the other. The reason for this is simply that, if a concept becomes intelligible by means of a dual reference to what it includes and what it excludes, then what it excludes is equally required for its functioning. The notion of a kind of conceptual collapse from an original concept into what is sometimes loosely called its "opposite" is simply a way of suggesting that, without a clear concept of what is excluded as well as what is included, the concept fails to have the required precise boundaries and appears to slop meaninglessly across the whole domain within which it functions.

But this cannot merely be assumed to happen. It has to be shown and, in the process, some precision has to be put on such notions as "inclusion" and "exclusion."

In the case in question, "pure being," as I have defined it, specifically marks out the region within which everything that can be talked about has something in common. It excludes every case in which differentia appear. But, if we do not have a concept of differentiation, it fails to mark anything out. There cannot be a point of intersection if there are no disjunctions. And there cannot be affirmations if there are no possible denials.

Thus, to work, the concept of "pure being" requires a concept of "pure disjunction." Without that, it becomes an empty concept. The converse is equally true: the notion of "pure disjunction" cannot work unless there is a scheme within which things are unified. This is merely another way of stating the argument which I used at the end of the last chapter against the possibility of an extreme pluralism: Things cannot be different unless there is some respect in which they are the same.

It should be noticed, however, that the way in which these concepts "collapse" is dependent upon their having a rather complex internal structure. It is because the notion of identity requires the notion of difference and vice versa that each of the concepts can be seen to fail without the other. "Pure being" focusses on unity and excludes diversity, while "pure disjunction" focusses on diversity and excludes unity, but neither, for that very reason, is, itself, simple. It is this "focussing" activity which gives some sense to the expressions "include" and "exclude" though neither of the concepts so far possesses enough detailed structure to raise such expressions beyond the level of metaphor.

In any event, we pass from "pure being," as I have defined it, to "pure disjunction" and not from "pure being" to "nothing" except in the most literal sense of "no thing." There seems little profit in saying, as Hegel did, that "pure being is nothing" and vice versa. What is true is that the two concepts I have tried to construct would, if taken in isolation, fail alike to perform their functions. One would give us the featureless notion of a perfect identity without disjunction and the other the featureless notion of a perfect diversity. Neither permits us to function with a domain consisting only of one concept and neither will function without the other. Each, if taken separately, does yield the notion of a blank, vacant, impossible world. To that extent — but only to that extent — they are alike.

We can reinforce this point and also begin to see the way to the next move, if we notice that the two concepts, "pure being" and "pure disjunction" are, if one may use the expressions untechnically, extensionally identical and intensionally distinct. Both of them, that is, mark out the same domain — everything. Everything which is must exhibit the unity with everything else, which is exhibited by "pure being," and the disjunction from everything else, which is exhibited by "pure disjunction." It may seem that they cannot be identical in extension just because one of them seems to be both an ontological and a logical notion while the other seems to be purely a logical notion. But, in fact, both concepts transcend this distinction. "Pure disjunction" is the notion which makes possible both the kinds of distinctions which are essential to words and propositions and the kinds of distinctions which may or do hold between things in the world. But, in itself, it is mere absence of unity and cannot be characterized as either of these distinctions.

VIII

What happens, therefore, is that the two concepts, viewed as an isolated system, finally fail to do any work. One of them gives the notion of a featureless unity and the other the notion of a featureless diversity. By this time, however, we can see what is excluded by the concepts taken singly or together: the notion of determinateness.

The reasonable conclusion is that what provokes the collapse of a system which is imagined to contain only these concepts is simply their perfect generality. It is because "pure being" draws attention to everything at once that it fails to draw attention to anything. And it is because "pure disjunction" excludes everything at once that it fails to do what any other negative concept would do — to draw attention, positively, to something.

There must, thus, be some scope for the notion of determinateness if there is to be any scope assignable to "pure being" or "pure disjunction."

The conclusion, thus far, has obvious similarities to Hegel's inference in the *Logic*, but it differs from his in important ways. Hegel proceeds from "pure being" to "nothing" and thence to what he calls "becoming." Presumably, he wants to call attention to two important features of his developing dialectic. One is what he specifically calls the "movement" of one of the original subject matters into the other. The second is the fact that the domain over which these most general concepts hold sway is neither perfectly static being nor yet perfectly static emptiness but always something in which there are features of each. He is here serving notice that he is going to describe a world throughout which some important kind of logical tension holds and that he is going to argue that this is the only kind of world there is. I shall try to show in the next chapter that the issue of "dialectical movement" which is being raised in the first of Hegel's points belongs, in fact, to a different level of the system. Hegel's second point also cannot, I think, be shown here. For the "unity" of "being" and "nothing" is not, as he in any case admits, perfect, and it is not literally the subject matters which collapse into each other.

It would seem more natural, then, to regard the next general concept in the system as determinateness. What we require *is* the notion of determinateness, particularity, or limitation. We can regard this notion as arising naturally out of the others as a result of the consideration that we have shown the need for the concepts of "pure being" and "pure disjunction" and we have also shown that they will not work unless the system they comprise is expanded to include exactly what they exclude. This needs some refinement, however. They exclude not merely the concept of "determinateness" but every other concept as well. But each additional concept is excluded because and only because it involves the concept of determinateness. They are excluded, that is, through it and because of it.

IX

It should be noticed — or admitted — that "determinateness" is not, as such, a kind of synthesis between the other two concepts. To get something which looked like a "synthesis" one would have to proceed to a significantly richer concept which might well be called (following, in fact, the next move in Hegel's scheme) "determinate being." And that will require further explanation.

The line of thought, in this case, goes from the original concept (pure being) to what it excludes (pure disjunction) and, then, by noting their deficiencies, to what they both exclude, determinateness.

Determinateness does not, however, function as another concept of the same order. Being determinate is a way of being something or other — being specifiably blue, or having a specific length, or being a particular kind of animal such as an elephant. It is a concept which relates specifically and only to the form of things. It is not merely that it cannot be regarded as intelligible by itself (that condition probably holds for every concept) but that it cannot be regarded as a separate subject of discourse even within a rather limited domain. "Pure being" and "pure disjunction," as I defined them, can be regarded as special cases in that they stand at a level of generality which is beyond the reach of discussions about form and content. When we begin to talk about determinateness, however, we are involved inevitably with that distinction. To get a working concept, therefore, we have to expand the notion to that of determinate being.

This concept can be assembled from the previous concepts together with their precise negative references. Determinateness is what they exclude. What they include is the notion of a subject matter which can be the object of reference in discourse and the notion of separate identity which is implied by the concept of disjunction.

The notion of determinate being is, therefore, a genuine synthesis, assembled out of the negative and positive references of the earlier concepts. Commentary on the procedure which has been used and the rules which seem to govern it will be offered in the next chapter. For the moment, the task is to try to make the procedure intelligible by exploring its consequences and by feeling our way toward the next move in the dialectic.

X

Though we are still importantly in the domain of Hegel's language and within measuring distance of the conceptual structure he employed, I have made enough changes (induced I hope by the flow of the argument) so that the discussion will have to proceed pretty much independently from here.

It is rather difficult, in any case, to follow Hegel just here. It is difficult to know how to construe sentences like, "In determinate being, being and nothing are immediately one: they are therefore co-extensive." For the synthesis which has led through Hegel's "becoming" to his notion of "determinate being" does not appear to be an obliteration of difference but the construction of a very complex concept whose components remain intelligible. Much that follows from this point to the category of "measure" seems to be perilous just on the ground that the nature of the syntheses, and the subsequent divisions, is not very clear. Inevitably, we shall, however, have to traffic in many of the problems which Hegel raises in this region. The concepts of limit and limitlessness and their relatives, finitude and infinity: the concepts which Hegel calls "something and another" and some form of the concepts of quality and quantity all arise in one way or another.

XI

To begin with, the notion of determinateness involves, as a minimum, the notion of quality, property, or specific feature. Equally, it involves the notion of something to which that feature is attachable.

It is doubtful that *all* the dialectical gymnastics to which Hegel subjects himself at this point are really necessary because it would seem that two notions — that of specific property and that of bearer of properties — follow simply from a consideration of the structure of the notion of determinate being as such.

What goes into the notion of determinate being is the conjunction of the concepts of pure being, pure disjunction and determinateness. It turns out, however, that these notions can only be held together in the form of the twin notions of property and bearer of properties.

For consider: if we attempt to render our discourse determinate, we must first deal with the notion of limit. "Pure being" turned out to be a concept which, though necessary, failed to distinguish anything in the world or in discourse just because it applied to everything equally. To get further than this we must introduce the possibility of properties which can apply to some things and not to others. As soon as one introduces concepts like yellow, large, squiggly, beatified, stupid, whorish, or large prime number, we have done this. But properties in this sense are only intelligible on condition that they have bearers. If a man says he has seen "a yellow," the proper answer is "a yellow what?"

This is not just a fact about our language, but rather about the domain of determinate being — the domain which is occupied by possible or actual entities which have specific limits and boundaries and are actually distinguishable from one another. It is not, for example, that redness and greenness are incompatible with each other — it depends upon what universe one is imagining and what things are supposed to be in it and how they are imagined to be red and green whether incompatibility arises or not. If being coloured is a way of occupying a spatial surface and different colour words are supposed to designate different ways of doing just this, then they will, indeed, have no function if both can apply to the same surface region of the same thing at the same time. But notice how many expressions about bearers of properties we have had to introduce in order to get to the notion of incompatibility. Where there is no potential incompatibility, there is no effective notion of limit or of determinateness, either.

There is, of course, a considerable danger of getting notions which are altogether too rich for the purpose at this early stage of the discussion. We need not, yet, get involved in rival theories about the nature of "things" on the one hand or about the nature of properties, classes, and universals on the other. All this argument points to is the fact that, in order to get a concept of determinate being, one has to structure one's discourse in such a way as to provide for a two-stage way of talking. We have first to mark out something which we want to talk about, then to assign specific properties to it.

Neither enterprise, by itself, will provide an intelligible reference to anything which lies in this domain. (If the notion of a property without a bearer fails to render an idea of a determinate entity, it seems obvious that the mere notion of a bearer of properties is in even worse shape. There are, however, evident difficulties about all this: for instance, to speak of a "mere bearer of properties" is to speak of something which has the property of being a bearer of properties so that we cannot quite express what is required in this way. These difficulties — or, at least the obvious ones — will turn up in due course.) The immediate result of this is that, if one conceives of the world referred to in discourse primarily as the domain of determinate being, it appears that there is a natural minimal unit of discourse and a natural structure around which logic ought to pivot.

XII

Presumably, the traditional subject-predicate form of propositions draws upon this fact. Equally, there is a tendency for later propositional logics to be cast in symbolic form in a way which suggests such translations back into English as "For any x ..." and "There is an x such that..." The xs specify members of some assumed universe of discourse and what follows the dots is a combination of reference to xs and the names of properties. Such forms, though more flexible and less committing than their Aristotelean predecessors preserve, in an obvious way, the two stage reference system.

The consequences of this development in our system of thought are numerous and dramatic. Once we begin to talk about a domain of entities which have distinct limits and which are associated with their properties in an intimate way, while remaining distinct from each other in a clear way, we can begin to develop highly complex logical schemes.

Because they are distinct and their properties are distinct, it appears to follow, automatically, that each of them can be said either to have a given property or not to have it; that no such entity can both have a given property and not have it, and that each such entity can be said to have a fixed identity and to be identical with itself and with nothing else. These features of such entities are perfectly general and apply to every one of them singly and all of them collectively. Classes and groups of such entities can be conceived on the same pattern, though paradoxes may be generated in special cases when the scheme is generalized to its limits.

Equally, if the scheme is conceived this way, we can hold that the properties in question apply not only to the propositional forms we adopt and the ways in which we choose to talk about things but to the things themselves. For, at this level, there is no way of distinguishing between the application of the principles to features of discourse and their application to features of reality.

Statements of the traditional laws of excluded middle, non-contradiction, and identity can be provided in either form as the need arises. For, so long, at any rate, as one stays within the domain of determinate being, it makes no sense to ask whether there might be things with contradictory properties or things which neither had nor failed to have a given property. Failure to measure up to these rules would be, after all, just what we would mean if we were to assert that we had on our hands an example of "indeterminate being."

What one can do at this level, of course, is to begin to develop the kind of theory about logic which seemed to be implied by the quotation I used in the first chapter from Professor Quine and the similar expression in *Principia Mathematica.* These very general features of propositions and of things do suggest to us that there are some propositions — like "Either Socrates is mortal or Socrates is not mortal" — which are true just because of the way in which logical particles are arrayed in them.

One can, indeed, hold the same view as a result of one's logical intuitions or because it seems a convenient postulate and then, of course, one need not hold that the properties in question hold beyond the domain of propositions and are actual features of the world. For it is only this way of sustaining such logical schemes and not anything intrinsic to them as statements of logical principle which ties discourse and the world in this way. But that would pose problems even for the professional logician if he should ever step outside his rather esoteric private preserve. In order to imagine a world which was not mirrored by his logic, he would have to have another set of propositional forms and limiting conditions. The notion that reality and logic somehow diverge has always been one which is difficult to grasp and, by definition, impossible to state.

It will be possible to carry this discussion further in the next chapter. For the moment, however, it is enough to be able to see that the domain of "determinate being" appears to be the traditional region of our logical discourse. It seems likely, therefore, that it will be possible to show that the traditional logic is not, literally, in opposition to the kind of "dialectical logic" which is being exhibited here but that it appears, in this context, as a stage in the development of the dialectic.

XIII

What is important, in this chapter, is to begin to see the direction of the development of the dialectic. So far we have merely been exploring some of the sub-concepts which can be seen as features of the concept of "determinate being" when the logical work of that notion as the synthesis of the two earlier basic concepts is explored. (The discussion, evidently, pivots heavily on an implicit theory of concepts which begins to take form when one searches for the kinds of consideration which are relevant to the exploration. This background theory, together with the significance of the dialectical problem as such is one of the signs of the fragmentation of the system into levels — the problem which will provide the central focus for the next chapter. The discussion here, however, is necessarily confined largely to an analysis of the concept of determinate being and to how the dialectic is to proceed from here.)

XIV

The direction of the dialectic becomes clear as soon as one begins to look at the consequences of the ideas already introduced. One of the consequences is the introduction of a problem about the notion of limit itself and about the generation of a system which provides for the possibility of the kinds of limits actually required. Both Kant and Hegel were fascinated by facets of this problem, as many other philosophers had been before, but what is important here is to see the way in which it arises in just the context provided by the notions I have already introduced.

In order for there to be the kinds of discrete things which can occupy the domain of determinate being each must be clearly and distinctly separable from all the others. But how is this achieved? Usually, of course, by reference to something else. The boundaries of France are intelligible by reference to a map which shows Germany, Belgium, Spain, the various seas and so on. Conceptual entities — brotherhood, friendship, enmity and so on — have their limits fixed by the functions of neighbouring concepts. A single entity would be, in a special sense, indistinct. If France were the name for everywhere, we could not fix it on a map, though we might fix it by reference to non-spatial entities. If we pass from "everywhere" to "everything" we either lapse back into the featureless domain of "pure being" or we begin to make distinctions between the idea of a totality and that of its components. But if each entity must have its limits established by some other entity, we seem to be on the way to a vicious infinite regress. For we cannot simply hold that the entities used as references are, in turn, limited by those which refer to them. That is true, but the cluster of entities thus established must, in its turn, be limited by reference to something else. We can fix all the countries of Europe on a map of the world and the world on a map of the solar system. But that, too, must have its limits.

We need not, I think, be committed to any obvious view about the ontological consequences of this difficulty. It suggests, at once, the antithesis of Kant's first antinomy: "Let us first take ... for granted that the world is finite and limited in space; it follows that it must exist in a void space, which is not limited..."[1] But the point of my argument is that this consideration applies (as Hegel seems certainly to have noticed) not just to space but to every orderly collection of determinate and limited entities. To demand limits is to demand to know what it is that limits. It is Hegel's problem of "something and another." Essentially, the difficulty is that the notion of limit demands a completed system of reference which will render the limits assigned to things intelligible but it makes such a system impossible.

---

[1] *Kritik der reinen Vernunft* (Immanuel Kants Werke, Band III, Berlin: Bruno Cassirer, 1913, p. 306.) The translation quoted is Meiklejohn's (London: Everyman, 1934), p. 260.

We cannot infer from this that the extent of physical space is limitless and the number of things in it innumerable or, indeed, that any of the systems of concepts which invoke the notion of limit and mark out regions of determinate being are subject to infinite expansion. What we can infer is that the crucial notion involved in the concept of determinate being — the notion of limit — is one which, if pressed, lands us in trouble. It is not that the world is necessarily very puzzling or even that "pure reason" left to itself creates conundrums like Kant's antinomies but simply that the concept of limit poses special problems.

Thus, whenever we look at "the world" (which, *here*, just means the subject matter of all our intelligible discourse) through a glass shaped to bring out the features of determinate being, we find that it fades into fuzziness at the edges. This does not necessarily mean that the objects which correspond to the requirements of determinate being — things in physical space may be, par excellence, such entities — are "unreal." It merely means that they are best regarded only as aspects of the real.

The point about the limits problem can be seen better if we notice that there are parallel problems about the other features of determinate being.

XV

The notion of a world of discrete entities each of which is quite distinct from all the others involves some notion of a "totality" of entities. But seen simply within the domain of determinate being, that notion poses notorious problems.

One of them is the paradox usually ascribed to Russell though it has relatives elsewhere, some of which are described by Russell and Whitehead in *Principia Mathematica*. Russell specifically introduces it as a problem which one meets when one wants to talk about "everything."[1]

The language he employs involves the notion of "class" — a notion which has not, except by name, appeared in this discussion. But this does not matter very much since a concept of "class" which will do here can be compounded out of notions which we already have: determinate entity, property, and plurality. A class, most commonly, is a way of ordering any plurality of determinate entities by reference to a property which they share. These ways of ordering become themselves, of course, determinate entities of a special kind and, in that way, may differ importantly from properties. The notion of "sharing" may be taken, provisionally, as metaphorical pending inquiry into its implications. We can also, for now, waive questions about the conceptual richness and the technicalities of talk about classes as such.

This much said, we can let Russell speak for himself: "The comprehensive

[1] (Second edition, Cambridge: Cambridge University Press) Chapter II, pp. 62-65; and *Introduction to Mathematical Philosophy* (London: George Allen and Unwin, 1919), p. 136ff. The quotation which follows is from the latter work.

class we are considering which is to embrace everything, must embrace itself as one of its members. In other words, if there is such a thing as 'everything,' then everything is something and is a member of the class 'everything.' But normally, a class is not a member of itself. Form now the assembly of all classes which are not members of themselves. This is a class: Is it a member of itself or not? If it *is*, it is one of those classes which are not members of themselves, i.e. it is not a member of itself. Thus of the two hypotheses — that it is and is not a member of itself — each implies its contradictory."

The paradox can be stated in a number of ways, but let me try to state it in a way which can be seen as immediately relevant to our difficulties here. We have seen that the domain of determinate being consists of entities which acquire their identities by reference to each other. The complete system of such references can be called "everything." Such a system can be regarded, amongst other things, as a class — that class from whose membership nothing is excluded. But it, itself, is something. By the rules of the domain of determinate being, if "being a member of" is a property, then each entity either has this property or it doesn't. But one of the members of this class will be the class of all classes which are not members of themselves. For there must be such a class if there is such a property as membership. (Classes need not have members, they can be null. Hence to admit that a given property can be talked about is to admit that the corresponding class can be talked about. We have already admitted classes, in the required sense, and therefore have to admit "membership.") Russell's dilemma follows. If such a class is a member of itself we deny that it is the class named. If it is not, we deny, equally, that it is the class named. Now we face the dilemma that the totality must have such a class as one of its members but cannot have it as one of its members because there can be no such class. We need not even regard this as a violation of the law of contradiction (which we have not yet talked about). We can simply regard it as a condition which prevents statements about the totality being effectively maintained.

Before we examine Russell's own and other proposed solutions to this difficulty, it is important to see that the difficulty, here, is not just that we are tripping over words. In *Principia*, Russell and Whitehead describe the family of paradoxes involved here as paradoxes about totalities. They are often called paradoxes of self-reference. A close relative, after all, is the common "liar" paradox. If I say "I am lying," then, if what I say is true, it is false and, if it is false, it is true. It cannot be included in its own reference, just as the class of all classes which are not members of themselves cannot be included in *its* own reference. But to talk about the totality of things does involve, necessarily, an internal self-reference and some way must be found of getting around this difficulty. (We can, indeed, set up a paradox more directly than Russell did though it involves more disputatious material:

If the concept of totality *refers* to everything else and *not* to itself then there is a wider concept which refers to both. But if it refers to itself *and* to everything else then there still must be another concept, namely the concept of that conjunction. The difficulty here seems to be that the notion of totality cannot be something added to the notions of its membership and yet it must be. For if it is "added on" then it does not, as advertised, have "everything" for its membership. But if it is not "added on" then it is not, as advertised, a proper class, or in Russell's word, "something.")

Russell's solution, of course, is well-known and is generally known as the theory of types. Its original formulation was very complex and numerous attempts have been made to simplify it. In essence, however, it amounts to a proposal to the effect that we should, as Quine puts it,[1] "think of all entities as stratified into so-called types." Thus there will be, if you like, levels of things and similar levels of discourse. If entities can be "stratified" into groups such as individuals, classes of individuals, classes of classes and so on, then discourse can be stratified similarly. Given this arrangement, we can make a rule that assertions may not refer to themselves in an offensive way. They may only refer to the next lowest "type." If they are to be referred to, it will be in an assertion cast in terms of the next highest "type." To quote again from Quine, "The rule is imposed, finally, that $(\alpha \in \beta)$ is to be a formula — $\in$ here is a sign meaning 'is a member of' — only if the values of β are of the next higher type than those of α."

Now this does, indeed, avoid the problem. But "avoid" is the right expression. Quine says, "The universal class V gives way to an infinite series of quasi universal classes, one for each type. The negation $-x$ ceases to comprise all non-members of x and comes to comprise only those non-members of x which are next lower in type than x."

Quine offers additional objections, but they do not concern us directly here. Russell's solution, in fact, is predicated upon the notion that it is not important or significant to be able to talk about the totality in the objectionable way. It is thus only intended to insulate language and thought from propositions which have the objectionable form while maintaining as much of the rest of discourse as seems possible. As such it succeeds. But our problem here is that, if the demonstration so far is sound, we *do* need to talk about the totality.

Quine has his own solution which needs to be discussed in the special context in which it arises. Russell originally treated the problem as a kind of natural phenomenon: talk about individuals, classes, classes of classes and so on arises naturally out of various kinds of discourse and particularly, in Russell's view, out of certain particularly well formulated parts of it which were what he thought of (whether rightly or not) as mathematics. In

[1] In "New Foundations for Mathematical Logic" now most conveniently available as Chapter V of *From a Logical Point of View* (New York: Harper and Row, 1963).

46

the same region are to be found various pieces of logical apparatus, overtly or implicitly. But this domain turned out to contain latent contradictions — expressions forbidden by its own rules. The problem was to excise the forbidden discourse with a minimum of dislocation and without distorting the basic framework.

Quine's "New Foundations" seems to read very differently. There is no doubt that he is concerned with the same domain and, in an important sense, with the same task. He says, indeed, that "A fair standard is provided by *Principia*; for the basis of *Principia* is presumably adequate for the derivation of all codified mathematical theory except for a fringe requiring the axiom of infinity and the axiom of choice as additional assumptions." But the aim of "New Foundations" is to simplify the *Principia* scheme by showing that it is derivable from a rather simpler set of quite arbitrary beginnings. Quine, in fact, offers some fifteen definitions, one postulate, and five rules. They seem to be offered simply on the pragmatic ground that they do the job.

On these terms there is no reason to suppose that one cannot get out of difficulties like Russell's paradox by building the rules so as to avoid the difficulty. And this is what Quine does, both in his original presentation in "New Foundations" and, subsequently, in a somewhat different way, in his *Mathematical Logic*. It is perhaps useful to see whether the point and nature of these rule changes can be seen here in a general way even though we cannot, obviously, stop to detail the whole system of logic in which they take place. As it happens, one of the five rules that Quine offered in "New Foundations" was, specifically, about the principle of membership as was his one postulate. The rule is originally introduced in a form which Quine describes this way: "[It] may be called the *principle of abstraction*; it provides that, given any condition '---' upon y, there is a class x (namely $\hat{y}$---) whose members are just those objects y such that---." Roughly, this means that for any designatable property, there will be an appropriate class and this is just the situation which led to Russell's paradox. Quine therefore proposes to remedy the original rule simply by adding the condition that *it* applies only to "stratified" formulas so that, whereas, in Quine's notation the original rule (called R3) read "If 'x' does not occur in $\varnothing$, $(\exists x) (y) (y \in x) \equiv \varnothing)$ is a theorem," the new rule reads "If $\varnothing$ is stratified and does not contain 'x'" and so on as in the original. Thus, there is not a *general* prohibition on so-called "unstratified" formulae and, as Quine says, many of the difficulties which result from Russell's formulation are obliterated. What now follows is that there is, he says, a "lack of any general guarantee of the existence of classes ... whose defining formulae are unstratified." Thus we cannot be forced to admit classes we don't want unless they meet the requirement of the rule. In a footnote dealing with a potential difficulty created by a theorem of Cantor's, Quine indeed says that if the difficulty did occur it would occur in the form of an assertion about the class "whose existence is disproved by Russell's paradox" and no such class is produced by his rule. Thus he takes Russell to have shown the non-existence of a certain class and his job to be to avoid a situation in which assertions can be made about it. But our difficulty is that we seem to be forced by the structure of the developing dialectic to talk about this class and we cannot adopt arbitrary rules as we please. It is true that Quine believes his system will still enable us to talk about the "universal class V to which everything belongs including V itself" but even if this is free of paradoxes itself, (and I suspect it is not), the arbitrary procedure for dealing with its sub-parts seems only acceptable on a pragmatic basis.

The same argument appears to hold in the end, against Quine's later proposal, in his *Mathematical Logic*[1] in which his original proposal is "supplanted by two rules, one of class existence and one of elementhood." But, "the rule of elementhood is such as to provide for the elementhood of just those classes which exist for (New Foundations)." This, skilfully, provides even more opportunity to say just what we want to say without getting into logical difficulties. But it still does so by providing arbitrary rules which have just the virtue and the defect of disguising from us the issues which seem to arise if we try to develop our rules in a non-arbitrary way.

I do not mean, of course, to decry such attempts which have done much to show how logical systems can be constructed nor to cast doubt on a performance whose brilliance it is not possible to convey here. The point I am trying to make is that there would seem to be no way, except a pragmatic one, to justify the highly esoteric rules which Quine produces any more than there seems to be a way to justify, independently of its ability to avoid the problem, Russell's elaborate theory of types. Indeed, it may be highly important to be able to say the things forbidden by these systems for in them lies one of the minor clues to the possibility of getting beyond the domain of determinate being.

XVI

The two difficulties we have so far seen in the domain of determinate being have to do with the notion of limit as a result of its implication of interdependence and the notion of totality which has so far proved unexpressible unless special *ad hoc* limits are placed on those objects of discourse which seem endemic to the domain of determinate being.

There is another difficulty suggested by the two I have been discussing and echoed, once again, in Kant's antinomies. For instead of saying that the description of the domain both requires a notion of totality and makes it impossible, except by arbitrary fiat, to get one, we might have said (as

---

[1] (Cambridge, Mass.: Harvard University Press, 1940). Second, revised edition, 1951.

the first difficulty anyhow seems to imply) that it makes it impossible for there to be either a finite or an infinite number of entities within it.

The first difficulty makes the point that there seems to be no way of establishing the domain with a finite number of entities — for we require an indefinitely expanding series of references to establish the separate identities of its members. But we can now ask whether, indeed, there could be an infinite membership. In some sense it is generally admitted not only that there could but that there is. For its membership includes whatever there is that can be talked about and meets the various conditions for membership in the domain. Individuable entities which can be talked about include, for instance, the so-called series of natural numbers. There are infinitely many of those — indeed, from some properties of that series various notions of "infinity" are commonly drawn. If one takes a series of numbers such as 1, 2, 3, 4, 5, 6, 7, and extends it indefinitely and another such as 2, 4, 6, 8, 10, 12, 14, and extends *that* indefinitely, two things are obvious: the second series is a "sub-set" of the first and it has the same number of components. It has been urged that a reasonable definition of an "infinite series" is one which has this property — the property of having a sub-set such that its components can be placed in a one-to-one correspondence with the whole membership of the original set. But this suggests that one could, for example, take away all the even numbers and still have just as many numbers as one started with. Cantor contended that infinite numbers, indeed, were just like this.[1]

It is said that Hilbert (whose fame is hardly less than Cantor's in mathematics) produced a sort of *reductio ad absurdam* of Cantor's claim that there were real infinite numbers and that they had this curious property — namely the property of remaining identical through operations of addition and subtraction. It took the form of a story about a hotel which had an infinite number of rooms. One day a traveller arrived and asked for a room. The desk clerk told him that each room was occupied and he began to leave. He was called back, however, by the manager who said he thought he could solve the problem. The manager at once picked up the telephone and pushed the button which connected him with every room at once. He told each guest to begin to move — the man in room one to room two, the man in room two to room three, and so on. "Now," he said to the guest, "I think you will find room one is vacant for you."[2]

The point of the story is that the hotel at all times had the same number of rooms. At all times, every room was occupied. Equally, at all times, it had the same number of guests. But it could always accommodate one more.

The difficulty, here, from the point of view of the problems of the domain

[1] See *Contributions to the Founding of the Theory of Transfinite Numbers* (translated by E. B. Jourdain, Chicago and London: Open Court, 1915).
[2] For one version of this, see J. A. Benardette, *Infinity* (London: Oxford University Press, 1964), pp. 113-119.

of determinate being, is that the hotel seems to lack just the crucial property — determinateness. How big does it have to be to have an infinite number of rooms each capable of accommodating a man? No size, of course. Is it bigger after the manager's telephone call? Of course not, it has the same number of rooms. (We can postulate, if we like, that all the rooms are identical in size — it makes no difference.) What is the aggregate weight of all its inhabitants? The question makes no *clear* sense. It seems that the number of stars or dogs or men or hotel rooms cannot be an infinite number in this sense unless we are prepared to change our rules and views about aggregating them. Nor does it seem that the manager in question *could* have installed all those telephones or had them installed unless by an infinite number of installers all acting in concert. For however many telephones were installed by a finite number of installers at work, they would only have been able to install a finite number in any finite time. However many they hooked up, there would always be another. Nor would an infinite amount of time necessarily have helped them — for however long they went on, they would always have had another telephone to install. It would be different, of course, if the properties of time changed because it *was* infinite. But then, how would we understand it? Infinities, in other words, cannot be *traversed* and cannot be aggregated in an ordinary way. And things lose some of their firmness when, like Hilbert's hotel, they become infinite.

On this basis it does not seem that there can be infinitely many numbers, either — so long as they are just considered as denizens of the domain of determinate being. For they cannot, say, be written down and then the space taken up by them measured. They cannot be thought of sequentially, either. The properties of an infinite *series* can be thought of. And infinite numbers, like Cantor's aleph-null can be thought about and *their* properties analyzed. But the sequence of natural numbers, considered as so many *distinct individuals* is another matter. For they, then, become as curious as Hilbert's hotel.

Perhaps there is a domain within which we can do better than this. But it is not the domain of determinate being.

XVII

For the moment, however, we must pass to another (and, at this point, the last) difficulty which is presented by the notion of determinate being. It arises from a consideration of the fact that we were forced to introduce the twin notions of "property" and "bearer of properties" in order to escape from the indeterminateness of the previous category.

The trouble now is that we cannot, effectively, unite these notions. If we think of them, for the moment, as "subjects" and "predicates" in a rather traditional way, it becomes evident that we can only speak of the "subjects" by assigning them "predicates," but that the "predicates" are only fully intelligible when they are assigned to their "subjects." In some way, all we can say about Smith, or a stone, or prime numberhood is exhausted by the properties we can assign to them. So that they must, in some way, seemingly either be identical with the list of these properties or else become not, like Locke's substances, "something I know not what" but "something, I *could* not *say* what." But they *cannot* be identical. Smith can be angry and stupid and fat but it is not in his fatness nor in his stupidity that his anger lies.

This is one of the peculiarities which may lead to one of philosophy's oldest and richest debates: shall we vest reality, as *perhaps* Plato wished, in a domain which is composed of those special things of which the names of properties are the names? Or shall we, as perhaps Aristotle wished, hold that the things which have the properties are the core of reality and the properties have their locale in them? If we choose the "Platonic" alternative we shall, of course, oddly have made individual things out of properties or universals — given them a life and world of their own in which they function as though they were individual things. But if we choose the "Aristotelean" alternative, shall we not, equally oddly, end up talking of individual things as clusters of properties? For what we know of them is that they are instances of or instantiations of such and such properties.

At any rate, this seems true at the simple level on which we are now proceeding. Much later, I will try, in the appropriate place (Chapter 6), to talk seriously about the "universals" problem.

For now, the point is a simple one. We found that we had to indulge in a two-stage analysis of our discourse in order to get determinacy. We needed both properties and their bearers. Now the trouble is that everything there is is accounted for, either way, by the bearers or by the properties. But we lack, in this region, a concept which will unify them. They have to have, and cannot have, the right kind of unity.

XVIII

So, finally, the domain of determinate being breaks down. Everything must have a limit, but there cannot be a limit to everything; we must have a concept of totality, but we cannot get one without doing violence to what we have already accepted; the domain must be finite and yet cannot be; properties and their bearers must be a unity but each swallows up the whole and the unity eludes us.

Determinate being is a notion which is necessary for understanding anything we can talk about but it must be transcended. How? If the dialectic works, we ought to be able to exhibit the next concept once again by the twin process employed before: we see what the concept excludes and we combine that with what the system has provided us with but so far been unable to employ.

Oddly, the difficulty which immediately faces us here is an embarrassment of riches: determinate being, since it embodies fixedness, excludes change, time, and process. Some notion of at least two of these is, of course, embodied in the dialectical system itself. Equally, however, determinate being excludes every kind of systematic unity. Again, the dialectical system itself provides, in some measure at least, an implied notion of systematic unity.

It would seem that it is to the problem of systematic unity that we should, however, turn at this point: for it was the absence of an adequate notion of unity in diversity which posed the problems which arose directly from a consideration of the crucial components of the notion of determinate being. Change, time, and process seem to belong to another level of the dialectic. The problem of unity stares at us at this level and seems the immediate cause of the conceptual breakdown. The change, time, and process issues will, what is more, turn up naturally at an appropriate point. It will turn out, in fact, that a crucial component of such notions can only be developed as a result of the discussion which follows about systematic unity. It will be possible shortly — and more clearly again in the next chapter — to exhibit the decision involved here in a clearer light. But the reader should notice that, as the dialectic becomes more complex, the problem of alternative steps in construction becomes more acute. Hegel appears to have been content to accept the possibility of alternatives: the number and arrangement of the "categories" is not the same in the *Science of Logic* as in the "Shorter Logic" which is the first part of the *Encyclopedia of the Philosophical Sciences*. The significance of this issue, however, cannot be estimated until more material is at hand.

Meanwhile, the reasonable move seems to be to proceed to attempt to produce a suitable concept of systematic unity. In order to see what ought to go into it, how it can be derived, and what its relation is to the rest of the system, we need to examine the procedure used in the earlier occasions of dialectical advance. We started with what I called pure being, proceeded to show that what it excluded was pure disjunction and that it was this exclusion which occasioned its failure to work. We then noticed that, collectively, they failed to work because of what they collectively excluded, namely determinateness, and that the synthesis of these notions, called "determinate being," did solve the immediate problems.

We now find that determinate being breaks down into a number of subdomains, the chief of which appear to be that of the bearers of properties and that of the properties themselves on the one hand, and the domain of the limited and fixed and that of the unlimited and unspecifiable on the other. All of these require unification for intelligibility but no unification is provided within the domain. Thus the argument for proceeding to a discussion of systematic unity rather than to the other domain — time, change, and process — is, principally, that the exclusion of systematic unity is the precise cause of the breakdown.

Here, however, we have another choice to make. Is the new concept to be related to determinate being in the way that pure disjunction was related to pure being or in the way that determinate being, itself, was related to both the earlier concepts? Apart from general questions about uniformity of progression within a dialectical system, this question genuinely makes a difference. For the choice is between regarding the new concept as a synthesis of the fragmented components of determinate being and regarding it simply as what is referentially excluded by determinate being. The concept required, presumably, will be different depending upon one's view though the difference in this particular case might well seem minimal since we could imagine a concept called "systematic unity" doing either job. Actually, however, it seems to be the case that what we are faced with is simply the collapse of the concept of determinate being. We have exhibited, if anything, just its failure to do any work without some complement. Its fragmented components do not seem, literally, capable of any "synthesis" and cannot be given quite the degree of dialectical independence which we might reasonably assign to the earlier major components — though the question is not so easy to decide as one might wish and it is hard to set it in a clear light.

One might say that it is easy to imagine that philosophers should try to view pure being, or determinate being, as the whole of reality and produce pictures of the world, in the first case like that of Parmenides and, in the second case, like a modern logical atomist. But though some philosophers have thought plurality somehow the decisive factor in our understanding of the real, it is hard to think of anyone whose view it is that reality is pure disjunction. Furthermore, both sets of properties and bearers of properties have been imagined in some sense to be exhaustive of the world, at least by some philosophers at moments when certain features of the universals controversy occupied their attention rather single-mindedly. And the notion of a real which is finally unexpressible just because it outruns the conceptual reach of what I have called determinate being is perhaps not so uncommon.

Internally, in the system, however, the components which feature in the breakdown have no independent derivation: they were simply produced by analysis of the features of determinate being. Each of the major components developed earlier had, as part of its derivation, reference to what one of the other components excluded, and thus represented a new feature of the system. Accordingly, if we were now to search for a synthesis of the fragments of "determinate being" we could only produce a whole which was either identical with the original or a mere re-arrangement of it.[1]

---

[1] It will turn out, when we come to develop an account of the most pervasive structural properties of the dialectic that the "cause of the breakdown" is just that each member of a pair of dialectical concepts focusses a certain level of generality in a particular way. In so doing the concept excludes an alternative focus — as it must if it is to do any work. But this alternative is part of the significance of the given level of generality and thus, it turns out, is required for the completion of the function of the original concept. This is

XIX

What we need then, to make any progress, is a concept which will reflect those features which are excluded by determinate being *and* are the cause of the conceptual breakdown.

What we want, almost literally, is to turn the notion of determinate being inside out — to find a kind of counterpart of it which emphasizes just what it suppresses and suppresses just what it emphasizes. That such a concept will have defects which are the counterparts of those of determinate being seems likely enough, but this we have, surely, already come to suspect. We know there is more to come.

A concept of systematic unity appropriate to the purpose here can be constructed quite simply. It will help to use a concrete example here, even though parts of it will be misleading just because it is a concrete example and the domain of determinate being and the counterpart I am trying to construct here appear to have for their membership only entities whose descriptions are limited by certain logical requirements and exclude certain features having to do with time, change, and process which are normally features of concrete objects. Leaving that aside, however, suppose that we want to talk about badgers and that we want to focus our attention on a certain badger. In order to do this we have to find some way of making our references perfectly precise, not only so that we will talk in such a way as not to confuse our badger with a skunk or some other quite closely related animal, but also so that we do not confuse it with any other badger. We can, of course, achieve the first object by being quite clear about the colour, odour-producing properties, size, habits, and so on of badgers and the second by making sufficiently accurate references to the spatial and temporal locations of the animal concerned.

But these are rather provisional procedures and only work because we have certain kinds of systematic knowledge and make certain kinds of special assumptions:

We sort out distinguishing characteristics by reference to what we know about the other animals which observers are likely to meet and which might prove confusing. No one actually tries to assemble *all* the facts about badgers. Some of them are irrelevant and, in any case, there is no limit to the facts about anything. We can describe what the badger looks like under lights at different intensities and multiply our distinctions indefinitely, or we can describe how it reacts to drugs, environmental changes, and other animals and go on multiplying our facts without logical limit.

Nor are there special "core facts" which are *just* about badgers or just about *this* badger. We can say it is two feet long, weighs twenty pounds, and

the kind of relation which we have seen to hold between pure being and pure disjunction and which holds, here, between determinate being and systematic unity. But all this can be made more intelligible in later chapters.

is brown and grey. But its length can only be stated in relation to something else, a foot-rule, another animal, or the shrub in the garden. Its weight is another "relational" concept and its colour is a dispositional property having to do with its potential relation to light rays or an even more complex relational property involving it, light rays, and our eyes and minds.

Given an individual badger it may be true of it and of it alone that it occupies a given region of space and time. But this is a rather arbitrary notion as we seem to be learning to our cost. For it is only for convenience that we say that its limits coincide with the outermost points touched by its body surface. Is the plant which grows the badger's food less a part of it than the glandular secretions which digest the food? The badger can stand some change in the surrounding plant life or in its digestive processes but it is related in much the same way to both. It must be able to dig a hole, find something to eat, and water to drink, and have darkness in which to play and hunt. It and its environment are indissoluble and there is no easy way of saying where the badger ends. If the sun shines longer and its hunting day is shortened it is affected in much the way it would be if it lost its claws or some of its teeth.

We are gradually driven to the view that to talk about badgers is to choose a way of ordering and marshalling all the facts about the world. Some, like the facts about the present state of the surface of Mars, recede into comparative insignificance, and would surely not deserve mention in a study of the nature and prospects of badgers, while others, like the availability of young rabbits for eating, become of pressing importance. But the badger environment includes them all and there are only shadings into unimportance and no absolute lines of division into what is and is not a part of the badger environment. Nor can we ultimately distinguish the badger from its environment. In this respect, what goes for badgers in general goes for any particular badger. To talk seriously about a particular badger is to talk about a particular way of marshalling these facts.

If we generalize from this example we can see that there is an alternative to the scheme for talking about things which I called determinate being.

Instead of regarding things as separable individuals, collectively instantiating the whole domain, we can think of the domain as being divided into a set of ordered perspectives, each of which contains the whole but differs from the others in centre of focus. There will be one such perspective for each of the original components. Each of them will have the same content, but a different focus.

The point to notice, here, is that we still have a kind of "determinateness," but entities are no longer separate from each other in the same way. They all have the same properties, but they are ordered in different ways. The environment of rabbits is the same world as the environment of badgers, and rabbits and badgers are not, in this scheme, *finally* separable. But we can distinguish the perspectives of each. Typewriters are related to the whole of the same world, but are neutral to more of it than rabbits and so the typewriter "focus" is less interesting.

It is important to explore this in a little more depth. Though the pressures of fact have tended to make us more willing of late to take the "environmental" view about rabbits, badgers, and sparrows, it is not necessary or interesting to think about typewriters in this way. But this should not mislead us into thinking that it is just because there are special facts about living things that we *can* take this point of view. To identify a particular typewriter, so as to make absolutely sure that you haven't mixed it up with anything else in the world, you would have to have a complete system in which everything there was or is has its place. To refer to the typewriter positively, you need, negatively, to refer to all the rest of the system. There is thus, a typewriter perspective which focuses everything in just this way. The typewriter place in such a scheme is determined by all the other places and they are its environment.

XX

It is now interesting to notice how the original problems about determinate being disappear and others take their place.

We do not any longer need to fear the "boundary" and "limit" problems. There are as many perspectives as we care to choose but, since all of them have the same content, the choice is relatively unimportant. Things have no sharp edges, but we no longer care — we have another way of identifying them. We do not need a *totality* of entities because the totality is built into each entity and the totality of focusses cannot be another entity in the way that, say, the "class of all classes" might be. We need no longer fear infinities for the same reason that the "limit" problem is not worrying.

But there are difficulties which may have been made less obvious than they should have been because of the misleading properties of the concrete example. This scheme gives us the needed notion of unity, but the notions of individuality which give it body were, in fact, drawn by making use of examples which sound more natural in the preceding domain. Given that we have a reason to talk about rabbits, we can see that we may want to expand the rabbit notion to the rabbit-and-environment notion and thence to the notion of a world as rabbit-environment. But what gives these perspectives their significance? How, in this domain, in which everything has the same content do we make the initial distinctions? And what significance do they have?

It turns out, surely, that they are just two sides of one coin. Anything can be looked at from the standpoint of determinate being as a particular thing and from the standpoint of systematic unity as a way of focussing the world, a kind of perspective on the whole. Determinate being demands a notion of systematic unity and vice versa. Each attempt to deal with one of

56

the domains leads to a legitimate demand for the other. Everything which could be talked about has a place in each scheme and is, in itself, neither one nor the other.

Collectively, moreover, this "everything" is a little queer. It is not just that this two-stance way of looking at things is somehow unsatisfactory on the ground that we cannot see a perspective from which to grasp both, but also that, as will emerge in the next chapter, we are still at the level of entities whose nature is purely logical. Anything which can be an object of reference has a place in both these domains. Only entities which fail to meet the purely logical requirements of either or both are excluded (square circles and married bachelors, for example). So far we are without the apparatus with which to distinguish the actual from the possible though we can distinguish the impossible. Furthermore, we cannot yet account for the change and process which are endemic to the developing system itself; much less can we account for the activity which would make such a system manifest. Indeed, a latent conceptual clash is already becoming obvious: both determinate being and systematic unity are static notions but the system in which they have a place is not. Collectively, they seem to provide a place for every entity about which we might want to talk, but scarcely for every mode of talking.

Before we can go further, however, we must try to tidy up the system and explore its levels and its rules. That is the business of the next chapter.

Chapter 3

Levels, rules, and domains

We have already encountered a fragmentation problem: the concepts I have used and introduced seem naturally to order themselves on a number of different levels. There is a kind of central core which has formed the primary locus of attention and which includes such concepts as pure being, pure disjunction, determinate being and systematic unity. Reflecting on this and bound up with it are a cluster of concepts through which the rules of the system become intelligible. Growing out of these in turn is a theory of concepts as such and, with it, the concept of the system itself. If we move in the other direction — toward the subject matter on which the core concepts function — we find at least two other levels. On one of them we can develop specific rules for dealing with the "logic" of the members of each domain represented by core concepts. On the other the members of those domains themselves appear.

The charts which often accompany editions of Hegel's works and commentaries on them are usually confined to what I have called the "core" level and represent it in two dimensions. Hegel was certainly aware of the levels problem but it does not always emerge clearly in his logic. There is a tendency to regard the concepts which form the core as simply "developing" in some rather mysterious way or, alternatively, to regard the whole thing as the working out of a single, rather mysterious, "triad" principle. I have already argued that Hegel regards the dialectical movement, which is a property of the system, as one of the "core" notions and introduces "becoming" in a way which makes the dialectical advance more mysterious than it needs to be. Again, there seems to be a major difficulty posed by the division of his dialectic into triads within triads: The *Logic* consists of a major triad composed of Being, Essence, and Notion. Within each component are numerous levels of sub-triads. Thus there is one direction in which movement is fairly straightforward from Pure Being to the Absolute Idea and another in which there is an indefinite fragmentation. How far can one go from triad to triad by way of further specification downwards?

How far downwards must one go for intelligibility? And exactly how are these directions related to each other? I leave these questions to Hegel scholars but their answers depend partly on the development of an adequate theory about the "core level."

What I propose to do in this chapter is to develop, as far as possible, given the material now at hand, the necessary theory. In the course of that, the general principles of dialectical development will become as clear as I can make them and the rules of procedure I have been using will be shown to depend upon them. At the same time, some general features of the system and of the theory of concepts which it seems to entail should begin to emerge. After that, I shall look at some of the questions which naturally arise about the membership and logical governance of the categories I have been talking about: pure being, pure disjunction, determinate being and systematic unity.

II

The reader will have noticed that, so far, four different procedures have been in use and the possibility of another has been suggested in the course of the development of the system. One of them was used to locate the original concept, a second to develop its internal structure, a third to develop its dialectical counterpart, and a fourth for what I called the "synthesis" of the relevant references of the two original concepts.[1] A fifth was suggested — by way of reference to the structure of the system itself — as being necessary for any further advance in the system.

Evidently, the first procedure has and should have only one application since its function was to produce, somehow, the original concept. The third and fourth procedures, which embody the notions of dialectical alternation and synthesis (however unsatisfactory those words are to convey what has been going on) ought, presumably, to be basic to the whole system. So should the second procedure which is more like the more common kinds of conceptual analysis. The need for a fifth procedure suggests, obviously, some difficulty in the system which needs to be clarified. In any case, all these procedures need to be given precision and some of them, at least, should either be stated in the form of rules and general principles or shown to be capable of leading to the development of rules and general principles. The relations between all these components then need to be explored.

---

[1] This "fourth procedure" is the most crucial of the whole enterprise. It is important to notice that what is available for synthesis is not the concepts which express the categories but the uniting property which they share ("being" in the case of the first two categories) and their joint specific exclusion reference ("determinacy" in this case). The result of this synthesis is, therefore, "determinate being." An attempt to synthesize the categories (or the concepts expressing them) *in toto* would surely result in a contradiction and, in any case, would produce a category which, if it were not absurd, would render its predecessors redundant. But this will emerge in the later discussion.

The procedure for getting the first concept involves three premises: (1) that rational discourse is possible; (2) that, if it is possible, there is some one most general concept which is entailed by all parts of it; (3) that there is a way of locating it which may fairly be regarded as "objective"; and (4) that the first three premises are capable of being defended in a way which does not already presuppose that we have a developed "logic."

The first premise follows from the fact that we can talk about the problem in the way that I did in the first chapter. We find, that is, that we cannot question the fact that we are engaged in rational discourse, for such a question would presuppose what it was supposed to put in question. But we find, equally, that whatever "theory" about logic is put forward, we can, in fact ask questions about it and demonstrate that the process is intelligible. It also follows from this that the fourth premise is not in conflict with the first. For we can ask the kinds of questions which occupied the first chapter independently of holding any *one* of the theories there put forth even though any *particular* question may seem to entail some theory about logic. We can entertain the possibility of a variety of theories about logic, in other words, by playing them off against each other and thus see the plurality without special commitment.

In fact we can see, at this point, a crude kind of dialectic developing of itself: for the doubts raised by any particular theory naturally suggest the alternatives which that theory excludes.

The second premise presumably follows from the way in which the first is defended: if there is a domain over which rational discourse holds sway, then it must, at least, have one uniting property — the property of being just that domain. If there is no such domain, then rational discourse is not possible. But we have already shown that it is possible. The concept of this domain is the one that the system demands as its starting point.

This does not guarantee that the requirement of the third premise can be met. The procedure used, however, was to look for the most general kinds of distinction which could be made within any constructed domain over which rational discourse would hold sway — such as the distinction between form and content — and then to search for a concept which met this requirement. That this procedure is also not in conflict with the fourth premise can be seen from the fact that all logical systems are designed as ways, in part, of making exactly this kind of distinction. A concept which is beyond this distinction, therefore, must necessarily be free from special commitment to any of them. It is also, for that reason, perspective neutral and cannot, therefore, be "subjective" though it will only be "objective" if that expression merely means "what is not subjective" and not "what falls on one side of the subjective-objective distinction." It appears, however, that it is only this looser sense which is needed. It remains true that a concept of the generality required cannot, literally, be expressed in our ordinary discourse — it cannot be given precise form or used to make distinctions in the world. But it can be seen to be entailed by our ordinary discourse.

This procedure, then, seems to be defensible and to lead to the kind of concept which I called "pure being." To get beyond this we require two other techniques. One of them consists simply in the analysis of the structure of the existing concepts by means of an exhibition of its conceptual function and an analysis of what would be required for this function to be dischargeable. This is what I referred to as the second procedure — the way of getting at the internal structure of each concept — and there is nothing difficult in principle about it. The "function" of a concept in this sense is just the "logical work" that it does. An account of this can be derived from the reasons which are given for introducing it in the first place. The "function" of "pure being," for example, is to provide an account of the unifying properties of the domain to which rational discourse applies. We can then ask what is needed for this job and the answer will be as precise — or imprecise — as the reasons for its introduction.

The other technique required for getting from one concept which forms part of the "core" of the system to another is predicated on three general doctrines: (1) that no system capable of any logical work can have only one concept or, alternatively, that a concept always entails a system of concepts; (2) that, within any system, the explication of the functions of a given concept will always suggest the need for at least one additional concept and (3) that in the "core structure" of a dialectical system, the concept immediately required can always be constructed from a consideration of the specific "exclusion" references of the preceding concept or some preceding set of concepts. Together, (1), (2), and (3) cover two different procedures — the one used for getting from "pure being" to "pure disjunction" and again from "determinate being" to "systematic unity" and the one employed in passing from "pure being" and "pure disjunction" (taken together) to determinate being. These will be dealt with, here, as far as is necessary, as separate cases: evidently a special justification is required in order to sustain the distinction between cases in which one passes from a single concept to its successor from those in which one passes from two or more concepts taken together to their joint successor. Where concepts are dealt with collectively, a justification will also be required for the particular clustering employed.

III

Stated baldly in this way, the doctrines upon which the procedures employed depend appear to be suspended above the system like the stage machinery hanging over a play. That is not intended. They are supposed to develop as the system develops but, since they *can* be stated independently and since they do function over wide ranges of the system, they also have a measure of independence.

This suggests that the reasons for them can also be stated in a more general way than appears immediately in the development of the system, and it should be possible to develop them in a way which will make it possible to decrease their dependence on any particular part of the system. If so, this would have two desirable effects: one of them would be to make the system partially independent of particular mistakes in reasoning in passing from one phase of the core level to the next. (Otherwise the whole system would collapse like a house of cards if a single mistake could be shown in its development. This is important if only because no one can reasonably expect a human being to produce a completely error-free structure of this complexity.) The other (equally important) advantage is that, if some measure of independence can be established, it will be possible to develop rules, or approximations of them, by which stages in the dialectical advance can be checked.

Admittedly, in any logical demonstration, there comes a time when you either see the point or you don't. If you don't see that a syllogism is valid, you can be shown Venn diagrams or Euler circles. If that doesn't work, you can be informed of the formal rules for validity in such cases and if that, in turn, doesn't satisfy you, the rules can be traced back to the theory of the syllogism. If you accept each and every stage but still don't see that this particular syllogism is valid, the game is up. Each stage, however, does have its demonstrative advantage and is apt to reveal a kind of error which its predecessor would not. Thus there is an advantage in producing rules or even — as in the present case — approximations to them.

IV

The first doctrine is a general statement about conceptual systems of a certain kind — namely those capable of performing any logical work, task, or function — and is to the effect that such systems are necessarily pluralistic. There are a number of ways of approaching this problem. The obvious one in this context is simply to point out that our conceptual functions can only be delineated by designating what it is that a concept excludes as well as what it includes. Thus there must always be at least two concepts involved, actually or potentially. It can be added that the only possible exception to this rule would seem to be a concept so general as to prevent the possibility of any notion of exclusion. But we have seen, in fact, that what appears to be the most general concept imaginable — the concept of pure being — does not prevent this possibility.

It is important for our present purpose to be able to show that the doctrine can be developed from just the system we are dealing with but it can, of course, be justified independently. For all logical systems involve some notion of exclusion and depend upon this fact for their intelligibility. To say everything is, equally, to say nothing and this is one way of stating the general principle of non-contradiction. (However one puts it, to say every-thing is to say whatever it is that cancels out what you mean to say.) Hence there are no one-concept systems.

No doubt there are other ways of justifying this doctrine. The particular ways I have chosen, however, are useful here because they help to introduce the general notion of dialectical alternation.

The second doctrine is equally straightforward and appears, in any case, to follow from the first. If, that is, there are no systems of the required kind which have, as their membership, only one concept, it will follow that the functions of any one concept cannot effectively be carried out unless some additional concept is forthcoming. Hence an analysis of this function, if adequate, will show signs of deficiency. (It does not follow that we will always be able to see the deficiency. There might be any number of reasons preventing us from carrying out the analysis.)

The third doctrine is more troublesome. Issues and concepts which seem peculiar to dialectical systems as such are obviously involved in it and such notions as "exclusion reference" and "concept immediately required" suggest difficulties.

It will be useful, as a preliminary, to enquire as to how far the properties referred to are shared, generally, with all or a wide range of conceptual systems and in what respects they are peculiar to what I have called the "core structure" of the kind of dialectical system I am trying to develop here.

All concepts, as I have argued earlier, have an "exclusion reference" and the possibility of conceptual systems as such seems to depend on it. Further-more, we can distinguish for any such case a "general exclusion reference" and a "specific exclusion reference." For example, the concept of "yellow-ness" generally excludes everything which is not yellow and specifically ex-cludes the concepts of other colours. The concept would not identify anything if it did not exclude everything else in a general way but, equally, it would not work if it did not refer specifically to the localized system of concepts which we use to distinguish colours.

Both these features seem to be crucial to the meaningfulness of discourse. To know what "yellow" means, you must be able to discover the general range of concepts in which it has its home. Given this, there is some hope of learning its meaning by some kind of ostensive definition but, failing this, no amount of "pointing" and no other combination of experiential and definitional activities will reveal it. (Consider the position of a man trying to learn what "yellow" means and having things pointed out to him. The pointing will not help until he discovers whether he is looking for geometrical shapes, biological properties, colours or whatever. By judicious choice of objects he may "learn" from the pointing that he is concerned with both colouredness in general *and* the colour yellow. But, initially, if he is given a road sign, a dingo dog and a box of matches to look at and he knows nothing else, he will have to decide whether the word is the name of a range of geometrical shapes, a cluster of organic materials, or a colour.)

Generally, then, there is a specific exclusion reference for any concept and what it points to is the range of concepts which belong to the same reference system. Since the concepts that we deal with are not often very precise, such references usually have some degree of ambiguity about them. Furthermore, for many cases, it is not possible to construct the remaining concepts or any one of them from such references. For some cases — numbers and components of things like a periodic table of elements — missing concepts can be filled by such references. Mainly, what one gets are clues and they are more or less useful depending upon the kind of system specifically involved.

Again, except for special cases, the notion of a "next concept" is not appropriate. Colours can be ordered given a theory about them such as one detailing their relations to wave-lengths of light but, just as colours, they do not seem to fall into a natural order. It may be that there is some natural order for every legitimate series of concepts, but there does not seem, a priori, any reason to believe this.

What we need if we are to sustain the doctrine that "in the 'core structure' of dialectical systems the concept immediately required can always be constructed from a consideration of the specific 'exclusion' references of the preceding concept or some preceding set of concepts" is a detailed account of some specific properties of such systems.

We must, therefore, look rather more closely at the components of the system now under construction.

v

I shall argue that the features we have to work with include these: (a) the core system consists of a sequence of concepts each of which refers, in a different way, to the whole of our possible universe of discourse; (b) the first concept lies on the highest level of abstraction possible within such a system; (c) its successor lies on the same level of abstraction but includes what the first concept excludes; (d) the first two concepts will require a joint successor which lies on a lower level of abstraction;[1] (e) there is a pattern derivable from (b), (c), and (d) which will be repeated throughout the system; and (f) the last concept in the system will lie on the lowest level of abstraction appropriate to such a system.

If I can sustain the position that (a) through (f) are actually features of the system, it will be possible to argue for the following conclusions: the system in question, unlike many apparent systems of concepts, does have an order. The notion of "next appropriate concept" will, therefore, have a meaning.

[1] The expression "abstraction" — and its implied correlate "concreteness" — present one of the crucial problems of the system. They must be understood, if at all, in just the sense introduced into the discussion which follows.

Each concept which is a member of such a system will have an "exclusion reference" to the rest of the system in a quite determinate way. The manner of this exclusion will tend to reveal the next required concept and, at any rate, the materials will be at hand for the construction of such a concept.

Let us, then, examine (a) through (f). It is obvious that "pure being" and, say, "determinate being" do not differ in extensional reference. It is the same world or the same universe of discourse whose unity is expressed by the notion of "pure being" and whose capacity for a specific kind of plurality is expressed in and through "determinate being." This completeness of extensional reference is in no way undermined and *could* not, indeed, be changed by the pattern of argument which leads from one of these notions to another. If it did, we would have made some kind of mistake in identifying the specific exlusion reference of the original concept, just as if we thought that colours had specific exclusion references to numbers, or biological concepts to religious ones. For apart from their specific characters, the only general characters which concepts like "pure being" and "determinate being" have consists of their general reference to the whole region over which discourse runs. Hence (a) seems reasonable enough. At this point (b) —the assertion that the first concept lies on the highest level of abstraction possible within such a system — seems to need no special defence. It is another way of stating that the requirements for finding a first concept for the system have been met.

The expression "abstraction" and its implied correlate "concreteness" do, however, need explication: pure being is not "abstract" in the sense that it represents some isolated features of a world which can be considered on a single level. And the last category, dialectical individuality, will not turn out to be "concrete" in the sense that it displays the whole of reality exhibited as a totality on a single level. Rather, the position is this: pure being emphasizes the unity of the universe of discourse and of things by calling attention to the links which form the most general features of words, reference techniques, and things. Dialectical individuality, at the opposite pole of the system, emphasizes the unity of things by calling attention to the ways in which their unity is determined by a kind of individuality which establishes their inter-relatedness. The most general structural properties of systems are exhibited at one pole and the internal features of individuals at the other. The point, in part, is to show that the two poles require one another — that the apparent dichotomy is intelligible as a dialectical unity.

Whether this is a meaningful notion or not depends, of course, on whether the system can be developed. If it can, the meanings which properly attach to such expressions as "abstract" and "concrete" will be inferrable from the progress of the system. If not, the situation cannot be rescued by defending the procedures being detailed here.

Initially, of course, we do require some approximate notion of what is involved. And it can be seen that there is a distinction between structures of the categories and what is structured by them. Pure being emphasizes structure to the exclusion of all else. The last category must emphasize what is structured and yet show the appropriateness of all the structures.

Given (a) and (b), there should not be much difficulty with (c) — the assertion that the second concept of the system will lie on the same level of abstraction. Given that the first concept requires a second to make the system work, the second concept will be found in what the first excludes at the level relevant to the system in which it has its place. What it excludes will either be at the same level or at a lower level of abstraction. But any lower level of abstraction would include, in a different way, what the original concept included and would not be, therefore, what the first concept specifically excluded but rather part of what it excluded and part of what it included. It could not, therefore, literally be what the first concept required to make it work at its own level.

From (c), it is not difficult to move to (d) — the assertion that the original concepts will require a joint successor and that this successor will lie on a lower level of abstraction. For the original level of abstraction will have been exhausted. At the same time, it is certain that the system will be incomplete at this point since the two original ways of conceptualizing the universe of discourse will be opposed to one another — one emphasizing unity and the other disjunction, for instance, or one determinate plurality and the other systematic unity. The solution to this clash, since it cannot be found at the original level of abstraction, will have to be found at a lower level. Now the two original concepts will necessarily have something in common — whatever defines their level of abstraction at least — and will also, therefore, have a joint specific exclusion. These features will be the clue to the next level of abstraction and they will have to be taken conjointly.

We can now pass to (e) and show that this pattern will be a continuing one. From a "synthesis" of the sort envisaged by (d), it will obviously be possible to create a situation in which (c) occurs again unless we are at the last concept of the system which should reveal itself by the absence of the possibility of an appropriate "specific exclusion." It will, of course, only do this if there are no more possible concepts of the sort the system requires but this is a notion which it will only be possible to deal with at the end of the investigation. This end would be, however, as asserted in (f), by definition, the lowest level of abstraction in the relevant system since, if it were not, further concepts would be forthcoming.

VI

It is now possible to argue for the necessary conclusions. Obviously, the notion of "next appropriate concept" will have a meaning. It is almost equally obvious that the kind of procedure made possible by the properties of the system will always provide materials for the "next concept." How it does so, however, will always depend upon the analysis of the function of the concept in the specific sense of function given earlier. Thus no two transitions will be alike. One evident difficulty, however, is that there is always a danger of "jumping" levels of abstraction — of missing a stage or stages in the dialectic. But this depends simply on the success of the analysis of the functions of the specific concepts and on the plausibility of contentions, following from those analyses, that the required specific exclusion references have been found. Equally, there is a difficulty which arises from the fact that the series of levels of abstraction might not be finite. The issues involved in this kind of question seem, however, best left until we have a better developed system to work with.

VII

There remains, however, at least one immediate complication. At the end of the last chapter, I suggested that, to advance the argument, we would have to rely on certain developing features of the system itself. The concepts with which that discussion finished — determinate being and systematic unity — appeared to be concepts of static states. The system, itself, appeared to reflect an orderly process of change. A significant way, therefore, of reflecting the content of our universe of discourse seems to be reflected by the system but not, as yet, in any of the "core concepts." Furthermore, this may be a reason for the state of affairs which the "core structure" seemed, at that point, to leave us with: determinate being and systematic unity seemed to be mutually entailing but also mutually exclusive and there seemed no effective way of unifying them. In the four procedures which I have just been outlining, however, there is no evident account of how one might go about drawing solutions from the "higher" levels of the system.

It is, nonetheless, natural enough that it should be necessary upon occasion to draw upon this source. The "specific exclusion references" upon which development in general depends derive their meaning and, indeed, their possibility from the fact that all the concepts belong to a family of concepts which, together, form a system having specific properties. In the early phases of the system, no single pair of concepts reveals enough of the properties of the system itself for these to be specifically relevant. As the system develops, however, its properties and those of its members become sufficiently precise for the interconnections between them to become evident. In the end, the properties of the system *have* to be reflected in the work done by its component concepts. For the system in question is simply an organized cluster of ways of looking at the whole of the universe of discourse. It must appear as a unified series of perspectives.

This way of stating the case may seem to involve us in another of those "totality" paradoxes which I discussed in the last chapter. Is the whole system another perspective added to those which it organizes or is it one of the perspectives which it, itself, purports to organize? If the first, they are not all systematized in the required way and, if the second, the system is not what it purports to be. But, in this case, there seems to be no reason to embrace either horn of the dilemma. The concept involved here is not one of the concepts subsumed under itself. Nor is it a wholly separate concept of the same order. For all its properties will be reflected in its members by the way in which it governs their development and they, in turn, will be reflected in it. We can look at it either way: from the point of view of the concepts subsumed under it, there is nothing in the system which is not reflected in one or more of them. From the point of view of the system there are no ultimately separable concepts which go to make it up for each is only intelligible by reference to all of the others. There will or should be a last concept of the series and it must be, in a sense, a summation of the others. But it will turn out that it is not a replacement for them and it is not a replacement for the idea of the system itself. These problems will, however, turn out to have a natural solution in Chapter 6.

Essentially, then, the hinted-at "fifth procedure" does not really introduce any important modifications of principle. What it does introduce is the necessity for some account of the way in which we distinguish between those occasions for which it is appropriate to proceed on the "core level" and those for which it is appropriate to draw on the concept of the system itself. The distinction lies in the details of the analysis of the conceptual function involved. If there is an evident failure of the concepts which comprise a certain phase of the "core" to complete the system (if, that is, we are left with unresolved conceptual clashes), then we need to explain that failure. If it can be explained by reference to the internal structure of the core concepts we have available, it should be possible to construct the next concept out of the resources immediately available. If, however, it turns out — as it began to seem at the end of the last chapter — that the failure depends on some additional reference, then that reference will have to be sought from the structure of the system itself. For there is no other source of information if the system is to be self-contained. The reason for giving priority to references that stay within the core system is that otherwise information which exists at this level will be smothered. If, like Hegel, I had introduced the notion of "becoming" at an early stage in the system, the full implications of the appropriate concepts of "static state" could not have been adequately developed. It should be noticed, however, that, once again, we are thrown back rather heavily on the details of the specific conceptual analyses involved.

VIII

We are now in a position to form an estimate of the general theoretical position at this stage of the investigation. First of all, the progression described does seem to be straightforward and one-directional within the core structure itself. There should be an orderly progression from the first to the last concept of the system and such digressions as may be necessary by way of reference to higher levels of the system ought not to raise any special theoretical difficulties. The "triads within triads" problem which seemed worrying in Hegel's system ought not to occur, at least within the core structure. Whether or not it will be possible, in fact, to get from the first to the last concept in a finite number of moves remains to be seen though, of course, I hope to show that it is. Again, the question about whether the number of concepts exhibited in any particular analysis of the core structure could be taken as final is a question which ought to be deferred. I rather think that it cannot, but I shall reserve my argument about it.

One ought, I suppose, to consider right here whether we should regret the fact that the principles and procedures I have been discussing fail to provide a set of sufficient conditions for successfully building a system. Obviously, none of the procedures provides guarantees of success unless the necessary conceptual analyses are carried out correctly and, since those involve taking account of the specific peculiarities of specific concepts, no set of rules does more than provide a set of necessary conditions. It is not hard to understand the theory of conceptual functions which I have been suggesting but that, too, cannot be reduced to a set of mechanical rules.

Such a situation might be regarded as an occasion for regret just because we are accustomed to thinking of "logic" in a way which suggests mechanical rules. But this, of course, is a mistake. It may be useful to revert, for a moment, to an issue raised in the first chapter in order to make this point. Quine's apparently harmless example of the sentence about Socrates "Either Socrates is mortal or Socrates is not mortal" illustrates, in part, what is involved. I suggested that, as it stands, we do not know whether it is true or not. For "Socrates" is the name of an assemblage of properties or a cluster of potential subjects of predication, and "mortality" does not apply to all of them in the same way. Therefore, "Socrates" in this sense may be both mortal and not mortal. Only an adequate conceptual analysis will tell us just when we have reached the "atom" to which the "logical particles" can be safely attached, and the "either ... or" formulation is meaningless without some theory about what conditions those atoms must meet. Furthermore, we can never make such schemes work in any argument without the necessary analyses of particular concepts. The position, therefore, is not unlike the one we have here. The general principles and specific procedures suggested are useless or meaningless without the specific analyses which will make them work. And so it is, I think, with all reasoning. No doubt the general principles I have been trying to extract could be laid down with more elegance than I have displayed, especially if they were divorced from the specific lines of argument with which we are, here, necessarily involved. But that is a matter of taste and practicality at least in part.

Admittedly, the specific conceptual analyses may be open to endless debate. That is always true. But what matters is that we should be able to see what kinds of reasons count in such debates. What we need is openness to argument and reasonable canons of relevance. If I have not provided all the material for these requirements then I have, I hope, at least indicated how it may be possible to do so.

The point is that the absence of a set of mechanical rules which are sufficient to coerce agreement or, if you prefer, sufficient to guarantee an error-free result, is not a special disadvantage of the logical activities which I am championing here. Admittedly, there are degrees of coercion and margins of error and they are obviously not the same for all reasoning activity. The name "calculation" is often used for those species of reasoning within which the degree of coercion possible is relatively high and the margin of error which can be expected of those who follow the rules exactly is relatively small, and a system of logic within which one can "calculate" is often, nowadays, called a "calculus."

One may imagine the reasoning operations which take place within such a "calculus" as being, in these respects, much like those which go into the arithmetical operation of addition. Even in addition, of course, there is a margin of error. The rules are precise enough and the concepts involved all belong to a small and special class which can be readily identified by the users of the rules. But not only do people actually make mistakes in adding (and so do machines), the underlying theory is by no means so simple or even so complete as might be imagined and the detailed analysis of number concepts is, itself, open to various kinds of dispute which are not so different, after all, from those which have been engaging us here. Furthermore, as the Socrates example shows, no kind of logic is, in operation, so simple as to make its working very like operations such as addition.

Equally, it must be admitted that many kinds of reasoning which hardly approximate to "calculation" are capable of producing agreement and capable of bearing most of the logical burdens put upon them. Legal reasoning, for example, depends rather heavily, amongst other things, on the correct analysis of particular rather peculiar concepts and on the ability to apply them to particular states of affairs and in unexpected combinations. It is fairly easy to define larceny, for instance, but much harder to decide whether some specific act is larcenous. If a man buys a chest of drawers, finds a sum of money locked away in a secret compartment within it, and appropriates the money to himself, is he guilty of an offence and, if so, what offence? The answer depends on just how one analyzes, defines, and manipulates the concepts involved. Yet it is possible to obtain a wide range of agreement about the result. Legal systems do work, within limits; lawyers can give advice to their clients with some measure of certainty; and our feeling that the law is, at bottom, outrageous, can usually be kept under control.

On one side, then, there is no system of reasoning which meets the precise paradigm of "calculation" — at least if the whole of the background theory of construction and application is investigated. On the other side, the absence of mechanical coercion is not necessarily fatal. Indeed, as the discussion in Chapter 1 tended to show, there is a tendency to approach arbitrariness as mechanical rules take over the field. Consider addition again: to what extent are the rules simple because they are merely conventional and to what extent are they grounded in such things as a theory of "natural" numbers? (*One* reason that some numbers are thought to be "natural" is that we "find" them and do not make them to our own measure. At any rate, there are others which are more obviously "created" by our own mathematical techniques. If this distinction finally makes sense, then we are, to some degree bound by certain rather basic number concepts. But these give rise to genuine problems in number theory and represent one region in which the "background" to simple operations like addition is not so simple and the rules of reasoning are in no way mechanical.) Generally, whenever we come up against a region where the reasoning problems cannot be solved by arbitrary invention and convention, we leave the domain over which mechanical rules hold sway.

What we want, usually, is some kind of balance: openness to the giving and taking of reasons is more important than mechanical rules; arbitrariness is worse than the messy business of having to deal in special ways with particular concepts. But we need enough order, at least, to be able to find our way around. Whether the present system involves a reasonable balance, the reader must decide. If the balance needs redressing, the reader, hopefully, will find a clue about how to go about if from just the errors which have convinced him of the need. At least, that is how a dialectical system *ought* to work.

IX

At any rate, as the system develops, further opportunities for clarifying the issues and the procedures involved will certainly arise. Meanwhile, if the structure is to become intelligible, we must attempt to deal with those issues which arise, metaphorically, below the core level. I have talked about a number of ways of conceptualizing any universe of discourse. Each of these categories provides a kind of domain over which various logical rules appear to hold sway and within which may be discerned or constructed accounts of the entities around which our discourse usually centres.[1] The

---

[1] It is important to bear in mind that the "core system" consists of concepts expressing categories, concepts which express the uniting properties which link pairs of categories so as to form a single level of generality, and concepts expressing specific exclusion

immediate question is just this: to what extent does this or any other dialectical system enable us to say anything about the contents of these domains?

The question is important in its own right because, if it is not answered with reasonable clarity, the system will remain not only mysterious but also irrelevant. It is also important because of the indirect opportunity it offers for the assessment of dialectical systems.

To begin with, the dialectician must seem to face a dilemma which is not merely awkward but potentially fatal: he must seemingly choose between holding that his system is one within which he can develop the whole range of concepts which rational discourse requires or can sustain, and holding that there is a radical dualism between those concepts which belong to such a logical system and those which have their roots independently of it and are sustained by experience or intuition or arbitrary logical construction. If he holds the first view he stands convicted in the court of common sense of a kind of ratiomania. He must also seem to stand convicted of sheer blind wilfulness by all those who have good reason to think that we cannot deduce or produce accounts of the whole world out of the shaky threads of our reason. If he chooses the second he is, however, equally doomed. For we are then back at the very position which the dialectician set out to deny: that "logic," of whatever kind, is a self-encapsulated system, neutralized from the rest of discourse. He will also face the charge that his "logic," as much as anyone else's, finally fails to make contact with "reality." For there is apt to be a fairly general agreement that the hard core of reality lies somehow within the domains marked out by the concepts which form the core level of a dialectical system such as this one. (And *that* will in all likelihood be agreed to as much by Platonists as by nominalists. The "forms" admired by Plato seem not to be, for the most part at least, forms of the categories of things but forms of things and attributes.)[1]

---

references. Within the context of the core system the specific exclusion references will always be expressed by concepts which also reflect a way of focussing the whole universe of discourse but do so on a different level of abstraction. Uniting properties and specific exclusion references cannot be turned into additional categories simply because they lack sufficient structure to provide an intelligible perspective.

[1] The *way* in which genuine individuals come to have an ontological primacy is, of course, something which has to be explained as the system develops. But there are two dimensions to this problem. The system, itself, obviously moves from very abstract ways of viewing the totality to very concrete ways and the "poles" between which the system oscillates will turn out to be pure being and dialectical individuality. The entities brought into sharp focus in the last category — dialectical individuality — are thus primary in the sense that it is dialectical individuals which are being viewed through the spectacles of all the categories. Each category, however, makes it possible to identify domains within which these individuals emerge more or less clearly but in the guise appropriate to that category. The categories permeate these identifiable particulars and vice versa but the particulars are the "things" which we would ordinarily say exist or do not exist. The distinctions are not, indeed, hard and fast since — as will emerge shortly in the detailed

The dialectician, therefore, is in no position to embrace either horn of the dilemma. Nor is he in a position to ignore it. He cannot easily embrace both horns at once and his only hope, therefore, is to dissolve it — to show that it rests upon a mistake of some kind or another. Ultimately, of course, he must show how such concepts as "experience" fit into the scheme and what happens when they are given their proper place. Again he must try to distinguish between developing the required concepts and revealing the "truth" and indicate how these activities are, finally, to be united. If he fails in these endeavours, his system collapses and the game is up. (Though he may, alas, succeed in these endeavours without, finally, succeeding in sustaining his system or showing it immune from doubt.)

Immediately, however, we can, luckily, begin to unpack important parts of this difficulty in a much simpler way.

To begin with, the difficulty cuts differently at different stages of a dialectical system. The present system, for example, was deliberately constructed so that its initial concepts would lie at a level of generality at which distinctions between thought and reality, universal and particular, actuality and possibility, and, indeed, form and content do not arise. Even if the arguments for the starting point I used are not, ultimately, conclusive every such system will, presumably, have phases which lie at this level of generality. Initially in this system, then, and somewhere in *all* systems which do the same logical work, there will be points of reference at which there is no gap to be filled by concepts more specific than those of the core system. The distinctions which give rise to the problem must arise, if they are to be justified, within the system as it develops. If the difficulties can be overcome, it will have to be by noticing in detail how the distinctions which give rise to them actually arise.

X

Detailed examination of the initial categories of the system may, however, begin to reveal the origins of the tensions which seem, ultimately, to produce the dilemma. Consider, then, the concept which I called "pure being":

It is, evidently, the concept of a domain within which no distinction can be made between the domain itself and some set of entities which could be said to be its members. It is not merely an undifferentiated unity. More than that, it does not admit of a distinction between the concept of its defining properties and the concept of their instantiation. There is no distinction between the intension of the language referring to it and the extension of that reference. For such a distinction would introduce the kind of structural complexity which — if my argument in the second chapter is sound — the

discussion of the domain of determinate being — some of them (logical entities for instance) are mirror reflections of the categorical properties themselves. But the distinction can be maintained so long as its own dialectical features are remembered.

initial concept in a system such as this cannot have. To distinguish between the way in which such a concept is structured and the way in which it refers to the world would introduce a fundamental duality which would destroy its function.

It remains true, however, that the concept of pure being, if it is to be intelligible at all, must represent a way of looking at the world. It is, of course, not unlike Parmenides' "being," the "what is," of which nothing more needs to be or can be said. Parmenides can be regarded as having made an important discovery — the discovery that all propositions must, after all, refer to what is or to what is not, and that the true propositions about the world necessarily refer to what is. If they did not all have some common reference this could not be said. To think merely of the common reference of all of them is to think of being. In an important sense, obviously, there is nothing *else* to be referred to. There is only fragmentation to be indulged in. And all fragmentation carries with it an element of falsification. The reason that this is not, as Parmenides may have thought, the whole story is that there are various ways of exhibiting the world as a unity and the special kind of logical priority which belongs to discourse about "being" is not necessarily either an epistemological or an ontological priority.

Part of the point of this discussion is that it is important to realize that propositions do not have a single, unequivocal, reference. They all have a common reference to "being" but nearly all have additional references as well. Indeed, I want to argue that propositions which are directly "about the world" (as opposed to those which are about other propositions and so on) generally have references to all the domains which are subsumed under the categories of a system such as this one. For if there is a series of logically linked concepts each of which is a way of focussing the whole of reality, the propositions about components of the real must refer to the appropriate sub-components of each of the domains. This complex range of references is not the result of sloppy construction or conception: it results, logically, from the nature of the reality which is being referred to. A consequence of it may be the appearance of contradictions: it may appear (as it apparently seemed to Parmenides) that the real cannot be both pure and undivided being and also a fragmented series of disjunctions, both static and changing and so on. But variety of reference changes this appearance if the variety can be shown to be necessary.

"Pure being," then, can be regarded as intelligible if we are given the necessary structure within which to talk about it. Interestingly enough, it can even be regarded as an object of experience. The kinds of mystical experience in which particularity seems to be transcended by an all-embracing unity can surely be interpreted in this way. For just as pure being seems best regarded as the common reference of all propositions about the world so the feeling of the mystic seems most commonly not to arise from some particular feature of his experience but from the sense that all particulars are being transcended. It seems more often the transformation of ordinary things into a special unity than the presence of extraordinary particulars which impresses him. For the same reason that it is not in point to demand the peculiar propositions which specially refer to pure being, so it is not in point to demand of the mystic the peculiar objects of experience to which he has had access. Consequently, he is generally reduced to embarrassed silence or vague generalities. At this level, then, there is not even a special problem about the relations between reason and experience: Given the appropriate concepts, there is no peculiar problem about either.

Evidently, pure being is not very interesting unless one has some special reason (such as the overtones of value which mystics generally feel in the presence of and while retrospectively contemplating their experiences) for thinking that it represents a particularly important way of conceptualizing reality. Such questions must necessarily be postponed in this discussion.

XI

Equally, pure disjunction seems to be mainly of interest because of the logical peculiarities which it involves and because of its importance as a transition category in the present and similar systems. Most of what I have said about pure being applies, *mutatis mutandis*, to pure disjunction.

It is not hard to see again that all propositions which are about the world refer to disjunction as well as to unity. For they have in common the very fact that they make distinctions. To say that all propositions have a common reference implies that they all, equally, have references apart. Otherwise there would only be one proposition. Another way of putting it is to say that "pure being" would, indeed, be empty were it not the notion of a unity which transcends a diversity. It is by contrast to disjunction that it acquires its intelligibility. Again, however, pure disjunction is not something referred to by a special class of propositions but a common reference of all propositions. We thus do not get, still, a disjunction between the domain itself and its members.

It may be argued, nevertheless, that pure disjunction is not merely the other side of the coin introduced as pure being. For it could be urged that negation forces the distinction between intension and extension and the argument I used seemed to introduce disjunction as simply the negation of unity. If there is any merit in the argument in question it becomes potentially of crucial importance here because it seems to be the case that the separation of thought and reality depends upon the separation of extension and intension. Hence we might expect to find the origin of the wedge at the point at which negation is brought into consideration.

This requires some unravelling.

It seems reasonable, at first sight, to suppose that expressions used to convey negations and so on do not function by themselves or in combination with other expressions in such a way as to mark out anything special in the world. The two sentences, "Smith is not an elephant" and "Smith possesses the property of not-elephanthood" seem to draw attention to the same state of affars except that the second suggests strongly that "not-elephanthood" is a property like "elephanthood" and it is difficult to imagine why anyone would believe such a thing and how, if anyone did, he would pass from naming the property to giving an intelligible account of it.

One does not need, of course, to imagine the reasons actually given for such doctrines. McTaggart, for instance, thought there were negative facts mainly because he thought that the correspondence theory of truth was correct.[1] Some negative propositions are true and must correspond to something. What needs imagining is why he did not think that this argument, if it was a good one, was, in fact, a reason for not holding the correspondence theory of truth. For the second part of the problem is one that (surprisingly, seeing that he was a recently practising dialectician himself) McTaggart does not seem to have given much attention to: How shall we give an intelligible account of negative "facts" and of the properties on which they depend?

Consider what it is to possess "not-elephanthood": There seem to be four choices. We might say that something possessed it if it did not exist at all; if it did exist but possessed some property incompatible with elephanthood; if it existed and happened not to be an elephant; or if it existed and possessed every property except elephanthood. The third of these *seems* to be the usual case for which the alternative is something like "Smith is not an elephant." But then this is merely a picturesque way of saying that the list of Smith's properties does not include the property of being an elephant and "not-elephanthood" does not, in any plausible way, figure as an additional property. It would appear that one of the other choices would have to be substantiated in order to make the "negative property" analysis seem reasonable. None of these, however, seems likely to work.

If Smith does not exist, then he is not an elephant. If we think of "*nothing*" as a word which has a referent, then we can say "Nothing possesses not-elephanthood" — not meaning "For any 'X' whatever, 'X' is not an elephant" but rather "Whatever 'nothing' is, it is at least not an elephant." But, surely, if "nothing" can possess properties, then it is something. And that is absurd. Giving extensions to negative expressions *this* way is clearly self-defeating and people who have wanted to ontologise about "nothingness" must (one hopes) have had something else in mind. What one might have in mind will develop in a moment. For now, however, this choice seems to be out.

The second choice sounds more plausible. If Smith has some property

[1] For McTaggart's views see The Nature of Existence (Cambridge: Cambridge University Press, 1920), Vol. I, pp. 62-63. I have discussed this and related issues at some length in The Concept of Truth, Van Gorcum, Assen, 1969, p. 71ff.

which excludes the property of being an elephant in such a way as to be incompatible with it, it sounds as though one might wish to say that there is more to the story than that he just happens not to be an elephant and we might call this "more" the property of being a "not-elephant." Thus if we knew the truth of "Nothing *can* be both a man and an elephant" and "Smith is a man" we could infer that "Smith is not an elephant" and we might want to say that the right thing to say about the situation is "Smith possesses the property of 'not-elephanthood.'" Furthermore, this may be a common case. For, usually, possessing some properties does exclude (in some sense) the possession of others and it may even always be the case that properties always have instantiations except where something else gets in the way. (There are no tigers in England except in the zoos. But suppose everything were right for tigers — the climate did not exclude them, the zoological history of the place was correct and so on. Then wouldn't it be surprising and even impossible that there should be no tigers?) The point, however, is not about the pervasiveness of such cases but about the interpretation of them. And these cases seem just to amount to (1) the possession of some property of a quite ordinary sort and (2) the justification of some inference or inferences about the exclusion of other properties. The property of excluding seems to be genuine enough for some or even all properties, but it is not the same thing as the negative properties originally proposed. I shall argue in a moment that the solution does lie this way, but the distinction needs to be preserved.

The fourth case is subject to the same analysis. It is true that if anything existed and possessed every property except that of elephanthood we might want to say that it was a "not-elephant" in a stronger sense still. But this seems to be an impossible case unless one introduces special restrictions. (One might claim to mean by "every property" just "those properties which are instantiated in the world" and one might introduce some way of talking about things so that the expression "the whole world except the elephants" could be said to designate an entity or a bearer of properties. But the advantages of this, if any, would accrue only in some very specialized and curious systems.) In any case, this is just a specially strong instance of a case in which some quite ordinary properties are combined with the property of excluding some further property.

The upshot of this seems to be that, if negation, as such, could reasonably be believed to have extension as well as intension, we would have expected these examples to have turned out differently. For to say that negation had extension would seem to license us to take some entity — "nothing" for instance — as part of our ontology or to take some set of negative properties to be properties in an ordinary sense. It might be the case, of course, that the extensive references of negations are simply to some general domain, and propositions might refer to it in the way that they refer to "pure being" or to "pure disjunction." It seems essential, for instance, to think of Hegel's "nothing" in this way. But it seemed for the reasons I offered in Chapter 2 impossible to construct such a domain. Thus the conclusion seems to be that negation, as such, has no extension. Negations are however meaningful and so seem to have intensions.

This seems reasonable, admittedly, partly because of an unstated assumption: the assumption that we ought not to assume extensions if we can find satisfactory alternatives. The examples, after all, turn on the notion that we can analyze the required references in such a way that they can be seen not to require special negative entities. More precisely, the general principle involved can be stated this way. Whenever we have knowledge, we can examine the assertions which set it out in order to sort out the referring expressions they contain or implicitly make use of. If the referential objects cannot be restructured so as to be described in terms to which we have prior or other commitments without distorting the knowledge in question, we are entitled to claim that the original terms have extensions. If we can perform this restructuring we are not without further grounds entitled to make such a claim. The "ontological status" of such referential objects may be the subject of further investigation (though generally they will have *some* ontological status given that we started with genuine knowledge and that the logical structures in which the assertions are clothed are not divorced from reality in some way). But if we find terms whose references can be restructured, we have terms with intensions but no extensions unless the terms themselves can be replaced by others which do not have the consequences concerned. Thus it becomes possible to have a class of seeming referential objects which will not have ontological status. This is one way in which the separation between thought and reality might arise.

The alternative, here, however, is to restructure the terms involved and to maintain that what is required is not the concept of negation but the concept of exclusion. "Pure disjunction" is what is excluded by "pure being" and vice versa. The exclusion, in this case, is a logically necessary one. "Pure disjunction *is not* pure being" can be translated into "Pure disjunction *excludes* pure being." The properties of the domain of pure disjunction, furthermore, can be constructed in terms of exclusion. For the discreteness of reference which is the basis of the generalized pluralism implied by pure disjunction stems exactly from the exclusiveness of the positive content of all references. Indeed, the whole of the dialectic process depends upon the notion that, ultimately, negation is never "mere negation" — it invariably involves a positive counterpart. Thus, in the chain of core concepts which form the main subject of discussion in this book, there is a process of positive exclusion reference which makes it possible to proceed. Obviously, we can introduce restrictions of convenience (and often must) and use a simple concept of negation. Such a notion, furthermore, seems the natural one in the domain of determinate being where, as I shall try to show shortly, the problems of the dialectician seem to begin in earnest. But there seems

78

no reason to introduce what Bosanquet liked to call "bare negation" as an ultimate notion unless it turns out that we ought to think that the proper explication of "Smith is, not an elephant" and similar cases is simply "It happens that Smith lacks the properties of elephants" and not "Smith has some properties which exclude his being an elephant."

At any rate, the dangerous wedge is not immediately at work on us. In addition, given this analysis we can see why it might be tempting to think of "nothing", conceived of as "exclusion," as having a kind of ontological status or, at any rate as being a genuine referential object. For the exclusion of one thing by another is a genuine feature of this and any possible world. Any other kind of world would be exhausted by the notion of pure being and, if the argument in the last chapter holds, that cannot be the case. When we think of pure disjunction we have our attention focussed on the world simply as a set of exclusions, as (if I may use the expression tentatively) the antithesis of the unity which is pure being. No doubt, just as there are mystical experiences so there are disjunctive ones — a kind of overwhelming sense of the plurality and (as plurality) the unintelligibility of things. Again, no *particular* experience is the special bearer of this vista of the world just as no particular proposition specially refers to pure disjunction.

That this is a possible view about all experiences is evident from the consequences of certain kinds of empiricism. If one follows the arguments in vogue not so long ago one comes, indeed, to just this kind of result. It was maintained, for instance, that there are or ought to be "basic propositions" which are genuinely grounded in experience in such a way that each of them expressed the content of one and only one experience and each proposition could be decisively confirmed by a single experience. Such assertions might be imagined to take such forms as "red, here, now" where the reference is to a single experience component and, if it is forthcoming, the proposition is confirmed. "Red" in such an expression is, of course, not the name of a property which could be imagined to recur over many experiences (for then one experience would not confirm it) but, as it were, the logically proper name of a single experience. Now if all experience could be construed in this way, every experience would be perfectly atomic and those language units which referred to it would simply refer to this general disjunctive property. That one cannot build a language capable of dealing with experience in quite this way seems to me obvious enough, but that one can build a picture of the domain of pure disjunction this way seems to me equally obvious. This kind of empirical atomism would thus be regarded as an attempt to assert the primacy of the domain of pure disjunction just a Parmenidean or a mystic might (in their different ways) be imagined to be asserting the primacy of the domain of pure being. Neither party, of course, is simply wrong. Each has focussed upon one of the perfectly possible (and indeed necessary) frames of reference from which accounts of the world can be focussed. But each seems to be the victim of the doctrine of unique reference which does seem to me to be quite wrong.

Thus, again, experience and logic do not, so far, seem to pose special problems for the dialectician. But this is only because the distinction between the domains we have been talking about and their contents cannot be effectively forced and because the distinction between extension and intension can, this far, be avoided.

XII

This discussion has left us with some useful equipment: The development of a concept of negation as exclusion is almost certainly important to the larger enterprise. The notion that assertions have a multiplicity of references is equally important. But it cannot be argued that much has been done to resolve the conditions which seem to produce the dialecticians's dilemma and, in particular, the passing references to experience cannot be expected, at this stage of the development of the system, to add much by way of enlightenment.

More excitement can be expected as we pass to determinate being.

Here, obviously, there is a distinction between the domain and the entities which compose it. The entities concerned include everything that can be referred to within the limits prescribed by a limited set of logical criteria. Because these *are* the limits, the domain is quasi-Meinongian in that there is no way (initially) of distinguishing between referential objects and objects with ontological status.

It should be noticed immediately, however, that the descriptions of the entities concerned cannot all be generated simply from the logical rules. Once we are able to form concepts of specific properties which have the necessary logical powers — which will, when assigned to entities, provide the requisite determinateness — we can begin to form descriptions of the members of the domains. But they are not, generally, given by the rules.

Seemingly, then, this is one of the places in which the limits of reason begin to show themselves and one of the potential cracks which develop between logic and reality. These cracks appear here even if we are prepared to give the title "real" to all the apparent members of the domain of determinate being.[1]

---

[1] I shall later — see Chapters 5 and 6 — offer specific defences of the doctrine that to say that something exists or is real (in the most general sense) is just to say that it is possible to have knowledge about it. Thus giving or withholding the title "real" turns out to be something for which we can find criteria. The system gives a special sense to the expression "ultimately real" in that we are always talking about dialectical individuals. Ultimately, everything which merits this title has to be whatever it is that can be viewed adequately through all the categories. Members of various domains will, however, have an ontological status which shifts from domain to domain. Thus, in determinate being, everything which meets certain logical criteria has a place and such "entities" are all

XIII

Before we can get down to the investigation of this problem it is essential to get ourselves clear about the logical conditions which are imposed upon descriptions of members of the domain, or which (if there is to be a difference) restrict the members themselves.

The conditions which we can derive from the argument which established the concept of determinate being in the last chapter include at least these:

(1) Each such entity must be describable as a "property" or "set of properties" together with an appropriate "bearer." (Without bearers, properties fail to exclude universal application; without properties, bearers fail to be identifiable.)

(2) Each such entity, in order to be determinate, must stand in a relation of exclusion to every other entity in the domain. Thus each such entity must stand in a clear relation to every property which could characterize such entities. For any given property, it must be possible to say that any given entity has that property or fails to have it.

(3) By inference each such entity must be unique and must, therefore, have some property which no other entity has.

(4) There must, therefore, be a kind of "logical space" within which all the entities which compose the domain have their places and no two such entities can occupy the same place.

(5) No such entity can be in time. If it were, there would be a distinction between those occasions when a given proposition correctly referred to it and those when it did not. There would come to be, that is, a distinction between referential and other objects, a distinction which the minimum requirements for the establishment of the domain do not provide. Anyway, if any such entity were in time, it would cease to be the case that, for any given property, it could be said either to have it or not to have it. For there would be future times at which this would make doubtful sense. (It would imply the truth of one of two propositions about the future.) It would also imply that temporal states were discontinuous in a sense in which, in the next chapter, it will be shown that they cannot be.

(6) From the preceding conditions, it can be seen that propositions asserting the membership in the domain of entities will be related to one another in certain ways including those which are expressed in the traditional "laws" of identity, excluded middle, and non-contradiction: i.e. if every

equal considered just as components of determinate being. Some of these "entities" will, however, turn up in the process categories simply as possibilities while others will be components of actualities. There is nothing puzzling about the fact that as we move from the abstract to the concrete, we find ourselves able to make additional distinctions. Again, looking back at earlier categories from the perspective of later ones, we can see how we come to be more interested in some components of determinate being than in others. Some of them, for instance, are components of actual processes and others are not.

entity must either have or not have every given property, two of the laws are at once sustained. Identity is a condition of the possibility of reference.

(7) The concepts which are implied in the general structure of the domain of determinate being also enable us to establish that, between propositions referring to entities in this domain, enough additional relations can be constructed so as to correspond generally to the requirements of certain standard logical systems.

It is important to try to establish this. Quine's account of the requirements for a system which will do the work of *Principia* suggests that we need three (and only three) logical notions: membership, alternative denial, and universal quantification.[1]

(a) Membership: We saw in Chapter 2 that the rudiments of a theory of classes containing a notion of membership functionally like Quine's could be constructed out of the materials at hand and was seemingly required.

(b) Alternative denial: This notion is symbolized by Quine as (——/---). The line before the upright stroke and the dashes after it stand for any statements, and the whole statement is normally read "Not both —— and ---." It requires the concepts of negation or exclusion together with the notion of conjunction and some situation which exhibits their combination. But the structure of the domain with which we are dealing requires, by reason of the conditions for discreteness, that any proposition which can refer to any member of the domain must be able to enter into these relations.

(c) Universal quantification: This is a more tendentious notion. For it first requires the possibility of propositions which are generally symbolized in such forms as (x) $(fx \supset gx)$. The first "x" is taken to mean "for all x" or "whatever x may be" and then the proposition goes on to say something like "If x is an f then x is a g." The necessary conditions for any such propositions are met if and only if there is some basic unity in the domain over which it functions such that there are *some* relations which will hold between them no matter what they are. This condition appears to be met by the domain of determinate being if only because the whole domain is unified by the set of limiting conditions we are now discussing. If, of course, one's logic is imagined to be further limited by a requirement to the effect that propositions with the universal quantifier are a standard form of proposition such that all propositions must continue to make sense if they are altered only by its addition to them or substitution for another form within them, the issue becomes more difficult. But it seems obvious that the domain of determinate being would meet this further condition as well. For the argument in Chapter 2 suggested that a two-place reference system of just the kind in question was essential to the intelligibility of the domain.

In general, systems like *Principia* were presented as including three rather

---

[1] *From a Logical Point of View*, Chapter V (New Foundations for Mathematical Logic), p. 81ff.

basic kinds of relations between propositions taken as affirmed or denied: implication, alternation, and conjunction. But, in the restricted senses in which they were introduced, they turn out, of course, to be reducible in ways which do not require these to be regarded as separate notions. "*P* implies *Q*," for instance, is taken, in the standard truth table setting out the possibilities for such structures, to hold for every case except the one in which *P* is true while *Q* is false. Hence "*P* implies *Q*" can be as well read "not both *P* and not *Q*" thus dispensing with the separate notion of "implication" as a basic piece of logical equipment. Similarly "*P* v *Q*" generally read "*P* or *Q*" was taken only to mean that not both of them could be false. Hence it can be read "Not *P* implies *Q*" and "implication," in its turn, can be replaced in the way suggested a moment ago. Nor does "conjunction," of course, provide any special difficulty. For it, again, was defined simply as the truth table case. Using Quine's "not both —— and ---" symbolism, we can substitute for "*P* . *Q*" where the "dot" is read "and" and implies a conjunction of truth values, the form $-(P \mid Q)$. Material biconditionality — the condition in which two propositions are true together or false together (as "*P* if and only if *Q*") — can be dealt with similarly.

This much equipment was regarded by Quine as adequate for the job done by *Principia* which was thought, in general, to be adequate for the provision of mathematics and much else besides and can be considerably expanded without the introduction of what Quine (then, at any rate) regarded as additional fundamental notions. (For instance, existential quantification, inclusion, and a function for the "=" symbol are introduced by Quine in the form of definitions which depend only upon the three basic notions he claims.)

Our concern here is not with what such a system is capable of doing (much less with such matters as the correct definition — if there is one — of "mathematics"). It is simply with showing that such a system, and, no doubt, various alternatives to it which hinge on the same general range of concepts, are natural structures within the domain of determinate being. Thus it is not merely the case that, with a structure like the present one all or at least much of the common apparatus can be constructed. It is also the case that such apparatus can be shown to arise within such a system as this one not out of arbitrary postulates but out of the necessities of the system. The only conflict (if it is a conflict) between the dialectician and his colleague who proceeds as Quine does is that the dialectician will regard such logics as parts of a more extensive and more embracing system. Even the apparent quarrel which we saw arising over the paradoxes which the theory of types and its substitutes were intended to evade need not be regarded as a kind of decisive struggle. If anyone wants to erect a wall around the domain of determinate being in the form of arbitrary structures which keep it from collapsing into paradox, there is no reason why he should not do so if it adds to his convenience. He may then fail to see what lies beyond the wall but, then, he may have no interest in that.

(8) Additionally, it can be shown that the relations between entities in the domain of determinate being will not accommodate referential propositions between which substantially richer relations of implication hold. Since the conditions above require both uniqueness and perfect discreteness amongst such entities, no one of them has a description such that the description of any other follows directly from it. This is, roughly, to say that no independent notion of implication arises directly from the formative conditions which govern the entities in the domain. Some device, like the one suggested above, which makes of implication a derivative notion is thus required.

(9) It is somewhat different with the logical space which the set of such entities collectively occupies. The distinction arises in this way: The argument in Chapter 2 urged that discrete entities must have limits or boundaries. This, in turn, requires that there should be other entities which provide the limits and, ultimately, a complete set of such entities. The discreteness of the entities makes this notion of completion impossible. This is one of the reasons for thinking that whatever logic is adequate to "the real" in the most general sense must make provision for more than determinate being. Equally, though, the description of any particular entity is such that it does not provide the basis for an inference to the next entity in the system. Thus, though there *is* a basic and independent notion of implication latent in the *structure* it does not apply to the particular entities which compose the domain. They maintain their atomicity. The principle of implication applies only to certain conditions which govern the "logical space" or the framework within which they become intelligible. And it does not provide us with information about that framework. It tells us only that there will be one.

XIV

We can now get down to the business of trying to see what the entities which compose the domain of determinate being might be like and how they could be discovered. To repeat, they cannot generally be deduced from the structure of the domain as such. Nor, given that we could provide a description of at least one of them could we expect to deduce the descriptions of all the others.

Before we jump to the conclusion that we have, finally, reached the gulf between logic and reality, we should work our way cautiously toward the edge of the alleged precipice.

To start with, of course, we *can* deduce that the domain is not empty: For some of its members will be logical entities whose place and status *does* follow from the logical rules. Some of them, that is, are propositions, classes of propositions, classes, classes of classes, logical constants, and so on — entities whose existence is substantiated by and mirrored in the rules themselves. We may ordinarily think of such things as very different from the entities which come to mind as "having being" and "being determinate" — rocks, trees, horses, books, packs of cigarettes, and distant stars. But, qua members of the domain of determinate being, all of them are simply referential objects and, what is more, most of the things which come to mind simply do not meet the obvious conditions for membership in the domain.

To try to get this clear, it is perhaps as well to revert yet again to the worn example about "Socrates is mortal." It is not clear, as I argued earlier, that "Socrates" as usually interpreted, names anything which can be said to be "either mortal or not mortal." We almost certainly do not have, in the example, an appropriate bearer of the predicate. Nor, for that matter, is "mortality," without refinement, a proper property for *any* "Socrates-like" bearer within the domain.

In fact, "Socrates" may very well not name anything which could be an appropriate bearer of *any* property which could function in this domain and "mortality" as usually understood is quite clearly not the name of any property which could function here. The argument which I offered in passing, earlier, was simply that "Socrates" was the name of a very complex compound and, while the body of Socrates, for example, is quite certainly mortal, one might well have more doubts about such things as the mind of Socrates, the personality of Socrates and so on. Additionally, of course, "Socrates" is the name of something which seems to be persistent through a period of time and cannot easily be understood apart from that property. But essentially temporal properties have no place in the domain of determinate being. "Mortality" obviously names a temporal property.

Evidently, we can try to replace complex bearers and properties by simple ones and temporal bearers and properties by a-temporal ones. We can, for instance, choose to regard Socrates as a collection of irreducibly simple particles and his temporal transactions as spatial ones. (The latter operation can be undertaken by introducing such devices as a four-dimensional continuum in which no distinction, in principle, is made between the dimensions.) On such a view "Socrates is or Socrates is not mortal" can be rendered: "The collection of 'Socrates' particles can be so arranged in space that, for any point in a 'Socrates line' in any dimension, it will always be true that there is or is not a 'Socrates particle' at that point." If we wish to get closer to the usual meaning of sentences like "Socrates is mortal" we can specify one unique dimension and one linear direction within that dimension and then maintain that "Socrates is mortal" means that there will be found "Socrates particles" at every point between two given points and at no point outside those given points while "Socrates is immortal" would mean that beyond some given point we would invariably find "Socrates particles."

Technical difficulties might or might not lead us to regard the sentences concerned as shorthand for a set of sentences each of which was about a single particle. This would probably depend upon our theory of classes, our view about whether classes of particles counted as proper referential objects, and our theory about the correct analysis of the expression "Socrates."

The point of this is simply that unless we can get bearers of properties and properties themselves into the requisite conditions of simplicity and a-temporality, they cannot be made to fit the required logical mould. Complexity makes it (generally) doubtful whether a given property does or does not attach, or more correctly makes it possible that both assertions are true. Temporality is likely to render a given predication indeterminate between truth or falsity. (The law of "bivalence" — the contention that every proposition is either true or false — is not, of course, identical with the law of "excluded middle" — the contention that every bonafide bearer of properties either has or does not have any given bonafide property. But indeterminacy with respect to property possession does run counter to the law of excluded middle.)

But all this is not so great a limitation on what can be said as is sometimes imagined since temporal expressions can be accommodated to a kind of logical space in the way that I have suggested. Problems about the unique direction of time (if they really arise) can be dealt with just by taking it as a matter of fact that some regions of the "logical space" are inaccessible. "Particlisation" is presumably a matter of combining the requisite conceptual equipment about logical simplicity with adequate devices when necessary for referring to classes of particles.

The difficulties which do arise when one attempts schemes of this kind are apt to be more subtle. For instance, anyone who says "Socrates is immortal" probably has in mind the persistence through a long stretch of time of something like Socrates' mind, his cognitive powers, or his personality. There are certain to be difficulties about the concepts of mind, knowledge, person, and time in this context and it seems doubtful that these problems can be adequately expressed within the required mould. There will be similar difficulties for anyone who says "Caterpillars develop into moths" or even, I fear, "Rocks persist for a long time."

It is, perhaps, important to look at some of these problems both with a view toward getting straight about the domain of determinate being, and with a view toward bringing us nearer to an account of experience which will enable us to come to grips with the alleged gulf between reason and experience which seems to develop at this point.

The difficulty involved in talking about entities like "the mind of Socrates" in terms of determinate being has to do, of course, with the process of particlisation. It is not that it is impossible to find a model on which one could do this. One could adopt, for instance, the "bundle theory" which derives from Hume. On this model, "the mind" can be regarded as a collection of ideas and impressions. Impressions can be regarded as single, simple (unanalyzable) sensations and ideas may be (in principle perhaps) analyzed into similarly simple components. Each of these can be regarded as the bearer of a single, simple, defining property and as being exhausted by that property. There might be very great difficulties in carrying out any such programme but these could be ascribed to ignorance, sloth, and lack of suitable logical apparatus.

The difficulty is that, though one could construct the rules for such a programme and imagine that they were scrupulously followed, the result seems utterly to miss the kind of point which someone who wanted to enquire into the alleged immortality of Socrates would most probably have in mind: Most probably he would have in mind the peculiar fact that Socrates is aware of what he knows, that the components of his mind and the objects of his knowledge stand in a rather peculiar relation to each other, and that the cognitive field of Socrates forms a special kind of unity. To replace these referential objects with the essentially passive, static, and atomic entities which necessarily form the referential objects which can be accommodated to the structure of determinate being is to miss the point.

To elaborate a little, the man who wants to speculate about immortality is impressed, initially, with the seeming discrepancy between the phenomena of mental life and the domain of other and more ordinary objects of nature. To speak of the components of Hume's bundles as being aware of each other makes little sense. (The visual sensation of redness is not, surely, aware of the buzzing sound in my head, but something is aware of both of them at the moment when I am considering, seeing that my head is full of red flashes and loud buzzings, whether I ought to consult a physiologist or a psychiatrist, or just turn over and go back to sleep.) The fact that this awareness can be regarded as another set of sensations does not help the problem. For the fact here is that the Humean and his opponent are not disputing over the facts but are jointly confronting the truth that there are alternative ways of structuring the facts.

Similarly (but I think more clearly) when we come to consider what Socrates (or anyone) knows, we face a peculiar problem. Either (within the "determinate being" scheme) the knowledge which is in my mind is identical with the object known or it is not. But neither alternative will do. If it is identical then it is not "in my mind" but is what it is and where it is. But if it is not identical, then there is, in principle, a gap between my knowledge and its object. If this is so, then I do not really, ever, know anything. Hence the "mind" which "has knowledge" cannot be just "another thing" (or collection of things) in the world but must, somehow, stand in a special relation — dialectical if you like — to the world which it knows. Again, there is a peculiar and complex unity (what Hume called the "theatre of the mind" but admitted that he could not explain or analyze) to our field of awareness and cognition. To "particlize" it both destroys it and makes it unintelligible. It cannot be just "another thing" in the world and yet it is no good putting it out of the world and condemning it to the ghostly life of a pseudo-thing either.

Now the man who wanted to talk about "immortality" will want to try to analyze all these features and to ask questions (as, indeed, Plato's Socrates *did*) about whether "the mind" considered in this way can be subjected to dissolution, corruption, or decay and about what its relations are to certain concepts of cause. What he will find is that when the relevant concepts have been transmuted so that they can be dealt with as "determinate being" (or integrated into propositions which can be carried in Quine's or Russell's logic), he can no longer ask the questions which interest him. For the referential objects he will then be faced with simply are not the sorts of objects about which he can discourse in this way. He will be told (and eventually may admit) that all the facts of experience and so on can readily be accommodated to the scheme proposed, but he will remain baffled. For the counterparts of ordinary concepts which will fit the proposed scheme will have been divested of just the structural features which are of interest to him.

It will go similarly hard with the man who wants to say "Caterpillars develop into moths," if what he wants to do is more than point to an arrangement of discrete states which can arbitrarily be taken (or not taken if one prefers) to form a special class of particles arranged to form a four dimensional continuum. Indeed, even the man who wants to say "Rocks *persist* for a long time" will find that he has been pushed into saying that there are a number of discrete states which can be regarded (for some purposes) as forming a unified class of a certain kind.

Most references to instantiated properties and their bearers will, then, undergo quite sharp transitions if they are coerced into the mould of determinate being. But they will not, thereby, falsify experience. One does not, literally, experience oneself as a continuous being, or see the caterpillar grow into a moth or notice that rocks persist for a long time. Rather, one has some experiences which can be made more or less intelligible by being integrated into various logical moulds. One may resist, for instance, Hume's bundle theory as being the "final word" but, if Humeans challenge one to specify some experience which will not fit the mould they offer, there is no *obvious* answer.[1] The position rather is that there are other intelligible

[1] Specific experiences may, indeed, lead one to prefer one theoretical construction to another but the justification of one's preference requires more than simple reference to the experience. For instance, research in neurophysiology has, in recent years, made it clear that one can distinguish between consciousness as such and specific objects of consciousness by reference to the results of structural alterations in regions of the brain. This does not make Hume's "theatre" a separate object of awareness from the events which are played out in it, but it may help to make the notion intelligible and it suggests that we may be right in thinking that there is an experience of conscious unity even though that experience does not fit into the Humean mould. Here we are relying (if we use this argument) on secondary experiences of neurophysiologists to help us decide between rival ways of categorizing our own primary experiences.

schemes which are open to us and that we may suspect that reason will force us to give them their due. (When we come to demand an account of knowledge, for example, we may see that the Humean scheme will force us to an unwarranted and perhaps contradictory skepticism. Or when we demand a coherent account of the caterpillar-moth relationship, we may find that reason will force us to another scheme. Generally, perhaps, as this book is designed to show, a consideration of logic will force us to trace a variety of logical structures and to try to find the connections between them.)

The point is that experience does not, by itself, force us to anything. It is neutral to the various logical schemes we force on it. In fact it is, in a peculiar way, transparent to them. It is not that there is "reason" on one side and a well-structured experience on the other, but that we know that we have experiences because we see what we can do with them when we get a well-structured logical scheme. So there is not a special gulf. It happens that we can see that there are many concepts which can be fitted, for instance, into determinate being (like the concepts of redness and red patch) but which cannot be deduced from it. We can form ideas of as much of each domain as the logical structures themselves and the experience we have happen to make available.

The fact that we cannot "deduce" all these concepts only results from the fact that, apart from the purely logical entities, which are merely, if you like, mirror images of the structure itself, determinate being is quite neutral to *all* its contents. For it is after all a domain of atomic entities between which there are *not* "natural" relations of implication.

If we look closely at this result, we can see that the alleged "dialectician's dilemma" does not and cannot arise under these conditions. The dialectician was pictured as facing two alternatives: either he claims that, within his system, all the concepts requisite for dealing with the world can be deduced or else he admits that there is some place in the construction of these concepts at which reason leaves off and experience, intuition, or arbitrary postulate takes over. If he opts for the first horn of the dilemma, he is a sort of ratio-maniac and, anyhow, his position is absurd if he is confronted with the need for concepts which are involved with words like "yellow" and "loud." If he opts for the second alternative, he is committed to the kind of dualism which, presumably, he has set out to avoid.

Given the situation with which we are confronted in our attempt to provide an account of determinate being, we can see that the dilemma is wrongly painted. For it depends for its force on the view that there is a highly structured rational system on one side and a well-structured concept of experience on the other. Such a well-structured concept of experience would imply that experience was, literally, something in its own right in the sense that it could be a referential object apart from the other referential objects in the system. It turns out to be the case, so far as determinate being is concerned, however, that, to get appropriate referential objects one has to regard experience as structured by the requirements which must be met by all entities within the domain. Experience can be so structured, but it is not "another thing" and there is not a special class of experiential concepts which are members of a logical order of their own.

This is not to say that there are *no* distinctions of a rather basic kind within the domain of determinate being. I have already indicated that there is, apparently, some distinction between those entities of a logical sort whose place is guaranteed simply by the logical structure of the domain and other entities whose "existence" cannot be deduced from that structure. I shall return to this issue in a moment. For now, however, the point is that there is not *here* a sharp distinction between "matters of fact" and "truths of reason" by way of structure. No duality of reason and experience arises in just the way that would make for the dialectician's dilemma.

Nor is it the case that we can readily distinguish between "necessary" and "contingent" entities within the domain. For anything that *can* be a referential object *must* have a place in the domain.[1] The distinction that does occur is between those entities about which we have knowledge as a result of our logical information and those about which we have knowledge only because we happen to have had the relevant experience. (If there are yellow patches to be referred to, we only know this because we happen to have had certain experiences and can construct the relevant concepts. But if there is a "class of all classes which are not members of themselves," we know this because the domain has certain logical properties. But if the concept of yellow patch is a possible one, then yellow patches have their place in the domain.) It is, no doubt, convenient to have this distinction in mind, but it is a fact that we can refer to classes just as it is a fact that we can refer to yellow patches.

Evidently, however, we are coming to a point at which it seems natural to try to talk about the gap between "thought" and "reality." For it seems to be one thing to maintain that yellow patches "exist" because their occurrence is testified to by certain experiences and another to maintain that centaurs "exist" because we can form a concept of them.

To begin with, however, we need to remind ourselves that "determinate being" is simply a domain of entities having a certain logical structure. Everything which can be talked about and which meets certain logical requirements belongs there. Considered merely as members of this domain, they are just "referential objects" of a special kind, the kind sometimes called logical atoms. We are entitled to say that they have some ontological status on two separate but interesting grounds. One of them, of course, is that the concept of the domain of determinate being is developed, in an

---

[1] But by reference to the counterparts of entities in determinate being — by reference, that is, to other categories and other domains — we may develop reasons for singling out some referential objects for special attention.

orderly way, from the concept of pure being and the concepts which follow it, and this, if you like, is the development of the idea of "reality." The other is that they are entities about which we have certain kinds of knowledge and this knowledge cannot be analyzed away.

Perhaps this deserves elaboration: People often *do* want to say things like "Really, there is no Sherlock Holmes," "Centaurs are merely imaginary," or even "Classes only exist in the minds of logicians." A counter-argument is, of course, "But people talk about Sherlock Holmes, centaurs, and classes and there are even true and false statements about them. Those people must be referring to something." The counter-argument is not convincing because its proponent must be prepared to go on and say something else. But it is a beginning. It is only a beginning because the proponent of the original position can readily go on to say "Sherlock Holmes originally existed in the mind of Conan Doyle and now exists in the minds of his readers and admirers. Furthermore, the idea of Sherlock Holmes was compounded of a lot of ideas about people which Conan Doyle happened to have. Centaurs are even less proper entities because the concept of centaur is an unworkable hybrid of ideas about men and horses. It is not even a sensible *concept*. And classes are just gimmicks made up by logicians. They happen to be convenient, but we must not read our own logical convenience back into the world." We can imagine all these points being suitably elaborated, but what they amount to is this: Often when we talk about xs it turns out that we are really referring, in a disguised way, to ys. We may talk about Sherlock Holmes when we ought to talk about the states of people's minds or the states of their imaginations. Additionally, if the "existence" proponent changes to a "logical" tack and says that because it happens to be the case that "The present king of France is not bald," there must "be" something rightly designated as "the present king of France," we can respond following Russell: Simply say "For any x, x is not both the king of France and bald." This way we can talk about the distribution of properties in the world without postulating a lot of strange entities.

Thus we have two things: Some sample reasons for rejecting claims to the "existence" of various rather curious entities and a technique for avoiding any logical difficulties we might get into by accepting the reasons. But the beginning made by the "existence" proponent was a beginning and can be followed up. He can maintain that he is *really* referring to Sherlock Holmes or the present king of France and that he will neither accept the factual contention that he is talking about the state of someone's mind nor the logical contention that the logical object of reference is really "the class of all of xs." (Russell, after all, did literally "change the subject" in the debate with Meinong.) For, in some sense, Sherlock Holmes remains as a "referential object" whether he is "in someone's mind" or not and "the class of all xs" is a special device which has to be argued for if one is claiming "equivalence of meaning."

If, however, we return to the place in which we belong for the moment — the domain of determinate being — we can perhaps see how these issues might really be settled. None of the referential objects there can be argued away as "apparent xs which are really ys," for they are just what their effective referring descriptions say they are. To say of something in this domain "I know that there is an x" is just a way of saying that you have the requisite conceptual equipment for referring to it. There will not, of course, be in it entities so complex as Sherlock Holmes or the Centaur or indeed any entities sufficiently complex as to permit a further analysis. It is true that we could use Russell's way out and talk about the class of all xs and the way properties are distributed within it because the domain does consist of a unified class of property bearers of just the right sort. But there will not be much occasion to try to reduce the membership of the domain by doing this.

It should be noticed that it is not because we can and do refer to things that it is important to admit all the proper referential objects to a domain whose members have some significant ontological status. (One might, after all, admit Professor Linsky's point that referring is not like hanging — only real men can be hanged, but unreal ones can be referred to. But this is to make some further distinction between referential and other sorts of objects and that possibility does not immediately arise.)[1] The serious reason for admitting referential objects (of the right sort) to such a status is simply that we have knowledge of them and we cannot analyze the appropriate claims to knowledge out into claims about knowledge of other sorts of things. To do that would be to maintain that "determinate being" was not a genuine "category" in the scheme. But that is what the whole line of argument is intended to deny.

The uneasiness which this kind of conclusion is apt to engender is natural enough but it rests on a misunderstanding. The fact that the "world" viewed under the guise of determinate being seems to lack many of the distinctions that we want to make in it is simply a reason for thinking that determinate being is not the only domain.

Equally, it would be foolish to underestimate the importance of such a domain. (It is valuable as we go along to try to form a clear estimate of the significance of each of the categories as a way of focussing the world. For there is a tendency amongst the post-Hegelians — and perhaps in Hegel himself — to assume that the later categories are inclusive in the peculiar sense that they obliterate the need for the earlier ones except as stepping stones.)

The significance of determinate being is that it is the region of discourse at which traditional logic, modern mathematical logic, and the mathemati-

[1] *Referring* (London: Routledge and Kegan Paul, and New York: The Humanities Press, 1967), p. 18.

cised versions of the physical sciences either do operate in practice or tend to operate in theory: By its nature it is the region of the precise, the determinate, the countable. Equally, it is a region in which a logic which provides for these features and a mathematics which embodies this logic mesh exactly with their subject matter so that, often, there is no clear distinction between the mathematical theory and the subject matter related by it. If the world could not be viewed in some such guise, such enterprises would be vastly different or perhaps impossible. (Something of this will emerge in the next section when we come to talk about systematic unity.)

Not surprisingly, difficulties *have* developed (at least in the minds of philosophers) about the distinction between "scientific entities" (like atoms, fundamental particles and so on) and "entities in the ordinary world." One reason for this, evidently, is that the scientific entities tend to approximate to the demands of the relevant logic and mathematics, and to appear "stripped down" to meet the demands of determinate being. They are referential objects deeply embedded in the referential powers of the appropriate theories.

Such entities do not correspond immediately to "observed things" in the "ordinary world" at least because the "things" in the ordinary world are constructed with a much more complex (if less rigorous) conceptual apparatus. But the "scientific entities" may be just as much "brought to notice" by experience as the ordinary ones, if we take the view of experience I was suggesting earlier. On the level at which the appropriate logic works, however, entities can be dealt with on the same basis whether our ability to refer to them is triggered by observation or by theory.

No doubt, if we want to, we can sort and distinguish entities within the domain of determinate being by assigning such priorities as seem to us convenient independently of their equal status as mere referential objects. But the criteria for such sortings will have to come from outside the domain — as I suggested in the earlier footnote on page 90.

Perhaps these issues will appear in a clearer light after the discussion of systematic unity. For now, however, the position seems to be that, thus far, there is no reason to think that we are involved in any fatal separation either between reason and experience or between thought and reality.

XV

Before we pass to a direct discussion of systematic unity, it will be as well to remind ourselves, briefly, of the reasons for introducing it. It will then be possible to formulate, at least roughly, the limiting conditions which it entails and to take note of the special difficulties which are likely to be involved in it.

Essentially, the difficulties which made it necessary to transcend determinate being were, on the one hand, the limits problem and its twin the problem of totalities, and, on the other, the problem of formulating an adequate notion of the kind of union which held between bearers of properties and the properties themselves. We were forced, in other words, from a concept of a fragmented atomic world to its dialectical counterpart, the concept of a world as a single, united, seamless system. (I will not, here, repeat the dialectical argument which made it possible [or seemingly so] to choose various alternative formulations of the solution.)

XVI

The limiting conditions imposed on assertions which refer to this new domain, then, will include at least these:

(1) All of them must refer to a way of ordering the whole of the domain.

(2) No such assertion can function by making distinctions within the domain if these distinctions are taken to specify separate entities.

(3) All such assertions, again, will have to be a-temporal. (There are two different kinds of reasons for this. One is that no temporal concepts entered into the structure out of which the concept of systematic unity was derived. The other is that temporal references would fragment the domain in a clearly unacceptable way.)

Other (more specific, but derivative) limitations will emerge as the discussion develops. Initially, however, it seems obvious that the real difficulty here is going to be to meet the conditions of intelligibility.

How can we say anything about anything without violating these conditions? How can we locate reasonable counterparts of statements which are quite sensible when taken as referring to determinate being? How are we to deal, here, with apparent references to time? And, finally, what will happen, here, to the "laws" of identity, non-contradiction, and excluded middle?

The first thing, indeed, to notice about the domain of systematic unity is that, within it, special notions of propositional reference are required. Heretofore, it has been possible to work with common sense notions and notions which are implicitly a part of fairly standard logical structures — expanding them only so as to take note of problems of reference to multiple domains. It was possible to hold that propositions, by reason of their structural features, could refer or be taken to refer to "pure being," to "pure disjunction" and to entities and features which can be discriminated within determinate being. But the central requirement of systematic unity is that we should be able to distinguish determinate features of the world without becoming involved in the atomizing process which the kind of discourse suited to determinate being involves. There are no longer any sharp lines of demarcation.

94

Suppose we begin, again, with an assertion such as "Socrates is mortal." Considered as an assertion about the world conceived as systematic unity, the problem about it is no longer to break it down into a series of assertions about the logically appropriate "Socrates particles" and then to de-temporalize "mortality" and give it a meaning which will make some class or set of these particles its appropriate bearer, but rather to show what the "Socrates perspective" on the world is like and how "mortality" fits into it. We cannot, within this domain, set "limits" to Socrates. For the conditions of systematic unity preclude the possibility of indicating where Socrates ends and the rest of the world begins. We can imagine Socrates as a causally dependent entity, whose occurrence presupposes that there is solid ground to stand on, air to breathe, and heat enough for ordinary bodily functions. These conditions are, in turn, dependent on the state of the solar system, the galaxy, and, presumably, the universe at large and, equally, on the stability of laws of physics, the continuity of chemical reaction in a fixed pattern and so on. Or we can consider Socrates as a creature with mind and knowledge — capable, if you like, of containing the whole world within the domain of his knowledge. Thus Socrates, so considered, is not a thing in the world but one of the modes of organization within the world, a specific kind of pattern which runs through the world.

Before we pursue this any further, it is important to try to make this perspective clearer by way of contrast with the domain of determinate being. It has sometimes been imagined, I think, by philosophers given to certain kinds of monism, or opposed to the kind of pluralism which is exemplified in the logical atomism appropriate to determinate being, that, when one talks in the way I have just been suggesting, one is calling attention, in a quite straightforward way, to *facts* which cannot be dealt with by logical atomism. But this is not quite the case. The causal connections in the Socrates example will, of course, appear in an account of determinate being but they will appear only as fortuitous arrangements of the appropriate logical atoms. Whether we are considering determinate being or systematic unity, the patterns involved will be essentially a-temporal. "Time" in both cases will appear simply as a dimension of the logical space involved. But the analysis possible within determinate being will make the pattern appear fortuitous, while, within systematic unity (since no ultimate separations are possible there) they will appear necessary. Roughly, if we can find a suitable analogy in the "time" dimension of the logical space for constancy, constant conjunction is the natural analysis of "cause" within determinate being, while *some* kind of logical necessity will be required to provide the essential analysis within systematic unity. But the appropriateness of each of these analyses depends simply on the conditions laid down for membership within each domain. The same "facts" in a different domain present a different picture. The result (if the dialectical argument leading to the postulation of each of these domains is correct) is not a contradiction between the components of which we must choose, but a pair of inter-dependent perspectives.

With this in mind, we can proceed to try to find out what "Socrates is mortal" might mean if there were reason to assert it within the domain of systematic unity. (It seems to follow, of course, that if there is reason to assert it at all, there must be reason to interpret it as an assertion appropriate to *every* domain. For otherwise, the core concepts are not just ways of focussing the world but postulations about different worlds.) Given, then, that Socrates, viewed this way, is a certain kind of pattern running through the world and uniting it in a certain way, what about "mortality"? Or, for that matter, what about any "property" which is assigned to Socrates in any ordinary assertion. Indeed, what about *any* property assigned to *any* bearer?

It will turn out that "mortality" belongs to a special and rather interesting class of potentially assignable properties but it is essential to deal with the general case first.

Within systematic unity the distinction between bearers of properties and the properties themselves must not be expected to remain in the form in which it appeared within determinate being. Assertions like "Socrates is mortal," "This typewriter is grey," "Some swans are white," and so on no longer pick out some entity or class of entities and make claims to the effect that some properties are instantiated in, born by, or identifiable in the thing or things concerned. Rather, they call attention to a way of patterning the world and the fact that the property or properties concerned are more-or-less fundamental to the pattern. This is not (immediately at least) easy to understand. But some examples will, I think, clear it up.

To see the point, it is necessary to consider and contrast a cluster containing at least two assertions. Suppose we take at random "This box is red" and "Socrates is an Athenian." To get at the notion of systematic unity we have to imagine both Socrates and the box as being fixed in their places in whatever scheme they belong to by a network of relations. The box is a box because it encloses a certain space in a certain way and it is *this* box because it is just this space which it encloses. If this region were not there to be enclosed in just the way it is, there could not be this box. Furthermore, it is capable of being conceived the way it is just because the other entities on which it is dependent are just what they are. To imagine it cut off from all or any of them, is to imagine it as something different — at least as not part of the particular systematic unity in which it functions. To say that "it" is red is to say, in effect, that this region of the system so delineated is red. But that is not quite enough since every property which is assignable to anything in such a system is assignable to the "box" viewed as a way of patterning that system. Probably, the system will run through green, pink, and mauve things as well and the box, viewed this way, is not sharply cut off from them in such a way as to enable us to say "Here, *this* is the box; the rest of those things are something else." What is being said (when we imagine the box as a feature of systematic unity) is that redness is somehow crucial to the box perspective on the world. It is part of what distinguishes this focus from every other. If we imagine Socrates as part of the same world as the box, then "Socrates is an Athenian" will mark out another pattern which includes all the same facts but suppresses or neutralizes some of them so that they become less fundamental. The box, no doubt, will figure as part of the chain of relations of dependence which determine that Socrates is what he is, and so is "part of Socrates," but the colour of the box will fade into insignificance so that even someone trying to "explain" Socrates in relation to his environment probably will not mention it. (It might be mentioned if it had some special aesthetic importance for Socrates or turned up in his life as a religious symbol.) Being an Athenian, likewise, is just one of the properties which figure in the world of Socrates and the box, but, whereas we would not say, on the ground that Socrates is part of the world of the box and not separable from it on ultimate terms, that "Socrates is red," we *would* say "Socrates is an Athenian." For being an Athenian is part of what we want to bring out in order to emphasize the Socrates perspective. Generally, of course, getting the emphasis wrong has the ring of absurdity. If we say the box and the Athenians are all part of the same world and depend on each other and, furthermore, cannot be understood apart from each other, we are involved in an argument which can be understood. But if we infer from that that "The box is an Athenian," the assertion seems not merely false but quite patently absurd.

What has happened, in a basic way, is this: in viewing the world under the rubrics of determinate being, we find ourselves with sets of atomic, concrete things precisely delimited by properties which meet certain rigorous logical requirements. These entities are, in the traditional sense, externally related to one another — their relations are added to them and leave them fundamentally unchanged. It is true that, to be intelligible, we have to regard these entities as arranged so as to have *some* relation to each other, to form the rudiments of a logical space. But this relation is pushed, there, at our peril since it leads to the totality problem and the breakdown or transcendence of the category. But in viewing the world under the rubrics of systematic unity, this discreteness disappears. It is not just that we get "internal" relations (in the traditional sense of relations which "make a difference" to their terms) but that we get a world of relations. This sounds more peculiar than it is. What it means, simply, is that all the terms turn out to be relational and what is left to us to do is simply to translate our talk about things into talk about patterns.

Thus, in general, the subject terms of assertions will have to be taken to designate a way of patterning the whole of the systems within which they function, and expressions assigning properties to those subject terms will have to be taken to indicate relative importance — to be devices for bringing out the focus which clarifies the pattern in question. Commonly, single assertions like "This x is a y" will convey little or nothing and assertions will become increasingly significant as they come in clusters which are larger and provide better focus. Characteristically, coherence is a touchstone of intelligibility in this domain and significance is given by creating a definite perspective.

XVIII

If we are called upon to analyze assertions like "Socrates is mortal," however, additional complexities come into play. For "Socrates is mortal" does not, like "Socrates is an Athenian," seem to call attention, here, to features of the Socrates pattern which are particularly crucial. It calls attention, instead, to something about the status of the Socrates pattern, presumably that *it* is not, ultimately, a fundamental feature of the system which it structures.

We are here, in fact, confronted with the problem of temporal reference. The "solution" to this difficulty within determinate being was to conceive time as another dimension not fundamentally different from the appropriate spatial dimensions. Thus within the "logical space" of determinate being, "Socrates is mortal" means there are Socrates particles in some ordered set of places (appropriately defined) and not elsewhere on the potential "life line" of Socrates. Now if statements referring to systematic unity are in some way "counterparts" of statements referring to determinate being, the "solution" offered will have to be a "counterpart" solution. But all statements referring to systematic unity refer to the whole of the domain so there is no evident distinction to be made between relevant parts of it.

What is open to us is simply to hold that, if Socrates is mortal, then the Socrates pattern is not fundamental to the system as a whole. That is, there will be ways of referring to the system which create patterns in which none of the features which are crucially emphasized when we talk specifically about Socrates will be emphasized.

Once again, we shall need examples to make this intelligible. But examples which are not too rich or obscured from the imprecision of the notions drawn from our ordinary ways of talking are rather hard to come by. The best procedure (as usual) is to start out with examples which are quite ordinary and then to see in what ways they might mislead.

Suppose we start with the red box of our earlier example and imagine it as an ordinary physical object about which we happen to have a number of beliefs which, if not exactly ordinary, are at least not particularly unusual. Imagine these to include the belief that the box exists or is part of the world at some times and not at others. Imagine, as well, that they include the belief that the box is composed of material particles of various kinds and

98

that these particles can be envisaged (under suitable circumstances) as matter or as energy. In addition, our beliefs may be supposed to include the belief that at all times in the past, present, and future of the universe this matter or energy is a part of the universe.

If all these beliefs were true, there would be a reason for believing that ways of patterning the universe so as to emphasize the particles in question would be more fundamental than ways which emphasized the box structure, and that ways which emphasized the "matter-energy" were more fundamental than ways which emphasized the particles. The box structure could be regarded as a "manifestation" of the more fundamental features and it could, if we wished, be regarded as being "immanent" in them in the sense of being contained in the possibilities associated with them.

If we are working in a system in which a temporal structure, proper, is not available to us we may still, if we have access to such notions of relative "fundamentality" generate a notion of time by regarding ourselves as successively attending to these patterns and ordering our attention. This notion of successive attention does not, of course, have any place in the scheme of systematic unity. But we can regard the arrangement of patterns in this way as a counterpart of temporal occurrence in the domain of systematic unity. It is true that it does not express the whole idea of time but, then, neither does the scheme available within the confines of determinate being. It is, after all, part of the point that all of these schemes pinch in some way. Furthermore, there seems to be enough connection between the notions of relative pervasiveness (which does duty in the determinate being scheme) and fundamentality to make it seem reasonable that these notions should function as counterparts of one another so that we *can* say that the two domains have the same contents but exhibit different ways of ordering them though we still need to develop for every kind of case a more adequate notion of "contents."

To be sure, if we think this scheme will work in general, we shall have to think that there will always be ways of dealing with temporality in the way in which we dealt with the box case. If this is considered as a matter about the "facts" of the case, it may seem doubtful that we always or ever do believe this. In the box case, anyone who accepted a "continuous creation" cosmology, for instance, would deny that the "facts" square with the analysis and it would seem doubtful that we could deal with "Socrates is mortal" in an appropriate way at all.

This suggests, however, that the example may be ambiguous in a certain crucial respect.

One way in which this is no doubt so is that the example I provided is drawn rather carelessly from our ordinary speech and affairs and painted as though we were in a position to deal with distinctions between actual matters of fact and "mere" possibilities — as if we were considering full-blooded accounts of actual states of affairs. In fact, the scheme so far developed is not rich enough to deal with these distinctions. For we have here only the dialectical alternative to determinate being and that, as we saw, is a domain within which, strictly speaking, we have only referential objects to deploy. The unities with which we have to deal in systematic unity must be similarly limited unless there is some reason to believe that a richer range of distinctions is possible here. But the limits which can be placed on the contents of systematic unity do not, in fact, add any distinctions of that kind.

This makes a difference to the discussion in the following way: When we talk, for instance, about the box pattern being less fundamental than some underlying pattern, or the Socrates pattern being less fundamental than a pattern emphasizing some set of conditions out of which we can imagine Socrates being constructed, the reference cannot be to some state of affairs out of which it may or may not be true that accounts of the appropriate range of efficient causes can be constructed. Indeed, when, in a preliminary example, I canvassed the notion of "causal dependence" as it might appear in an account appropriate to systematic unity, it was obvious that the relevant features of that account would have to be formulated in terms of a kind of logical dependence. For we should require both a richer account of time and a distinction between actuality and possibility to deal with "efficient cause" in the usual sense in which it means something more than causal conjunction and different from logical dependence.

What we are left with is the notion that, when some pattern is said to be less fundamental than another, it is because it depends upon some more general feature or features within which it can be said to be immanent or on which it can be said to be dependent. Additionally, it will have to be the case that the dependence relation is asymmetrical for otherwise the two patterns will be equally fundamental. Put this way, we do seem to have a general condition which must hold for any state of any possible world which would be expressed by sentences like "Socrates did not live forever" or "This red box is not a permanent feature of the universe." For otherwise the entity either would not be explicable (would not, that is, in the terms appropriate to the category of systematic unity be fixed in its place by a complete network of relations establishing its pattern as running through the whole of the system) or would be expressible in terms of a pattern fundamental to the system. In the first case, it could not be spoken of under the rubrics of systematic unity and, in the second, it would appear as a feature of the world at all possible times. If we found a case which did not meet the requirements because it *was* inexplicable that, of course, would be a special reason for doubting the soundness of the dialectical scheme. But we should realize that it would appear as something which "just happened" and stood in isolation from the rest of the world. For reasons given in the first chapter, it seems unlikely that any such case is intelligible. At best, such cases would be like miracles: It is doubtful if we would feel sufficiently

100

certain that we understood what was going on to want to use them as reasons to overthrow rational structures to which we already had some commitment.[1]

Thus we can find counterparts for temporal statements — however unsatisfactory they may be for expressing just what we want to express by them. Equally, we can find counterparts for causal statements. In each case the differences between statements expressed in the way appropriate to determinate being and those expressed in the way appropriate to systematic unity will be just those differences which stem from the differences of logical requirement between the two categories.

XIX

It is perhaps worth exploring these features a little further in the hope both of increasing clarity and of showing the significance of the two categories. One way of doing this is to look at a fairly simple statement of the classical problem of induction. Viewed through the logical spectacles of the schemes appropriate to determinate being, the problem appears like this: If someone attempts to infer from the occurrence of n instances of x, all of which have exhibited a certain characteristic, y, that a further occurrence of x will also exhibit y or that, given many xs, all, many, or even some of them will exhibit y, he is faced with a pair of rather unsatisfactory alternatives. He can say flatly that the position is that inferences from known instances of anything to instances about which knowledge is less complete are always formally invalid and that their inadequacy is always exactly proportional to the lack of knowledge of the additional instances involved. Thus, faced with the assertion "On n occasions, the sun has risen in the east and set in the west, therefore on the occasion which we shall call $n + 1$ it is reasonable to believe that this pattern will be repeated," he will simply deny that the belief is founded on any proposition which derives support from the assertion preceding "therefore." He can defend his position on the ground that the preceding information about sunrises and sunsets refers to occasions which

---

[1] It is worthwhile to note the implied problem here: The categories of a system like this one are linked together so as to form an explanatory unity. The properties expressed by the categories also permeate the members of the domains which they organize so that the implication is that whatever is ultimately real is part of a system of "total explanation." But the members of the various domains are also *conceptually* independent and so (if thought and reality do not part company) *really* to some degree independent of the structure of the categories. Thus the problem of the general applicability of the principle of sufficient reason requires independent investigation. Again, some of the categories require — as systematic unity does — a unified explanation. But they do not guarantee it. Thus, if the system holds, an independent investigation ought to be made to find out whether the problems besetting anyone who holds the principle of sufficient reason can be solved. The problem is discussed again in Chapter 6, but it forms the subject matter of what must be another book.

are all atomic in the sense that they do not bind each other or any subsequent occasion.

Alternatively, he can revert to a kind of probability theory. If he knows that there are a limited number of alternatives as with a coin which, when tossed, is presumed to come down either heads or tails ("on edge" being eliminated by definition) he can claim that we know something about future tosses, namely that the probability is one-half for either alternative. Here, roughly, we are not concerned with coins but with mathematical sequences of certain kinds to which coin tosses may be imagined to approximate. We thus find, in general, ways in which various classes of events can be arranged to approximate to the properties of manageable arithmetical distributions. Most likely, of course, this does not help with the sunrise case since we do not know what the alternatives are, what the definition of the "event" in question really is, or what the bearing of past occurrences to future ones (or known to unknown, to stick to the atemporal locutions) would be if we did have this information. In the coin tossing case, we do know that the chances of the result being heads rather than tails are not (merely by the mathematics of the theory) altered by the fact that the last n tosses have all been heads. We do know that, given a very large number of tosses, we would expect the distribution to be roughly equal, but this does not bear on the outcome of toss $n + 1$.

It need not be the case, of course, that this way of going about the problem always leads to an uninteresting result. For there may be cases in which we can contrast a "random" distribution of events with an actual distribution and infer that some interesting influence is at work. If we set a man to work guessing cards, we can assume, if there are five different kinds of cards, he will, if he guesses the way that we expect the "chances" to fall, be right once in five. If he consistently does better than that over thousands of attempts, we will begin to think something interesting is at work. Perhaps he is cheating, or he is telepathic, or he has hit on some flaw in our system for shuffling the cards. But it is not clear just why we should think this, or how we should interpret any distribution of outcomes within a finite set of outcomes or how, indeed, for any complex phenomenon, we could tell what a "chance" distribution was. For our actual information is still about certain mathematical sequences and, insofar as actual events have additional properties, we are still at sea. If we consider various possible changes in our mathematical schemes, we are more at sea still. This way of looking at the problem does, certainly, suggest a rather general possibility for dealing with a wide range of "inductions" but it is, importantly, a curious one. We can imagine ourselves constructing a scheme in which the chance distributions for all possible phenomena are worked out. We can then imagine associating various kinds of "causal influences" with various deviations from this expectation. Once we know these, we can project, again, the expected distribution and associate new distributions with additional causal influences.

102

If the possibilities were finite and the causal influences were known to be persistent in some way, we might imagine our information about the world gradually closing off the alternatives until we could say we had a rational foundation for something like "inductions" in the traditional sense. But "persistence," of course, gives the game away for the problem originally had to do with the atomicity of individual events (or particle positions in some four-dimensional continuum). Besides, assumptions about finitude would be difficult to justify and, anyway, the hope of simplifying the necessary account of the universe so as to get the whole scheme to fit the required mathematical mould seems forlorn.

The fact of the matter is that, although much has been done to make various probability theories useful as practical tools for various kinds of investigations they only "solve" the problem (as it appears in the determinate being scheme) insofar as we are willing to make various important *ad hoc* assumptions. So no alternative, on the premises which are natural to the determinate being scheme, is really very happy.

It may not be happier, but the situation is certainly quite different within the scheme appropriate to systematic unity. Consider, now, the sunrise case. Within "determinate being" we have to think of the problem as being one in which we are faced with the distribution of some set of entities over the appropriate logical space. The question becomes: If we know something about the occupants of some regions of this space, what can we infer about their neighbours? The answer is "nothing" unless it happens we know something (as in the coin-tossing case) about the special restrictions which limit the possibilities open to us in describing those neighbours. (If we know it is a tossed coin, we know it lies either heads or tails.) As a problem about the properties of a special systematic unity, we know, however, that we are dealing with a completely integrated system. To say "The sun might not rise in the east tomorrow despite what we happen to know about many past days" is to say that we have a pattern of rather low fundamentality such that, if we consider a sequence of possible patterns, so as to be able to distinguish between today and yesterday, some of the patterns may emphasize sunrise features with different geographical references and some may involve no sunrise features at all.

At this point, however, we can ask questions like: "Can anything *be* the sun and not rise in the east?" or "If anything counts as tomorrow, will it not have a sunrise?" In this context, such questions will have to be interpreted to mean "Are all patterns within which 'sun' features are prominent alike in the relevant respects?" and "Is it part of what is entailed by arranging our understanding of the world into patterns which feature days that there should be components identifiable as sunrises?" If the questions were rephrased so as to make them relevant to the determinate being scheme, the answers would be straightforward enough just because the various components of the situations concerned would turn out to be externally related to one another. But if we are to regard the relevant situations as systematic unities, it seems that the answer must almost certainly be that nothing can be the sun unless it does fit into the total picture in a certain way and nothing can be a "day" unless it begins and ends in a certain way. For we are not now considering the sun as a separable entity which *might* go its own way but as part of a total pattern which renders intelligible some features of our affairs which, even if they are presented to us in a fragmentary way, are to be understood (if at all) as perfectly general systems embracing everything. On this view we begin to see the sun as just part of an interlocking system which would have to be different in every respect if it were to change at all.

In one sense, the answer becomes "If there is a sun, it will, of course, rise tomorrow in the east." If it doesn't you were wrong in thinking that there was a sun at all and, in that case, your whole thought structure is wrong (though perhaps only to a minor degree). For, on this view the concept of sun is not itself separable; it is only intelligible as part of such wider notions as "solar system," "physical universe" and so on and, within those systems, it can have one and only one place. Thus, if there shouldn't be a sunrise, the latitude which remains is restricted by the openings that can be found by giving a range of meanings to "is" in expressions such as "There is a sun."

There seem to be two primary possibilities open for exploiting this latitude. To deny that there "is" a sun may be to deny that there is any place in any scheme which will provide a complete conceptual system for the concept "sun." On this view, "sun" becomes like "unicorn," the kind of thing about which you cannot form a satisfactory concept. The bits of it don't seem to hang together (in the way that the magical properties of unicorns may not fit with their presumed biological properties). Nor do they mesh with other concepts (in the way that unicorn concepts seem not to fit into evolutionary theories). Alternatively, and more likely, to deny that there "is" a sun may be to deny that there "is now" a sun. This is a way, in this context, of saying that the sun features in any total theory are not fundamental so that it is imaginable that we may now have reasons for attending to other possibilities latent in the more basic pattern. Once the matter is straight on either view, however, it becomes sensible to say "We know that it is likely (or unlikely as the case may be) that the sun will rise tomorrow." "Likely," here, will not mean "probable" in the probability theory sense discussed a moment ago. It will refer rather to our certainty in believing that we have got a concept of "sun" which will mesh so as to provide a complete set of concepts dealing with everything, or to our belief that the pattern in which this concept figures is relatively fundamental.

Now these ways of looking at theories are quite common and have probably played important parts in the history of science. It is not uncommon to give up concepts (like that of "ether") just because they won't fit with other concepts in any adequate way and become embarrassing in the way that "unicorn" would become to a biologist who, thinking that the

104

various mythical references indicate that there once were unicorns, struggles to fit them into his evolutionary theory. We could have kept the "ether" concept by paying various conceptual prices — perhaps by believing that the earth stands still. But that would have made it very hard to establish any intelligible pattern running over a wide range of astro-physical and other concepts. Similarly, since there are many literary references to them, biologists might have taken unicorns to be like dodos — interesting but extinct. But it is doubtful if they could have found a place for them or been able to maintain a consistent explanatory system in the absence of unicorn remains. Of course, our certainty in saying "There will be no unicorns tomorrow" is conditioned by the fact that we are not wholly certain about existing conceptual structures.

Again, the fundamentality issue is, probably, fairly common. One way of looking at earlier and later theories in physics is, sometimes, to regard the earlier theories as applying to affairs relatively localized in space and time while later theories are more fundamental in the sense that they hold over larger regions including those dealt with by less fundamental theories.

XX

Now, however, we need to look at the important disadvantages of viewing the world as a set of ordered "systematic unities" from the point of view of anyone involved in inductive theorizing or, indeed, theorizing at all. The main difficulty, of course, involves inference patterns. The bits of a systematic unity (if they can be regarded as bits at all) fit together to make a pattern which *is* the primary object of reference. But they have to fit together like pieces of a jig-saw puzzle: Each piece fits into the next one because that is how, together, they form a unity and not because of any general inference rule. The test, as with the jig-saw puzzle, is the final coherence of the scheme. And there is not a rule to tell us what that amounts to. If you can put together a "sun" concept, some "planet" concepts and the appropriate concepts of physical forces and so on to make a scheme that fits and doesn't do special violence to any concept to which you are already committed (by way of reason or experience or whatever), then you can congratulate yourself that you have a "theory." If you do do violence to some existing conceptual commitment, you can alter that commitment. If you find that you have two rival "coherent" theories then, obviously, you don't have a unique fit and you can cast about amongst your conceptual commitments until you find a reason to make some alteration which will give you a unique fit. Roughly, the stronger your conceptual commitments are, the more nearly the process of making everything fit will seem objective — since your latitude will be small — and the weaker they are, the more the process will seem subjective and rather like creating a work of art. In such enterprises much will depend upon whether some crucial anchor concepts can be shown commitment-worthy and whether the "logic" of the situation turns out to be binding.

In this respect, we should remember that we are, still, dealing with a world in which "referential objects" fill the domain. There can be many schemes, in principle, which can be made into systematic unities although we may think that, given all the levels of fundamentality, only one of them may represent "the real world." Generally, in constructing scientific theories, there is no way of choosing between rival coherent models. But the range of them may not be quite as great as we might think because there will be logical restraints. If the scheme presented in this book is correct it will be essential, for one thing, to have schemes which have counterparts in other domains. This may also lighten the burden in other ways since, although systematic unities have components which are necessarily linked by unique inferences, their counterparts in determinate being can be dealt with in terms of propositions about which there are general rules and this fact can be used to advantage at times — most obviously by arranging the counterpart statements to form standard deductive argument patterns.

It seems not unlikely, in fact, that scientific reasoning often operates both from the standpoint of determinate being and from the standpoint of systematic unity. If there is no opposition between them — if, indeed, they are two sides of the same coin — this should occasion no surprise. It may be, however, that some kinds of dispute between rival philosophers of science actually or potentially become unduly complicated and misleading because of the general failure to realize that they *are* two sides of the same coin. Of course, some of the special features of these schemes as I have delineated them do not often seem to figure in theoretical discussions. It is common to think of time as a dimensional feature of a kind of logical space. But the counterpart of time which I considered for systematic unity does seem strange. It may, however, not be so strange as it seems. Generally, for instance, if one has a theory of the solar system, the overall pattern of the scheme is regarded as more fundamental than the momentary locations of the entities concerned. What is required of the theory is that it should contain the possibility that the components are where we think they are at a given moment. Time does seem to become a buried feature in such schemes. Similarly, though it will turn out, I think, that salient features of certain theories about organisms (including evolutionary theories) require a much richer notion of time, it is worth noticing that the fundamental patterns to which evolutionary theories direct our attention are relatively neutral to the time spans over which the events they refer to take place. The explanatory power of such theories depends significantly on their ability to call attention to fundamental features which, since all organisms possess them in one way or another, form a unifying level. Equally significantly, such theories must be able to call attention to the variety of possibilities latent in the fundamental unity and to connections which show the possibility of an orderly development. This last stage does, presumably, set lower limits on the time spans involved but it is not usually required that upper limits should be shown or that the exact time span should be deducible from the theory. The *possibility* of construing the scheme in terms of a time span does, in fact, depend on our being able to show that there are various levels of fundamentality and that a variety of patterns lies immanent in our account of the most fundamental level.

XXI

Hopefully, we are progressing toward intelligibility though there is still the difficult problem of dealing with systematic unity in terms of such seemingly general and binding restrictions as the law of non-contradiction. Before we turn to that, however, it may be useful to look at the region of human affairs in which we would, most naturally, expect to find systematic unities: art. This may have some special merit, additionally, because it may help to make clearer the way in which experience can be interpreted within systematic unity. It may, also, cast a little light on the difficult problem of establishing what is at issue when we want to say that the same "contents" can be referred to by a variety of "counterpart statements" appropriate to various domains.

The difficulty here, in part, is that this is not the place in which to mount an aesthetic theory. Just as, in the last few pages, I was not trying to construct a "philosophy of science" but only to call attention to features which might be found in some scientific theories, so, here, I can only try to call attention to features which are not uncommon in works of art. This is not to say that they are, or should be, found in all works of art — though a case might be made for such a view.

Quite commonly, however, things which are valued as works of art have the following characteristics: They form a close-knit unity within themselves such that a change in any part of them would alter the whole in a significant way; they are to be understood as unities and not as collections of individual parts; they contain components, but these components are arranged to form a pattern which gives significance or emphasis to all of the parts in a determinate way; and they refer beyond themselves though not as propositions do — not, that is, to some particular in the world which they may be said merely to reflect information about. In addition, even when, as with music, they come to us spread over a region of time, they generally transcend that span if they succeed in their aim. The piece of music comes to us as a unity of intelligibility; the last line of the poem has meaning because we recall the first and the intervening lines.

Works of art which have these properties are thus in part microcosms of the notion of systematic unity and those of them which can be said either to refer to reality as a whole (as perhaps Milton's *Paradise Lost* does or the portraits of the human condition found in Shakespeare do) or to refer to effectively self-contained universes (as some music might be thought to) are, in a way, themselves counterparts to propositions construed in the way appropriate to determinate being. For just as those propositions refer to entities while containing in themselves structural features appropriate to their way of marking out objects of reference so works of art, sometimes at least, may refer to systematic unities and contain in themselves the appropriate internal structures. When we construct theories or segments of theories designed to reveal the aspects of things appropriate to systematic unity our activities, in fact, become significantly like those of artists. Equally, part of the fascination that works of art of certain kinds have for us lies in the fact that we recognize in them ways of bringing out aspects of reality which would otherwise be difficult to convey or impossible to discern.

But the situation is more complex than this: Perhaps a small lyric poem which may, overtly, be about a bird strikes a deeper chord than a paragraph in a field handbook because, structurally, it is a miniature model universe and, together with its overt references, it succeeds in fusing the particular and the general. It may be capable of making us feel a unity with its subject matter just because this complex of unified references transcends the ordinary distinctions.

Here, again, we can see that experience is itself transparent to the structure imposed on it. The poet is not just reporting "seeing a bird" though that, no doubt, is part of it. Given the structure available to him from the traditions of poetry or, conceivably, created for the occasion, he can turn it into something intelligible and capable of transcending its own immediate limitations. But the experience is not something over and above its various interpretations. Just as the work of art may symbolize the structure of the world — or its structure viewed through one of the basic unifying concepts we have been talking about — and is thus, itself, open to a range of meanings and interpretations, so the experience itself is rather like a symbol in that it has a range of possible meanings and is not, itself, something over and above them. Our way of "pinning it down" must be to explore the range of interpretations it is capable of just as our way of pinning down the poem must be to explore the range of systematic meanings to which it is open.

As we explore the categories established by the core concepts of the system, we ought to be able to see how the assertions which are appropriate to each domain are linked to their counterparts in other domains — to trace, that is, the effects of the successive logical requirements and the way in which they function to provide an intelligibly linked set of meanings. Why there should be any experience and how it comes to be the case that it can be regarded as providing a significant basis for a common subject matter are questions which must be dealt with much later in our investigation. The point that I want to make is that there is no reason thus far to imagine a kind of dualism in which there is experience on one side and reason on

108

the other. Experience only appears insofar as it has a logical structure and the "basis for a common subject matter" is not another and independently discussable kind of *thing*.

XXII

We must now, however, turn to the problem about the "laws of logic." In discussing determinate being, I was able to construct recognizable forms of the traditional laws of identity, non-contradiction and excluded middle. Part of the significance of this lay in showing that a dialectical system does not exclude such notions and, indeed, provides a domain over which they have their traditional force. The potential difficulty, however, is that it may well be imagined that, where such rules or laws do not hold sway, intelligibility is, finally, impossible. If that is true and if a successful dialectical system necessarily involves regions over which such laws cannot be made to hold, then the dialectic is impossible and is necessarily reduced to nonsense. On the face of it, we have, at this point in the discussion, two reasons for thinking that we have passed outside the scope of these rules.

Immediately, the domain of systematic unity seems to make impossible the kind of atomicity which these rules in their ordinary formulations seem to demand. In the background, the whole notion of multiple reference and category succession which the core concepts entail seems to be in conflict with the basic conceptual pivots on which the traditional laws turn.

I shall first try to formulate each of these objections as clearly as I can. Then I will consider whether or not there are other formulations of the basic laws or other ways of doing the same logical work. I hope to be able to show that there are and that in the face of them the original objections can be answered.

In order to get the objections at all straight we shall, first, have to look at the traditional formulations of the "three laws" and then try to unpack their meanings in a way which will expose the relevant issues. This is more difficult than one would suppose for though the "laws" are mentioned frequently enough in the philosophical literature, they are most commonly taken for granted or else it is assumed that the difficulty, if any, about them, is simply to make them clear. Occasionally it is suggested — as in the logics of Bradley, Bosanquet and Hegel — that the traditional formulations are specific forms of more general principles, but so far as I can tell, the clarity of the more general formulations is less than that of the specific forms and, in the cases cited I am not entirely sure of the relations between the two.[1] Part of the difficulty, after all, is that the "laws" are supposed to be basic

[1] See Bradley, *The Principles of Logic* (second edition, London: Oxford University Press, 1922), Vol. I, p. 141ff; Bosanquet, *Logic or the Morphology of Knowledge* (London: Oxford University Press, 1911), Vol. II, p. 209ff; Hegel, *Science of Logic* (Struthers and Johnson), Vol. II, p. 35ff; Miller, p. 411ff; Felix Meiner edition, Vol. II, p. 26ff.

preconditions of the possibility of assigning meanings and, if that is true, it should not surprise anyone that the consideration of them will be difficult since assertions about them will have to presuppose them. At any rate, I shall proceed independently and as simple-mindedly as I can. If some aroma of Bosanquet, Bradley and Hegel hangs over the discussion, that will not be altogether surprising; but I am not consciously borrowing what seems to me rather unclear.

At any rate, the traditional formulations of the three laws are, of course, simply these: "A is A"; "not both A and not-A"; and "A is either B or not-B." It is sometimes alleged (and sometimes denied) that the "laws" can be taken to apply directly to whatever entities are the objects of our references. (If they do apply to these objects, then there are properties of the things in the world which exemplify — and could not fail to exemplify — the laws.) It may be held that the laws apply to the internal structures of propositions and indirectly to the components of the world or that they do not refer to propositions at all. Finally, it may be held that they apply to certain connections between propositions and their truth values. If we regard the laws as referring to the structural properties of propositions, we will be able to allow the formulations which I have called "traditional" to stand, and simply interpret the capital letters as standing for the appropriate components. If one takes the last view (suggested by some common elementary logic texts as though it were quite obvious and non-controversial), then a different formulation is required. Ruby, in such a text, offers these formulations: "If a proposition is true, then it is true; ... a proposition, P, cannot be both true and false; ... and a proposition, such as P, is either true or false."[1] More subtle formulations can be advanced, of course, and confusions between the laws and an axiom of bi-valance (an axiom to the effect that there are only two "truth values" and that every proposition has one and at most one of them) could be eliminated by formulations such as: "A proposition in any context has, for all occasions of reference, the same truth value; no proposition has more than one truth value; and all propositions have at least one truth value" — assuming that this is what is intended. But merely to state these various alternatives is to make clear that it is not obvious what the traditional "laws" are intended to assert nor whether what they state is a requirement of meaningfulness — nor even whether they are true.

The difficulties will become more evident when we try to sort these matters out. First of all, whether the laws apply to things or to assertions must depend upon whether there can be "things" with "rational" structures of the required kind or not. If there could be, then we would have to enquire as to whether there must be. Obviously, if there can but need not be "things" of the required kind, the laws may sometimes apply to things and sometimes

---

[1] *Logic, An Introduction* (second edition, Chicago: J. B. Lippincott, 1960), p. 262.

only to assertions. If there cannot be such "things," the laws can apply only to assertions. If all "things" must be of the required kind, then the laws will have to apply to all of them. As to whether we ought to state the laws in terms of truth values or not, that will simply depend upon whether or not the continuities, disjunctions, and clashes apparently dealt with by the laws depend for their occurrence upon the relevant truth values or not.

Clearly, we cannot investigate these matters without a better understanding of what is involved in the "law formulations" about identity, non-contradiction, and excluded middle. But we can, perhaps, try to develop this understanding by looking at the way in which the formulations developed in the present system. We found that we could not continue talking without a notion of determinateness; that this involved a notion of identity which would make possible a sequence of successive (logically, not empirically) operations of predication; that it involved the notion that a given subject could not both be characterised by a given predicate and also not be so characterised (since that would, precisely, deprive it of its determinateness); and that a given subject *must* be characterised by a given predicate or else not be so characterised (for the same reason). The notion behind the laws, in that context, is, then, identical with the requirements for determinateness. In that context, too, since we have only referential objects, the ordinary distinction between "true" and "false" assertions does not immediately arise. (We can *later* see how to develop additional criteria which will give meanings to "truth" and "falsity" in a more ordinary way.) Initially, however, the position is that there is a distinction between intelligible and unintelligible assertions and the former *all* mark out genuine referential objects. Thus, in this context, the laws do not refer to the ways in which truth values attach to assertions.

Given this, we can see that the "things" which people this domain do have the required logical structures and the laws apply directly to them. For to have the right logical structure is what it is to be a thing of the kind which this domain requires.

Initially, then, we can view the laws as stating certain conditions for determinateness, as applying both to assertions and to things, and as being neutral to the "truth value" question. (Though we can easily see how, given truth values, we could generate formulations which we would apply to them. Moreover — and this is important for the question of later generalization of the laws — we can see how the laws might be expanded were we to need more than two truth values.)

At this point it is possible to state the difficulties which are imagined to arise (1) when we pass from determinate being to systematic unity, and (2) in respect to the core concepts of the system.

(1) In systematic unity we have a domain which is so ordered that all its members have the same "content" and yet are distinct so that (in some sense) any one is what it is and also *everything* else. This seems to make identity

impossible and to entail outright contradiction. Equally, the distinctions between predicates are such that it is not possible to say that a given member of the domain either has a given property or fails to have it. For the suggestion was that relational patterns replace "things" in the ordinary sense and that the distinction between members lies in the mode and degree of emphasis involved. This seems to make impossible the law of excluded middle. In fact, it would *appear* that we shall want to say "*A* is not-*A*," "both *A* and not-*A*" and "*A* is neither *B* nor not-*B*." If this means that continuity of reference is impossible, that assertion and denial can be indifferently combined and that predicates and their negations are sometimes or always non-applicable, it need hardly be said that we are in trouble.

(2) We have a series of categories each of which purports to be a way of focussing the whole of reality. Each, however, creates a domain of entities and the successive domains entail different modes of logical governance. It therefore seems to follow that each designatable entity will have a sequence of counterpart entities and that "it" will be the whole class of such entities. The various properties which "it" has will, however, be incompatible with each other. Each such entity will, therefore, be non-identical with itself (in some important respect); will have a description which entails contradictions; and will (since these features involve another, the possession of certain predicates in some contexts and not in others) have a description which runs counter to the law of excluded middle.

The options open to us are (a) to abandon the laws; (b) to reformulate the laws; (c) to reformulate our account of the features of the system which seem to run counter to the laws; or (d) to abandon the enterprise. But they are not clearcut. Options (b) and (c) can be combined and the distinction between (a) and (b) is not clear since we do not have any obvious criteria for deciding how much and what kind of reformulation amounts to abandonment.

It would seem, however, that we ought to stop short of (a). It is true that the laws only arose as part of the special requirements for determinate being and that it is only there that we have any commitment to them within *this* system. But the reason for introducing determinateness — the source of the laws — was that, otherwise, we would lapse into nonsense. The reason for going on beyond determinate being was, of course, fundamentally of the same kind: but the initial intelligibility must be shown to persist from one domain to the next. It would therefore seem that reformulation is in order and also that the reformulation must be exhibited as clearly falling short of abandonment.

In order to understand what reformulation under (b) or (c) would mean and what moves are open and closed to us, we shall have to traffic in an example. In order to make the matter more interesting (and the contrasts and clashes more forceful) I shall press a little further the example about "persons" and "minds" which I used in exploring the meaning of "Socrates is mortal"; but it should be realized that what is at issue is just some logical points which seem painfully simple at first glance and yet turn out to be rather complex and slippery on investigation.

What I will do in this example is to take two theories about how one should construe the human condition or, if you like, about what "persons" are. I will then show that, in the ordinary way, they are contradictory but that, given the "core concepts" we have already developed they are not. I will also try to show how, within one of them, various logical difficulties of just the sort we have been dealing with arise but that it *can* be made intelligible. Then I shall try to apply these findings to the required reformulations.

On one view, human beings consist of their bodies. Their continuing identity can be ascribed either to the persistence of appropriate particles or to the persistence of certain arrangements of some particles like them so as to form patterns which are identifiable. Their thoughts, feelings, and experiences, on this view, are located in the vicinity of these particle patterns and may be said to be composed of certain events such as the electro-chemical changes which take place in their brains and elsewhere in their nervous systems. The existence of any such person may be said to begin when a certain arrangement of particles can be said to be independent from that particle set which is its parent and to end when the pattern no longer has certain characteristically human shapes. In the ordinary way, such entities are regarded as localized in time but, if we wish to consider this theory as referring to the domain of determinate being, we need only construe the ostensibly temporal references as components of an appropriate logical space with suitable dimensions.

On another theory, human beings are not identical with their bodies. In practice, their experiences fan out over a wide area of actuality and possibility. On this theory, a man is to be regarded as being located over the region of his experiences. His experiences are not thought to be in his head and identifiable with his brain states, but to be where they seem to be. Where they are, he is. Furthermore, whenever he acquires knowledge, he may be said to spread into the required locus whether in space or in time. Thus if he can recapture the thoughts which Nelson had at Trafalgar, he extends backwards in time to the occasion of that battle. In principle, since he can know whatever there is to be known, given only the right conditions, he may be said to occupy a region identical with that of the sum total of designatable reality. His experiences of his body will, of course, be part of what he knows and part of what he is. They will also limit him in various ways and, so long at any rate as he insists on keeping them, they will tend to keep him in check. But he cannot be said to come into existence at a specific moment of time since he can transcend this limitation in various ways. And to speak of the dispersal of his body will be only to speak of a point of time at which certain limitations are removed and after which various modes of communication with him become impossible and further speculation about him is subject to rather severe limitations.

With minor amendments, this theory can be made to fit the requirements of systematic unity. We simply regard the man as a way of focussing the world and not as a thing in it. Time, as has already appeared, becomes for practical purposes of limited significance. It is true that the man's knowledge — and so the way in which his knowledge and experience can be said to represent the world — will change but we can regard this sequence, as I suggested in talking about systematic unity, as a series of more and less fundamental patterns of the world. If some of them are no longer suitable for the maintenance of personal identity we can (as I suggested in the 'Socrates is mortal' example) make the appropriate changes in our choice of designations.

Whether these theories, as theories about what it is to be a human being, are sound or not is not immediately important. They are both, identifiably, about the same thing — human beings. Each calls attention to some salient feature in our affairs. One of them calls attention to the fact that we have bodies, are dependent upon them, often identify each other (if not ourselves) by reference to bodies, and acquire, store and deploy our knowledge by means of our central nervous systems. The other calls attention to the fact that our knowledge takes us "beyond ourselves" in the first sense of "ourselves," that to locate ourselves "inside our own heads" is a peculiar thing to do since that does not seem to be the locus of our affairs, and that, once we have abandoned these notions, it is difficult, if not impossible, to re-impose suitable localizing criteria.

One might suppose (perhaps philosophers usually do suppose) that the conflict between these theories is to be resolved in one of three obvious ways: The first way is to say that a human being is composed of two separate substances or basic kinds of thing which are normally called body and mind. The first theory is true of bodies, the second of minds. But this, of course, does not work. For the first theory involves an account of "minds" — the view that "minds" are to be understood as functions of the central nervous system — and the second theory involves an account of bodies — the view that bodies are certain experiences of ours. We could restrict each theory so that it did not stomp on the toes of the other, but that seems to destroy the point. The second way is to urge that each theory represents an aspect of the human situation and that there is really one human being with two aspects, physical and mental. But, again, the aspects overlap. The third way is to say that there is some common subject matter which can be arranged in two different ways — as with Russell's neutral monism. But, if the theories are stated as I have stated them, the common stuff would have to have incompatible properties. Crudely, if there are these theories and either of them can be made to hold, the other, seemingly, will have to be abandoned or, in traditional terms, it seems that the philosopher will have

114

to be a materialist or a physicalist, or go a long distance toward a special (and very "mentalistic") kind of idealism.

But, now, given the logical structure that I have developed in this book, the problem seems to be that we have to combine the theories. If there are any human beings (whether in the full-blooded sense or merely as referential objects) and *if* the theories can be made coherent enough so that we know what we are talking about, then each has its place. One describes the human being as represented in the domain of determinate being, the other the same subject matter as represented within systematic unity. But, clearly, they are in conflict with each other on any ordinary interpretation.

Equally, the second theory, though it seems to exploit evident features of an intelligible situation which it would be difficult to describe effectively in any other way, presents difficulties. It involves a form of the notion of identity in difference. We want to say that, in some way, parts of the contents of people's minds — the objects of their knowledge — are identical with certain features of the world. In some other way, they are non-identical. But these "ways" must not be so construed as to make two separate "things." Again, a man's field of awareness and, indeed, the totality of his knowledge forms a unity. Yet its contents form a diversity. It will further follow that, though men, on this second theory, overlap with each other and could, in principle, have identical contents of knowledge and awareness, yet they remain separate in some important sense. Again, we have to be careful about talking about a "separate sense" in a way which will give rise to the notion of "separate thing." For that would enable us to save our notions of identity, contradiction, and determinate predication at the expense of destroying the notion of systematic unity.

If we look at the example and at the notions of identity, contradiction, and determinate predication which the original "laws" make use of, we can, however, begin to see the way out. As I suggested much earlier, we can understand, in terms of the second theory of the example, what is required for intelligibility. Instead of regarding our subjects of predication as "things," discrete from other things, we can regard them as perspectives, centres of focus, and patterns. They do not possess their properties but organize and emphasize them. This radically alters the usual notions about what is referred to in subject-predicate assertions. Subjects do not now exclude one another or have uniquely specifiable predicates. At the same time, there are ways of identifying them and referring to them. Thus we need not paint the situation as giving rise to necessary contradiction in description, as failing to make identity possible or as failing to provide for exclusive predication at all.

What *does* happen, however, is that some of the notions embedded in the traditional laws become susceptible to analysis in terms of degree. A given assertion always refers to whatever there is in the world — Socrates, the rabbit in the woods, the star Arcturus and the red box of our earlier examples.

And all these become the subject of predication. They do not become so *equally*, however. For the assertion may emphasize Socrates at the expense of the rabbit. Similarly, all possible properties are referred to by any assertion which serves to mark anything out within the confines of systematic unity, but not equally. For some are emphasized and others are obscured in calling attention to any pattern. In saying that a man who, in theory, knew everything, would become identical with the world but also different from it, we are, similarly, saying that it is one world but there may be many perspectives on it so that there will be differences in emphasis in our ways of regarding it as a unity.

The same kind of consideration can be used to rescue us from the apparent contradictions which develop as we pass from one core concept of a system like the present one to another. The contents are identical; the patterns and emphases are different. It is, if you like, the same world but there are different perspectives on it. Essentially, what this means is that there is a degree of identity — sufficient to produce continuity in discourse, but insufficient to produce the straightforward phenomena to which the traditional laws of non-contradiction and excluded middle apply.

What I have been doing is to exercise option (c) — the reformulation of the difficulties about systematic unity and about the succession of core categories — and to begin to suggest how option (b) — the reformulation of the traditional laws themselves — might be carried out. But this incipient suggestion needs careful watching.

If one begins with the law of identity, the problem seems simple enough. We need to provide what Bosanquet called "the pervading unity" which the law demands because, failing continuity, all discourse becomes meaningless. Except, perhaps, in the process of ostensive definition, no term in any process of discourse can by given (much less can it retain) a meaning by means of a single instance. For it to have a meaning is either for it to have an established referent or to have an established logical function. (These two requirements have led, by a fairly direct route, to the "verifiability" and "use" theories of meaning in their various forms.) But a referent established by a single instance can only be a proper name. To become more than that it must call attention to common features of two or more instances or occasions. And proper names are only "meaningful" in a more extended sense. Similarly, established *uses* presuppose a variety of contexts which can be compared. Now to deny that "A is A" is, on the face of it, to deny just these conditions. But we need to distinguish between the requirement of pervading unity and the requirement of perfect identity.

Perfect identity is required for determinate being because the entities are literally atomic in the sense of being incapable of inter-penetration. Failing that they would not be determinate. Perfect identity is impossible in the case of systematic unity and impossible in the case of the domains established by the successive core concepts of this system (when those domains are considered collectively) just for the reason that inter-penetration is essential. In systematic unity, we never do succeed in referring to anything without referring in some way to everything else. Nor do we ever succeed in establishing a mode of reference which precludes or actually avoids reference to everything else. Similarly, in considering the succession of categories, we have to admit that, since each demands the next in order that we might go on with rational discourse, and, since each is unintelligible without the others, we never succeed in isolating them perfectly. Nor do we really succeed in separating the entities which can be talked about in each domain. Thus perfect identity is impossible.

There are, however, degrees of identity — sufficient to establish the patterns of reference which we require and to distinguish the degrees of emphasis required. The pervading unity comes, in fact, from uniting disparate things and, providing that we have enough criteria to make the necessary identifications, we can establish the required continuity of discourse. We can even keep the form "*A* is *A*" if we wish so long as we remember that "*A*" will stand for some degree of relative identity — vis-a-vis the context specified — and not necessarily for some unitary entity.

When we come to contradiction, however, our difficulties may seem to be greater: If the function of the law of identity is to provide continuity of reference and use, and thus to give the minimal grip on intelligibility, the function of the law of non-contradiction is, surely, to provide an outer limit to what can be said. Violations of the law of non-contradiction either have the result that nothing is said or that everything is said. A proposition and its contradictory can be taken to be so related that one, as it were, undoes the work of the other. Or they can be taken to be conjoined in a more drastic way so that, since they cover every possibility, they assert everything. (Thus a minimum condition of consistency in any system is that it should exclude *something* which can be said in that system.) In fact, of course, to say everything and to say nothing is to do the same thing. An assertion which excludes nothing cannot *distinguish* anything, either.

In the face of this, we must ask: What happens if we admit relative identity or the notion of degrees of identity? Do we any longer exclude anything or do we leave the field open for just the kinds of conjoint assertions which *do* destroy the whole of meaningful discourse?

Let us, then, look at our example. We want to talk about Socrates or Smith and we have chosen some scheme exemplifying the properties of systematic unity for the purpose. We do want to say "There is a pattern in the world which can rightly be called Socrates and one which can rightly be called Smith." But, of any given region of the world we want to say "Well, that is *both* Socrates and it isn't." It is not, notice, that it is *partly* Socrates and *partly* something else. For then we should only have to sift our terms in order to get perfect identities and proper contradictions again. The point of it is that the world, on this view, has no parts, though it is susceptible of

117

ways of emphasis and there are intelligible patterns in it. But what we can do with the curious "This is Socrates and this is not Socrates" assertion is to construe it as a conceptual clash. Once we have got several relative identities — in the form of patterns or whatever — we can show that they clash and that their clashes are statable in terms of something like degrees of emphasis, degrees of fundamentality or whatever happens to be appropriate. These clashes will serve as a restricting influence on our discourse so that assertions will not become so soft as to be "open to everything" in the way that proper contradictions are. In moving from one category to another, the problem becomes one of diagnosing the incipient conceptual clashes, sorting out the ones which would be destructive of the system, and replacing them with a development of conceptual tensions which continues to resolve the problems. The whole notion of exclusion reference on which the early part of this chapter depended heavily, was after all, a notion of a relative conceptual clash as opposed to straightforward contradiction.

It may be, still, that the law of excluded middle will produce additional problems but similar adjustments would seem likely to solve the problem. Admittedly it is no longer just the case that "A is either B or not-B" for the possibility of there being lesser clashes than contradiction (and of there being whole conceptual systems over which *only* these lesser clashes take place) makes it certain that there will be cases of "A is B and not-B" where B is construed as a strict identity, and therefore that cases of "A is neither B nor not-B" will occur and will have to be dealt with in the same way.

There are, however, several possible lines of confusion here, at least two of which seem to be worthy of passing attention. In the ordinary way, the relations of predicates to subjects are such as to admit of three possible choices. A may be said to possess B or not to possess B, or B may be said to be non-applicable to A. If we say "No Mormons are ever drunk," we are saying that drunkenness is a property never possessed by Mormons, though our assertion is not quite of the same kind as "No walls are ever drunk." But this does not alter the fact that walls, like Mormons, are either drunk or they are not. Again, predicates may be supposed to exclude one another in a way which is quite different from the sharp separation of possession or non-possession imagined by the law of excluded middle. Predicates usually exclude one another if and only if they are rival determinates under the same determinable. Things cannot be red and blue, because the choice here is a choice between two ways of being coloured, and colour words have just the function of providing such choices. But nothing has to be either red or blue, while everything, in the ordinary way has to be blue or not blue. These distractions simply bring home the fact that, in its ordinary formulation, the law of excluded middle is intended simply as a device to ensure determinacy. Without such a sharp separation there can be only relative identity and conceptual clash. There will, of course, be counterparts of the traditional formulation in the revised scheme: It will

118

be true that every property is either emphasized or not in every pattern and that, relative to any given property, it will have a determinate degree of emphasis. These new formulae can be read (with the appropriate qualifications) as "A is either B or not-B" but it should be realized that neither "A" nor "B" has its original interpretation though it will be possible to develop quite well structured logical devices (if anyone wants to) to handle the new interpretations. Generally, however, in the revised scheme much will depend on particular conceptual relations and we shall be, again, in a realm of "informal" but not impossible logic.

The upshot of this investigation is then that the traditional laws are a particular polar form of rather more general principles. The more general principles remain intelligible and applicable and continue to have force, though the traditional particular forms are confined to determinate being and to certain classes of limiting cases which will be found in other parts of systems like the present one.

Inevitably, this is not the end of the story. We shall, necessarily, have more traffic with problems about identity as we go along. For the present, however, I conclude the problems presented can be handled, that systematic unity can be made intelligible and that we have no need, yet, to abandon the notion of a succession of core categories.

Chapter 4

The development of a system
— time, change and individuality —
pure process and determinate process

The situation which we face now is this: The core of the system so far developed consists of four categories, rather arbitrarily but not, I hope, insignificantly, called pure being, pure disjunction, determinate being, and systematic unity. They are to be understood, first of all, as coming in pairs — pure being and pure disjunction are "dialectical opposites" of one another, as are determinate being and systematic unity.

The two pairs are related in this way: Determinate being is the synthesis of the unifying property of the first pair together with its "exclusion reference" to the next level of concreteness. Pure being and pure disjunction, that is, lie on the ultimate level of abstractness. As ways of focussing the whole universe of discourse (and so the whole of reality encompassable by reason), they exclude all distinctions beyond the notions of unity and plurality. They are united, if you like, in referring to "being in general" and in excluding determinacy. Since the minimum possible way of distinguishing a general focus of the universe of discourse from the entities which can be referred to in it is represented by determinacy, determinate being takes us to the next level of concreteness. Determinate being — the domain of atomic referential objects — requires, for its intelligibility, its dialectical opposite, systematic unity. In systematic unity, we are still at the same level of abstractness, but the framework within which entities are discerned takes precedence over the entities themselves and attention shifts to relational wholes and relative identities.

In the intervening chapter, I have tried to elaborate the procedures for arriving at these concepts, to fix some of them into rules, to establish the nature of the logical rules governing the entities which can be referred to in each of the domains, and to face the logical problems generated by the concepts introduced.

What we now require is another synthesis. It is important to remember that the syntheses I have been using and will be using do not follow the traditional Hegelean pattern — at least as Hegel is most usually read. Determinate being was not the synthesis of pure being and pure disjunction but the synthesis of the uniting property of those two concepts together with their exclusion reference. Otherwise we would, in the ordinary way, have a combination of incompatibles without additional information.

What we need to know now, therefore, is: (1) What is the uniting property of determinate being and systematic unity? (2) What is the reason for believing that the two core concepts or categories with which we ended Chapter 2 do not complete the system? (3) What additional information is available to us? (4) What is the next level of concreteness? and (5) How shall we characterize the next core concept? Given answers to these five questions, we should be able to proceed as in the latter parts of Chapter 3 and explore the special features and problems of the new domains. If we can do that, it should not be difficult to proceed to the next core concept which, after all, will merely be the dialectical opposite of the concept we have been working with.

(1) I shall urge that the uniting property we are looking for — the link between determinate being and systematic unity — is best expressed by the notion of static state. First of all, they are both ways of conceptualizing states of affairs — specific and relatively determinate conditions of things. One of them emphasizes the entities at the expense of the systems within which they are embedded (and so provides only for relative identity of place within a system) and the other emphasizes the unified systems at the expense of the particular things (and so provides only for relative identity of things). They are united, then, in the property of providing determinacy in respect of entities and systems, though each exhibits as primary what the other exhibits as secondary. Secondly, they are united in excluding time — one because perfect determinacy of "things" excludes all notion of process or continuity through change and the other because determinacy of system involves a total system which precludes change.

We may, however, well ask how the concept of time, change, process or whatever can be derived within the system at all. At the last synthesis it was possible to derive determinateness from the original concept of the system because pure being involved something which could both be referred to and was perfectly general and this notion was only intelligible against the background of what it was intended to exclude. Its exclusion reference, in other words, had to be latent within it. In this case, however, the exclusion reference, although clear enough to us as enquirers who have, after all, the whole of ordinary discourse to draw from, is not obvious within the system. It only became obvious because we saw what happened when we tried to fit ordinary concepts into the reference modes of determinate being and systematic unity. What we do have to draw upon, to preserve the clear requirement that the system must be self-contained, is the development of the system itself. Obviously, *it* has been changing. It has progressed from the blankness of pure being to the complex and subtle distinctions which could be envisaged in systematic unity.

Evidently, then, the idea of being static is intelligible only in terms of reference to something which changes. It is by trying to see how the general properties of the system are reflected in the core categories — and how far they fail to reflect those properties — that we get the notion of "static state." But this will have to be expanded, in any case, under (3) below.

(2) Given, then, that we know what unites the preceding concepts, we have to know what is wrong with them as a final characterization of the universe of discourse. For this will give us the best clue to their "exclusion reference" generally and to the particular aspect of it which will lead to the formation of the next concept.

The short answer, is, of course, that time, change and process are excluded from the static state concepts but reflected in the system. Therefore, the system is incomplete. But this is too loose and general an answer and, anyhow, it is packed with notions which, *a priori*, we have no way of making precise.

The longer answer, therefore, starts from the difficult activity of tracing the precise difficulties in the combination of determinate being and systematic unity and then of beginning to elicit the most elementary notions which might go under such headings as "Time," "Change," and "Process."

One can start on this simply by noticing the difficulties in determinate being and systematic unity taken as a pair. The essential one is this: Though they do give us notions of what it is to be determinate with reference to a system, they give us quite inadequate notions of individuality. The atomic entities of determinate being can be analyzed into subjects and predicates. But the subjects are blank without predicates and the predicates are indifferent to all subjects. The whole domain can be considered extensionally as a collection of atomic subjects or intensionally as an array of predicates. But putting them together gives rise to the traditional problem of universals and neither seems "real" without the other. The unified patterns with their degrees of emphases do form organized relational wholes in systematic unity, but the cost of this is reliance on a merely relative identity and a world whose components fade into each other at constant risk of logical disaster. Neither of these schemes is, ultimately, intelligible without the other and yet, together, they do not form an effective unity though we may be able to see how their combined advantages may be deployed and how, rather pragmatically, we can exploit both sides of the coin.

Effective individuality, then, is the first part of the "exclusion reference" which we can infer precisely from the ways in which the two concepts in some ways make good one another's deficiencies and in some ways fail to make them good. The connection between this and time, change, and process is not obvious but it can be delineated.

It seems to me it is this: To be an individual is not just, as we have seen, to have some specifiable identity. The entities which serve as referential objects in determinate being and systematic unity have that. It is being an identifiable entity which provides an effective unity for its parts. And this involves change. For, if the parts are merely ordered in a kind of logical space (as in determinate being and systematic unity), the parts either will be externally related to one another or they will not be genuine parts at all.

I am aware that this sounds mysterious. But it is better to state it bluntly and then set about the explanation. The explanation is this:

The kind of logical space which is characteristic of determinate being is not a genuine unity at all. As we saw in the second chapter, it turns out to be impossible to form an effective notion of totality within such a domain. Furthermore, the component entities in such a domain themselves fail to form adequate unities. They are like the hardness, sweetness and whiteness of the Lockean lump of sugar: It requires not merely a "Something I know not what" to unite them but a "Something I *could not* know what." For the positions in a logical space of this kind have no intrinsic connection with each other. On the other hand, the parts which can be distinguished within systematic unity have no ultimate status at all. In this domain — which seems, again, to be the universe of a Bradleyan metaphysic — every attempt to make distinctions ultimately fails even though provisional distinctions may be rendered intelligible by the application of suitable logical devices. In other words, if one emphasizes the entities in a logical space, a finally unacceptable fragmentation is the result. If one emphasizes the system in which they have their place, individuation itself breaks down.

Time, on the face of it, is not like this. It has a unity of its own and this unity is so pervasive that, when one tries to break it down, it ceases to be time in any intelligible sense. Consider, for instance, the attempt to break time into moments and to associate these with such standard temporal concepts as past, present, and future. The present has to be whatever it is that is going on now, the past what was going on but isn't any longer, and the future what will go on but isn't going on yet. The natural inclination is to regard the present as a kind of succession of "drops" each of which falls between the past and the future. But if the present is separated this way, then change must either take place within it or it must lie within a more general time against whose background change takes place. If the former, then there is a "past" and a "future" within the "present" and this seems to be nonsense. If the latter, we have a series of times within time and within each of them the difficulty will take place. This leads to the same nonsense combined with a difficult and probably vicious infinite regress. The conclusion seems to be — however it is to be made intelligible — that time has a unity of its own.

Furthermore, time is not neutral to the entities which compose it in the way that space is. For time, again in the ordinary way, has a single dominating direction. It runs, obviously, from the past to the future. If it ran from the future to the past, it would have to run in on itself so that there would be two orderings of events. If, that is, Julius Caesar first crosses the Rubicon and then, a thousand years later, I return in a time machine and watch him do it all over again, his crossing takes place at two places in the ordering of events — once just after Caesar's decision to return to Rome and just before the creation of a new political order in Roman affairs and once just after my eating bacon and eggs for breakfast and just before I wrote my letter to the editor of *Nature* revealing my new invention. Even if we say it is the *same* event, its very duplicity of place in the ordering of time will make a considerable difference especially if, as I argued in the last paragraph, time has a fundamental unity of its own.

Now, what has this to do with the way in which components can be held together to form genuine individuals? Just this: If we can form an adequate concept of an individual as persisting through a region of unifying time and maintaining its identity while changing its components, we have developed a sense in which the individual transcends its parts — genuinely holds them together and has a being which, while depending upon those components, nonetheless *is* what gives them their unity. So long as we imagine the components of an individual as being simply dissectable slices of it, we can always replace the description of the thing by the description of its parts. It thus does not and cannot "hang together" in any fundamental way. But once imagine an individual as being fundamentally *in time* and involved in a process of change and you are in a position to *begin* to formulate the notion of a genuine individual.

It is perhaps instructive, as an illustration of this point, to look at Samuel Alexander's *Space, Time, and Deity*.[1] Alexander, there, traces the world through its material, organic and mental phases and endeavours to project it onward toward the emergence of still higher unities. But the point of the story seems to be that, although in Alexander's view, space and time come interlocked, the world proceeds from space-dominated discrete states to time-dominated integrated states. His apparently inscrutable statement — hesitantly made and, alas, less well developed in a direct way than the context seems to demand — that "Time is the mind of space" becomes intelligible from this perspective. He insists that he means to say that "Mind is a kind of time" and not that "Time is a kind of mind."[2] This *is* intelligible if it is the case that genuine individuality is time-dependent.

[1] (London: Macmillan, 1920).
[2] *Op. cit.*, Vol. II, p. 38.

If this is correct, it then follows that there is a link between the dominant exclusion reference of the static state categories and the internal difficulties which lead us to believe that they are not the end of the story.

We cannot, however, simply adopt wholesale some philosophical or common sense theory of time and incorporate it into a new category. We have, now, to look closely at the information available to us within the system and see what we can construct out of this exclusion reference together with the unifying property of the last two categories.

(3) The information available to us can, then, be summed up under two headings: What we know about the development of the preceding core concepts and what we know about the general properties of the system. The first we have already dealt with in a variety of ways.

The relevant part of the second body of information relates, evidently, to the tendency of the system itself to exhibit a kind of "logical time." It has, that is, the following features: Though it passes through a sequence of discernable stages, it nonetheless retains a unity of its own. It has a single dominating direction (though it will be possible to show, eventually, how the last phase of it *entails* the earlier phases). Though it is not separable from its components it does have an individuality of its own — it unites and dominates its components so that they are not merely externally related to one another. Thus it has the properties of unity, succession, direction, and individuality which seem to be characteristic of time in general.

It does not, of course, contain all of the properties of "physical time" nor all the properties of "psychological time." For the former requires entities which undergo the appropriate processes and the latter requires a unity and succession of awareness. If, however, we found things in the world which could be adequately described by use of the kind of logical structure involved, we would say that they were in physical time. And the kinds of mental activities which are involved in understanding and following out a system of this kind may be said to be characteristic of psychological time.

In any event, we do seem to have the conceptual equipment on hand to do the job which is required just here.

(4) A more difficult question, apparently, faces us when we ask: "How do we determine what the next level of concreteness is?" In effect, however, this question is about the decision which we have to make in order to determine how much of the information available to us we ought to exploit in order to construct the next core concept and proceed to the next category.

In order to do this, we must assess the position in a little more detail. On the first level we had only the notions required for minimal reference — unity and plurality. On the next level we introduced a distinction between domains and their components but all the components remained on a single level of distinction. All the entities which could be spoken of in determinate being and systematic unity were of a single kind — referential objects — whose status was simply determined by the logical restrictions appropriate to each domain. It would seem that, on the next level, it ought to be possible to make *some* distinction between the component members of each domain. The next most general way of distinguishing entities from each other would seem to be the distinction which we commonly make between possibilities and actualities — the distinction which we might think characteristic of the line between reality and existence if "existence" (as its etymology suggests) is used to refer to things which in some way or other "stand out."

A distinction like this seems to be required, in any case, when one introduces notions of time. For, then, possibilities and actualities can no longer exactly coincide. If there is change through time, the implication is that, at any one time, one has on hand only a selection of the things which are formally possible. Only some possible referential objects can be said to "exist" at a given time. Otherwise all moments of time would have identical contents. This does not mean that more things "could actually occur" or are "physically possible" than exist at any one moment. That is another question. For such hybrid notions as these have reference to further limitations and natural inhibitions in the stream of things and it may or may not be that these additional features are ultimately required.

Roughly, however, when one introduces time one gets a distinction between a background of possibilities and a stream of occurrents. Indeed, it is, surely, by reference to this distinction that it is possible, ultimately, to "make sense" of time.

The suggestion, then, is that the next level of concreteness must be one on which this kind of distinction can be made. For the next core concept must include time and the introduction of time forces this distinction.

To provide for *this* level, then, we need a minimal notion of time, change, and process which will avoid the preceding dialectical impasse, make the necessary additional distinctions within the universe of discourse, and carry over the necessary components from the static state categories.

(5) There are two choices open to us. Each will have a place in the system as it develops. But the immediate question is to decide with which to begin. The choices are these:

We can take "process" as fundamental and exhibit the carried-over "static state" elements as simply logical devices for making distinctions in it. Or we can take the notion of "individuality" as fundamental and exhibit "process" as derivative from it and embody the features carried over from the "static state" categories as natural features of the relationship.

The first of these gives us a kind of Bergsonian world.[1] Everything, on that view, is ultimately a flow which, as Bergson maintained, is not a flow of anything — for process, from that perspective is ultimate. The distinctions made within such a process will appear as features from the static

[1] See especially *L'Evolution Creatrice* (Paris: Felix Alcan, 1907). Authorized translation by Arthur Mitchell (London: Macmillan, 1911; and New York: Random House, 1941).

realms of logical possibility, obtained by "freezing" the process in our imaginations.

The second gives us — for reasons which I will elaborate in their more appropriate place — a stage in the development of the doctrine of the concrete universal in which individuality is expressed as necessarily involved in process and as requiring, for its explication, a complex rational system.

The question is, therefore: Which of the possibilities should we introduce first? In itself, of course, this does not matter very much. But, if the system provided no way of making the decision it would, evidently, have failed to the extent that category development had become arbitrary.

In fact, however, the first alternative does mesh much more clearly with the requirements of the developing system than the second and the second will, in due course, be seen to develop naturally from the inadequacies of the first. What we need, after all, is a fusion of the unifying notion carried over from the static state categories with the concepts of time and process. And this is what the first option provides. It retains the static state notions as background logical possibilities and simply adds to them a new notion of temporality. It does, in other words, just what we require to get over the immediate problem. The second concept introduces radically new notions for which the need cannot, at this point of the discussion, be seen so clearly.

This, perhaps, will be more obvious after the necessary examination has been undertaken.

I shall call the first notion "pure process" and the second "determinate process."

III

"Pure process" provides us with a perfectly natural (though rather frustrating) way of viewing things. If I can succeed in rendering it intelligible and in showing its relation to other ways of conceptualizing the world, the result may be some insight into the reasons which have made such schemes attractive to Bergson and others.

Inevitably, we shall have to traffic in examples and the traffic will take a form which will, by now, have become rather familiar to the reader: Out of the examples will come (hopefully) ways of sharpening our understanding of the concepts which are associated with the category. Once we have this improved understanding, it will be possible to hedge the examples themselves with the necessary cautions. If the required clarification results it will, then, be possible to see what special difficulties attend to the category under examination.

To begin with, it is probably useful to look at very simple examples of motion or change and their relations to space and time — beginning with cases which at least give the impression of "grafting on" the appropriate notions to those which we have already developed. We can then proceed to cases which introduce more radical distinctions.

Let us, then, begin with falling bodies and imagine them to be ordinary things — steel balls, falling rocks, or old car tires — dropped from moderate heights near the surface of the earth. We will imagine them, too, to complete their falls without any extraneous influences and to be tough enough so that they don't break up on impact. Under these circumstances, the objects concerned will exhibit a limited range of interesting features.

We shall have the same object in two different places. There will be a lapse of time between occupancy of the first place and occupancy of the second place and, in that time, the object will or will seem to occupy a succession of different places. Its movement will be explicable in terms of a limited number of physical laws such as the law of gravitation.

If we were still talking within the confines of determinate being, we could either talk about a single entity being extended over a four dimensional space or about a succession of particle entities (linked by some common property) so arranged that the set of them extended over a four-dimensional space. In the first case, the continuing "identity" of the thing would not arise as an issue. In the second case, we could establish identity by reference to the linking property. Now, however, we need to face the new question: What constitutes identity through time?

In determinate being, again, we are not faced with serious questions about the unity of space and time. Zeno's paradoxes cannot be forced upon us and space can be "particlized" to suit our convenience. When we add time as a genuine notion in its own right, the unity of time does become an issue and the unity of space may then pose a problem for us as well. The concept of motion, presumably, involves correlating points in space with moments in time. If space and time are continuous such divisions falsify its nature. But, if time is actually discrete, we will have the problems I mentioned earlier about the location of the implied change. Similarly, if space has *real* parts, there will be discontinuities and the appearance of entities in the successive parts will not be subject to the same explanation as will its appearance within a given part. (To some extent, Zeno's complaints stem from special assumptions about the nature and interrelation of certain kinds of "real parts" — parts which are infinite in number and need to be traversed in a certain order. But *any* doctrine about "real parts" would produce some difficulty in the form of discontinuity.)

These difficulties do not disappear if one abandons the implied view that space and time are real independently of the entities which occupy them. For even if they are simply properties of the entities which are usually said to "occupy them" the unity issues simply arise as questions about the ways in which these entities are related to one another.

Additional difficulties are posed by issues which come to light when one talks about explanations. To an important extent, explanations offered

128

within the domains of determinate being and systematic unity function simply as summary descriptions. In the kind of four dimensional continuum available in determinate being, a characteristic explanation in terms of the law of gravitation, for example, will sum up the actual or anticipated distribution of entities across a logical space — assigning high densities in some regions and low densities in others. We can, indeed, express such notions in graphs which are almost pictures of the relevant logical space. In systematic unity, a law (like that of gravitation) will point to an important level of fundamentality.

When we have "real change," however, the position shifts from one of summary description to something more difficult to state and more puzzling to deal with. For the explanations now relate to actual "goings on" which, since they stretch over past, present, and future cover different levels of reality and unreality. The "laws" we refer to therefore acquire a degree of independence and we must ask whether they are "added on" to our descriptions from the outside or whether they reflect something about the nature of the things in question. And they, too, may conflict with the "unbroken flow" image of time.

Finally, now, in a world where things are happening in a quite literal sense we have to face up to questions about the distinction between what actually happened to the thing and what might have happened to it. In determinate being, the distinction is merely between two referential objects, one of which is more interesting to us than the other. Here, we are faced with an account of a thing which, on the face of it, might have turned out differently. Even if we start out by restricting ourselves to the notion of an undifferentiated realm of referential objects, we can still ask about the distinction between what is said to have happened to the thing and what did happen to it — even in a story we can ask: "What if Hamlet had had access to a competent psychoanalyst?" and "What would Watson have done if Holmes had been dead wrong in his 'deduction'?" We begin, in other words, when we introduce time and change, to get things which we can envisage as open to an alternative array of possibilities.

The point of this discussion is to cast doubt on the descriptions from which we set out. It turns out that there is something somewhat queer about the notion that we can take a straightforward "static" object like a steel ball, drop it from a tower, follow its course on a space-time graph, and identify it when it hits the ground.

So long as one is content to transpose the whole enterprise onto a picture of a rather special kind of logical space, it all makes perfectly good sense. If, however, we genuinely want to introduce notions of time and change, we must expect to find difficulties.

Let us look at what happens if we take our various puzzles seriously. "Identity" through time, if it is taken in a strict sense, implies that nothing happens to the thing which is said to preserve its identity. But something

129

must happen to something else or "time" would not be discernible. Hence, if anything does preserve its identity through a region of time, it must be externally related to some other thing which, in fact, changes. But this produces numerous conundrums.

It sounds reasonable enough to say "Of course, this is the same steel ball. It was once in one place. Now it's in another." We mean to say, I suppose, that the places have remained the same, but the ball has changed its place, and the "once" and "now" presumably refer, in part, to shifting positions of the hands on a watch or the sun in the sky. But the "ball" is not neutral to its context, the places are not exactly the same, and the question "What moved?" is susceptible of a variety of arbitrary answers.

The "place," if it was identified at all, was identified by reference to something. If we exclude the ball from that reference, our decision, though probably pragmatically defensible in the light of our interests, is made only for the purpose of abstracting the ball from the situation. Thus the place without the ball and the ball without the place are artifices of ours. We can see this if we answer the question "What moved?" with the curious phrase "The places have moved, but the ball has remained where it was." For that — though inconvenient — is, logically, just as good an answer.

The conclusion that one seems forced to is this: We establish identity through time by a process of artificial abstraction. The identity referent is not the "ball in time" but the ball considered, abstractly, as a logical possibility to which we assign such properties as we find helpful in the situation. The "identity" still refers to the ball of determinate being. We use it as a sort of "pointer" to make distinctions within the unified flow of time.

If we face the "unity of time" issue itself we come to a conclusion of the same kind. We cannot really break time up into bits. To do so (as the earlier arguments were designed to show) will make change impossible. Nor can we plot change against a fragmented space. What we can do, again, is to develop a grid structure in the domain of atomic possibility and super-impose that on the unified time and space appropriate to change. We can and do ask such questions as "Where was the ball at time T^3" and get answers of the form "At point P^6." But, of course, if the ball was really moving continuously and not, as it were, jerkily from point to point and moment to moment, it wasn't *really* there, it was passing through. We can neutralize the effect of the jerky point-instant doctrine by postulating a mathematically dense set of points. But this does not really get over the difficulty. It merely shows that we can produce a conceptual structure which will open up a temporal series to practical exploration. But we are still, really, working with the structure of determinate being superimposed on the smooth flow of time.

Our explanations, similarly, cross the lines of levels of reality. The laws of physics which we use are, themselves, quite a-temporal and our explanations function still as though they were summary descriptions. But neither

130

summary nor description is feasible within the seamless unity of temporal flow. We do our work by abstracting from the continuity of time and laying out the results as if we still had the determinate being scheme.

Obviously, this becomes especially vexing when we want to distinguish between the existent temporal continuum and the static domain of possibility within which we construct the requisite concepts. For, here, we want, directly, and without artifice, to refer to the temporal unity. But it seemingly cannot be characterized without resort to the abstractions which falsify its nature. It appears that, like Bergson, we may have to say of it that it is just "a flow" and not "a flow of anything." In the falling objects cases, of course, we are not very worried by all this. What we want to know can usually be extracted by the standard artifices and we can rely on experience to help us to get "the feel" of the distinction between the existent entities and the ones that are merely real as referential objects — though how this trick is done is something that we shall have to look at a little later.

v

The issues become more pressing, however, when we pass to entities which we think to be time dominated. In purely abstract terms, we can imagine the falling balls cases reversed and the universe ending up just as it started. This would, of course, interfere with the second law of thermo-dynamics, but this is not the point. The physical considerations which lead to for-mulations such as the second law are thought of, in this kind of example, as being external to the ball-identity. If it is the same and the places are the same, the deed could be undone if the two places and the ball are imagined as abstracted from the rest of the universe even if (because of the increase in entropy) the surrounding universe is *not* the same. We could imagine a closed, reversible-clock oriented system (with special restrictions on ob-servation) within which no one could ever tell the difference. And the ball example did depend on some notion of abstractibility. But suppose we are faced with a sequence of events which contains the life of some species of lepidoptera which passes through egg, caterpillar, chrysalis and moth phases. Here, on the face of it, we cannot imagine the reversal of these phases. Furthermore, the thing only reveals its identity through time. It is unintelligible or it is something else if we are not given the requisite time span. Thus it is not, like the ball, potentially identifiable in a time-neutral context. Its very being is time dominated.

Indeed, our way of describing it is manifestly misleading. It does not, like the series of pictures in the biology text book, exhibit itself as a series of discrete jumps. We freeze it in its tracks in order to describe its phases. Our information about it is, in some crucial way, invariably distorted. For we cannot learn about it without freezing it into a set of point instants —

whether literally or conceptually. To know is to interfere. Somehow, though, as Bergson thinks, we do know what we are doing at least in the sense that we know that conversion of process into point-instant carries with it *some* degree of falsification.

We should not, of course, get carried away or misconstrue the function of this kind of discussion in the present context. I am merely trying to show what happens when we try to take time, change, motion, and process seriously as, apparently, we *must* do at this stage of the development of the present system. The examples are simply intended to call attention to various levels of complexity which are involved in doing so. It happens that examples are common enough in our ordinary and in our intellectual affairs. But I do not mean (as Bergson *did* mean) to set about the head and ears of the biological scientist and beat him with what, here, would turn out to be a crude weapon. One reason that it is a crude weapon is that our intellectual traffic with organisms takes place on a number of different levels. On a sub-molecular level, the techniques of physics can be used and on a molecular level biology can be, in important ways, integrated with chemistry. In both cases rendering the subject matter time neutral by dealing with it in terms appropriate to determinate being is, perhaps, no more "harmful" than dealing with the falling rock in this way. At the level of quite large organisms. there may well be questions which *do* require us to transcend those categories, though even there the intervening category of systematic unity provides another and partially countervailing perspective. All that follows, if I am right in taking the present system seriously, is that there will be some occasions when, if we really want the truth, we shall have to face up to whatever problems time-dominance creates for us. That will be true for all subject matters but whether these occasions are of importance for what we want to call "biological science" or not is a different question.

At any rate, the problems are even more acute if we use as our examples enquiries into the nature of thought. For, though organisms can be dealt with at various levels and the required time-dominance partially alleviated, thought seems relatively impervious to this technique. The order of words in a sentence is such that the whole intelligibility of the scheme is obliterated if it is reversed or if the words are randomly arranged. (Considerable *alteration* is, of course, possible and linguistic conventions about word order vary notoriously.) Arguments, even more, depend upon the premises being understood in a certain ordered relation to the conclusion and on the possibility of one's being able to remember the premises when one comes to the conclusion. To imagine any of these "thinking activities" as static or as being spread out in space rather than time is to imagine oneself hopelessly at sea. We can imagine that there are counterparts of assertions about thought and that these assertions have suitable referents in determinate being and in systematic unity, but they are particularly inadequate to their original task. Furthermore, temporal unity is particularly important in such activities.

For we can no more regard thoughts as a series of point-instants than we can regard them as static. Divided or regarded merely as a sum of parts, they become, again, nonsense. A sentence is not an assembly but a unity of expression. Arguments, certainly, can be dissected but they require for their validity a transcendent unity which actually links the components. The unity, again, is not a mere assembly.

Here, too, we can see quite clearly what we often *do* in the face of this problem. We do abstract the parts — in the making of grammars, dictionaries, and linguistic analyses — and reflect on the thinking *process* from the standpoint of the abstracted timeless possibilities which we assemble in these ways. But we are painfully aware that we cannot translate from these possibilities so as to know how to assemble a decent English sentence let alone a poem. The sterility of grammarians is a standard butt of centuries of humour as is the impotence of those who would teach others how to write or even to think in the creative sense of the verb.

VI

The point of all this is that it illustrates the plight of anyone who wants to manipulate the category of pure process: on the one hand he has a seamless temporal flow, a transcendent unity of time and process. On the other, he has a set of timeless possibilities, conceptual material brought over from the earlier categories. He can use one to cast light on the other, but he cannot really get them together effectively. Often, the combined illumination is adequate. But sometimes we want to talk about the process itself and, with this conceptual material, it becomes seemingly impossible.

Whether, like Whitehead, one faces this problem by demanding two significantly distinct realms,[1] or like Bergson one insists that the real is really the temporal, the problem remains. Whitehead's "eternal objects" are substantially like the domain of static possibilities I have been talking about and his "actual occasions" with their unifying links running through time are rather like our process. But Whitehead becomes mysterious when he talks of the ingression of the eternal objects into the world of actual occasions, and his language, like most language, turns out to refer most directly to eternal objects and only rather indirectly to the process itself. Like Bergson, he has to rely, in part, on acts of intuition.

The questions which we have to face, therefore, are once again: Have we created a monstrous domain within which nothing intelligible can be said? Are we, again, in danger of undermining requirements basic to all logics? Are inferences possible between assertions which belong to this domain? If we can answer all these questions, we shall still, once again, face our special logical dragon, the dialectician's dilemma. It will probably be easy,

---

[1] *Process and Reality* (New York: Macmillan, 1929).

once again, to refute the suggestion that reason and experience are parting company, but it does not look as though it will be so easy to undercut the growing distinction between thought and reality.

The real and immediate difficulty, of course, is that, though the situation forces us increasingly to try to talk about time and process as such, the only grip which we can get on things seems to be by way of essentially timeless entities.

VII

The natural way out of this is the following: We cannot, directly, conceptualize processes. But we can say what they are not. Furthermore, by deploying thought structures which refer directly to static states we can, by noticing their exclusion references, distinguish between various kinds of processes as we did in marking off the falling balls example from the one about the moths. We can, that is, specify the situation very exactly (physicists and biologists, needless to say, can specify the examples I was using very much more precisely than I can here.) Then we can say what it is that we do *not* mean to emphasize. As these features become more refined, so does what they exclude, and what begins to emerge are concepts of a different order having to do with temporal unity, direction, purpose and so on.

It is, I suppose, notorious that Bergson, for all his insistence that logic and language in general fail us when we come to talk about time, change, life and process, and for all his insistence that the genuinely real cannot be adequately conceptualized, nevertheless went on to talk about the *élan vital* of *Creative Evolution* and the "deeper self" of *Time and Free Will*.[1] In doing so, he was, of course, directly ascribing characteristics to realities whose essence was processual. And this must seem to be a contradiction. But the way out — though it is an imperfect one — is surely there through the notion of negation and exclusion reference. Bergson, himself, spends a good deal of time in *Creative Evolution* on the notion that negation always posits something and that, by contrast to the static realm of possibilities which we get by specifying what processes are *not*, we can begin to grasp what they are. He says, to be sure, that we must grasp the real "directly" and not be seduced by negation into the permanent limbo of the eternal realm of possibilities. But he does, I think, mean to suggest that by way of the contrast implied in negation, we can learn how to convey part of what needs to be said.

It is, perhaps, by thinking about the unity of time and process, its essential direction, its unfixedness with relation to any specific set of possibilities (since they never exhaust it) that Bergson was able to formulate his notions

---

[1] Translated by F. L. Pogson (New York: Swan Sonnenschein, 1910). For the "deeper self" see especially pp. 129-139.

of organic unity, life force, and creative freedom. For these, as he uses them, are essentially "reverse references" derived exactly from seeing what is excluded from the domain of static possibility. The difficulty is, of course, that they are picturesque and metaphorical — that being negative in orientation they resist precise formulation.

Nevertheless, they do enable us to form an "overall view" of what "pure process" might amount to and to avoid, ultimately, the threatened formal contradiction. To make this point, however, it is necessary to examine the kinds of notions used, for example, by Bergson against the background of some of the details of the exclusion references involved. It is also necessary to undertake this investigation in order to come to a position from which it will be possible to move to the next category — determinate process. It should be realized that the investigation here is necessarily limited to what is essential to establish the required intelligibility and to clear the ground for the development of the next category.

To start with, what we can learn about the unity of time is simply that it transcends every attempt that we can make to establish it by reference to the relations of the things in time. We can see, by developing law-like accounts of biological phenomena, that the components of a developing organism are inter-dependent. But the inter-dependence of moments of development still leaves us with a set of fragments between which relations are either formal and logical (and therefore timeless) or mere brute facts of constant conjunction. The unity which we require, however, has to be more than this and yet less than the blank unity of undifferentiated wholes. This new unity is, literally, the exclusion reference. It is, however, possible to give it positive content in experience, as Bergson thought, by calling attention to the fact that the distinctions that we make are abstractions from what must be a more unified whole. We can, literally, feel the unity by noticing the inadequacy of the abstractions.

This felt unity, similarly, manifests itself as a directional unity. We can see that dealing with the world of static logical possibilities isolates us from the forward movement of time. Equally, it isolates us from what Bergson thinks of as the creative force of the world. The possibilities are never equivalent to the temporal actuality since it cannot be frozen into them. Thus, when we have conceptualized the world as a set of static possibilities, we can no longer see how there can be any novelty in it. But the point about the novelty is exactly that it does not fit into the required conceptual mould. Possibilities neither come nor go and cannot be added to or substracted from. Their relations to one another are fixed and permanent. By seeing this disjunction we *can* form a notion of Bergson's *élan vital*, a directional force which brings novelty and unity to the static and disjunctive possibilities of what *he* thinks of as the world of logic and and mathematics and what I have described as the domain of determinate being. This unity, of course, can be transposed into the category of systematic unity and the novelty re-described, there, as the openness of such structures to analysis in terms of levels of fundamentality. But once temporalized, these notions do fuse into something recognizably like Bergson's *élan vital*.

VIII

On this view, then, assertions about components of the temporal world *all* become assertions about something like Bergson's *élan vital*. The limitations of this way of viewing things become apparent when we begin to ask about the reformulations required of ordinary assertions in order to produce their counterparts in the domain of pure process.

Bergson himself gives examples of this though he does not work them out as fully as one might wish. He argues, for instance, that "If language were moulded on reality, we should not say 'The child becomes the man,' but 'There is becoming from the child to the man.'"[1] The hypothetical "if language were moulded on reality," of course, means "if language were adjusted to process-reference." The point he is trying to make is that the "subject" child is not there once the man has developed and the "attribute" man in any case is contradictory if applied to the child. We should notice that none of the usual devices for avoiding the dramatic change of "subject" proposed by Bergson will work in this context. A sentence of the form "Smith has turned grey" is usually taken to mean that something (Smith's hair) has "changed" while something else (Smith's identity) has remained constant. Part of the puzzle, however, is that, taken as an assertion about "Smith's hair," it is incorrigibly mysterious: one colour has simply "gone" while another has "appeared." Taken as an assertion about "Smith" it demands that we produce some account of the sustaining or continuing property. But any attempt to provide one takes the reference out of the domain of process and into the domain of static entities. The new reference may only be static with reference to the particular property in question. But if it is in process we will require, in turn, another property which is static with respect to it. This process will either go on to infinity or it will lead us to posit a subject outside process. Neither alternative is acceptable. Nor is the possibility of abandoning the process reference altogether and simply translating the original assertions into assertions about sets of static properties which simply replace one another in an arbitrary and mysterious way as the grey colour seems to replace the brown in Smith's hair.

The shift which Bergson proposes is, therefore, demanded. And, to talk about pure process, or within such a category, we must be prepared to say things like "There is becoming from the child to the man."

We should be careful to notice the implications of this. Suppose that

---

[1] *Creative Evolution*, translated by Arthur Mitchell (New York: Random House, 1941), p. 340.

136

instead of saying, "The political, social and economic life of the rising middle class of the late middle ages developed into bourgeois capitalism," we say "There is process from the political, social, and economic life of the rising middle class of the late middle ages to bourgeois capitalism." There is a peculiarity in saying "There is process" instead of "There is a process" or saying "There is becoming" instead of "There is a development." But this peculiarity is inevitable since the expressions "a process" or "a development" destroy the unity of reference and would require the attachment of precise distinguishing predicates thereby recapitulating the whole problem. It is obvious, too, that the expressions which come after "There is process" at most designate some way of making non-exhaustive distinctions within the process referred to.

A consequence of this is that there is no way in which we can construct formal contradictions within these structures. The predicates applied merely indicate possibilities for discernment. Since none, in principle, is exhaustive, it cannot be shown that any other can be excluded. Admittedly — or luckily — the result is not the catastrophic one that anything whatever can follow the subject. That would, indeed, violate the limiting rule posited by the traditional law of non-contradiction and, equally, my attempted re-formulation of it. But the only restriction is that what follows the subject must be compatible with the application of the concept of process or becoming.

The difficulty, however, is not merely that this result leaves assertions within the domain unusually open so that it seems that almost anything one wants to say can be said consistently with almost anything else. It is, more importantly, that it is difficult to see how inferences can lead from any one assertion to any other.

These difficulties are, perhaps, less extreme than first sight would indicate, but they are serious for all that. Their extremity is, of course, moderated by the fact that, though the subject terms suffer from extreme openness, the predicate terms are bound by the usual rules of their own interrelations.

If we take seriously Bergson's proposed "propositional form" and imagine that all assertions should — within this domain — be of the form "There is becoming from X to Y" this becomes clearer. Consider, first, the more common propositional forms whether "All S is P," "Some S is P" and so on, or "For any x, if x is S, then x is P," "There is an x such that x is S and x is P." One of their characteristics is that the connection between designated subject and assigned predicate cannot be further characterized. Subject and predicate terms are simply joined by the "is" of predication. Any attempt at further characterization simply leads to something else on the other side of the "is." The presumption is, naturally, that there is nothing more to be said about this relation than is contained in the implied rules of the logical system in which it appears.

Now Bergson does not, in fact, pursue this line of thought but, in the context of a logical treatise, it demands to be pursued. To begin with, when one says "There is becoming from X to Y," "X" and "Y" are restricted by the demand that they follow the ordered relation which "becoming" enjoins. The force of "X" and "Y" is, certainly, reduced by the fact that they no longer mark out ways of "being" as "becoming" so as to exhaust the nature of that "becoming" and, therefore, no longer wholly exclude other predicates. But they may exclude some other predicates because the ordering would render certain additions unintelligible. We can imagine a "becoming" within which are discernible both "amoebahood" and "manhood" but can we imagine one which passes directly from one to the other? We can imagine a becoming, again, in which we discern both the oriental despotisms with which Hegel is inclined to begin the history of the west and the advanced liberal capitalisms which plague us and feed us at the moment. But can we, again, imagine one developing immediately into the other or an immediate reversal of the order? The degree of conceptual clash which such sequences envisage is, after all, very great (although it has not prevented politicians from trying to bring about equally unlikely transitions). The point is, however, that there are limits.

These limits are more forceful because Bergson's formulation (if it is taken with total solemnity and placed in the context I have invented for it here) entails a very special restriction: It requires that there is only *one* proposition. I said earlier that we cannot substitute for Bergson's "There is becoming ..." such expressions as "There is *a* becoming." For to do so would be to make distinctions within becoming of just the sort that the conceptual framework required prohibits. There cannot be several becomings. For then process is fragmentable.

If it is true that there is only one proposition, then all assignable predicates have to form part of the same system. They will be limited both by the demand that they be compatible with process and by the demand that they be linked with each other. Thus there is a drastic elision here of the universal and particular forms. But the logical consequence of this, far from being disastrous, helps to save the day by making assertions within the domain at least partially closed to alternatives and by providing at least the rudiments of structure which make inferences possible. The inferences, however, are between components of the single proposition and not between propositions.

This answers some of our questions, but it brings us nearer to the more vexatious ones.

IX

It is, now, obvious that experience — at least in the form of Bergson's intuitions — plays a crucial role in anything that we seriously want to say within this domain. What the conceptual framework does is to enable us to isolate the nonprocessual elements in experience, leaving us hopefully with

138

a loose concept of pure process which we can use to identify the required intuition. Whether we actually have such intuitions or not is, perhaps, another matter. The point here is that we should be able to understand the possibility of such an intuition and then the possibility of understanding the world in terms of it. Once again, however, it is not that there is an "experience" on one side and a rational structure on the other. It is just that the plasticity of experience is such that it is possible to formulate it in this way. The other ways of formulating experience are simply other rational structures and there is, still, no reason to believe that there is something called "experience" which is independent of *all* of them. Bergson often talks as if there was but the care which he takes to build the appropriate logical structure in which to enshrine his own vision surely makes this seem to be a misunderstanding. Experience once more seems to figure symbolically: like symbols it is susceptible of many interpretations but, like them, again, it is not anything apart from *all* of them.

We do not, therefore, have *that* worry though, again, if part of what we have to *explain* is why there should be any experience, we are not, yet, in a position to answer the question. As experience becomes more significant, that question *does*, of course, arise. For an arbitrary postulate "There is experience" would be at sharp variance with the attempt to demonstrate all the conditions for the logical structure we are dealing with. In the earlier categories, experience was not essential for the intelligibility of the logical structures themselves though it was convenient to look at them in terms of it. Here we could not, presumably, understand the demanded logical form "There is becoming from X to Y" if we had no experience. The possibility of explaining why there is experience, however, only arises when we get to the last category.[1] If the introduction of experience appeared here as logically destructive in some way — if we had experience isolated from the rational structure, for instance — we would have to explain it here. There seems no reason, however, to demand, now, more than we have. Every category, in the nature of the system, has some limitations.

What does concern us, now, however, is the growing separation of our concept of thought from our concept of reality. On the face of it, there is now a sharp distinction between the "existent" process phenomena and the merely "real" background domain of logical possibility. This makes it possible, for the first time, to be mistaken in the ontological status which one

[1] See Chapter 6. If, as is argued there, the last category exhibits the world as a set of dialectical individuals and the dialectical individual is intelligible only through its "reflection" in each of the earlier categories these reflections will have, in general, the characteristics — given that the individual is aware of them — of experience. They will be objectively "the world" but subjectively linked to the individual. Of course, this explains at most part of the form of experience and not its content, and does not answer all the questions which might be contained in the omnibus question: "Why is there any experience?"

assigns to a referential object — to think that what is *not* really *is* in some special sense in which "is" means "is existent."

We need, however, to ask what kind of mistake would be involved in such a situation. First of all, what is it, in general, to say that something is non-existent? Then what is it in this particular setting to say that something is non-existent?

In the special context which constitutes the argument of this book taken as a whole, we would not expect to find an answer which was both perfectly general and complete to such questions as "For any x, what does 'x is non-existent' mean?" For the answer varies from domain to domain. In any case, I have just given a rather special meaning to "exists" as opposed to "is real", and "is real" itself has a special contextual meaning. But the issues themselves have a certain generality about them. We must know, in some abstract way, what links the family of properties which are designated by these expressions from domain to domain and, inevitably, we must have had *some* idea of what we were talking about before we introduced these issues into their special places within the system. A general consideration of these issues might, for these very reasons, provide a way of checking up on what we are doing. If we could find a way of talking about such problems which did not lead to the special formulations on which this system depends, that would be a reason for thinking that there might be a genuine and formulable alternative to systems of this kind. Opportunities to check basic features of the general line of argument ought, in any case, to be exploited.

It is useful, just here, to begin with Bergson's opinion about Kant's general contention that "existence" is not a "real" predicate. Kant had argued, of course, that, if we compare two conceptions, one of a real thing and the other of a merely possible entity, they will turn out to be the same at least in the sense that, as ideas, we can discern no difference between them. Bergson takes this to mean that "Between thinking an object and thinking it existent, there is absolutely no difference."[1] Nothing counts as "thinking A" *and* "thinking that A is non-existent." For, if there were no A, one could not think about that, but only about something else.

Admittedly, there must be some way in which we can give an account of making mistakes in the assignment of ontological status. Bergson's own solution to this problem is to suggest that what happens when we correctly conclude that "A is nonexistent" is that we *add* something to the thought or concept of A — we think of A together with the exclusion of A by some other reality. But this is simply to postulate two levels of reality. "A" still has *some* ontological status, but is excluded at a particular level of reality by something inconsistent with it.

He thus uses a technique like the one which I have called "exclusion reference" to make the situation comprehensible: "For the idea of the

[1] *Op, cit.*, p. 310.

object 'not existing' is necessarily the idea of the object 'existing' with, in addition, the representation of an exclusion of this object by the actual reality taken in block."[1] And this kind of notion is, I have suggested, seemingly crucial to his whole mode of solving the problem of making a domain of "pure process" intelligible at all.

The argument moves rather quickly and introduces a great many complications which Bergson does not pursue. The complications are not necessarily relevant to the rather specialized task which he has set to himself, but they are necessary for the general review which seems to be required here.

The initial starting points seems to me a perfectly sound one. But the general principle behind it needs elucidation. It is quite correct that part of the reason for Kant's surprising conclusion about the likeness of the conception of the real and the contrasted idea of the merely conceived (Kant actually speaks of "possible" and merely conceptual, not "nonexistent")[2] is that each must perform a function as a referential object. If they were different one would not be related to the other in respect of being "the conception of" in the sense that Kant wants. The implication of this is that nothing can be "thought of" without being given *some* ontological status. If it had no such status then we would be thinking of something else.

This point can be put in this way: If we actually have knowledge of anything then that thing must have some place in our ontological structures. But this is only true because, otherwise, it would be the case that we had, in fact, knowledge of something else. Equally, and Kant would surely agree despite his insistence upon the noumenal world, nothing could have any ontological status if it were literally impossible for us to have *any* knowledge of it. (Kant is insistent that we have negative knowledge of the noumenal world in the first critique and, subsequently, of course, offers us additional knowledge of that special kind which is derived by producing the postulates of pure practical reason.) The reason that nothing could have ontological status if we could have no knowledge of it whatsoever is that such an entity could not function as a referential object. What cannot function as a referential object is whatever cannot be accomodated to any *possible* logic. But the only meaning which can be assigned to "impossible" is just "whatever cannot be accommodated to any possible logic." If we are denied this use of impossible, we cannot give any sense to "possible" either and, if we cannot make this distinction, no rational discourse can be envisaged.

Hence the property of "having an ontological status" is conjoined with the property of being an actual or possible object of knowledge in such a way that to have one property is to have the other and in such a way that, for logical purposes, we can interchange them. Our ways of defining

---

[1] *Op. cit.*, p. 311.
[2] *Kritik der reinen Vernunft* (Berlin: Bruno Cassirer, 1913), p. 414.

"knowledge," "logic," "possibility" and so on will determine the scope which will have to be given to this property.

Kant's error in his discussion of the issues arising out of the ontological argument seems to have been that he did not explore his own assertions about the variety of ontological statuses which can be assigned. He equates the "possible" and "real" hundred thalers at the level of referential objects but he does not explore the possibility that at other levels there may be a difference of ideas. The conception of a "real" hundred thalers, for instance, is the idea of a hundred thalers in a certain context — the idea of a hundred thalers which will buy a book or a loaf of bread. In this "system of ideas" there are important additional relations.

Thus what we have to explore is the idea of a variety in ontological status. Let us adopt the usage which I have been employing and call the most general level of ontological predication "reality." We can then agree that anything which can function as a genuine referential object is "real." Thus both Kant's "possible" hundred thalers and his actual hundred thalers are real. But they differ in *some* respects and one of them is that the actual hundred thalers has a special ontological status.

We can now begin to talk about the kinds of mistakes which can be made. At the most general level, we can only go wrong in believing that there "are" thalers or dragons or kings of France if we have made some mistake in delineating the class of referential objects involved. The conception of a dragon may be internally incoherent. Does it have a cast-iron stomach? Can anything both perform the functions of a stomach and be made of cast iron? Can you design a nervous system appropriate to fire-breathers? Is it the conception of an animal? If so is it an idea which we shall have to assimilate to an evolutionary theory? After a few of these questions we may come to the conclusion that we don't really have a conception of a dragon at all — that it is, perhaps, assembled from bits and pieces of other referential objects — fires, birds, snakes and whatnot. Or we may have seeming conceptions like that of the boojum, which fail on more elementary grounds. Boojums, for instance, seem to be altogether too vague (and necessarily so) for it to be said that we refer to them at all.

Thus, though every conception which is capable of conveying the sense of a referential object is the conception of something "real," not all seeming conceptions will succeed even in this. Furthermore, not all entities referred to will lie on the same level.

Before we can go any further, we shall have to examine our terminology and try to purge it of misleading suggestions. Kant seems to talk of what we would usually call "conceptions."[1] In the first quotation on this point,

---

[1] *Op. cit.* Kemp Smith's translation (London: Macmillan, 1933), p. 504, renders the word as "concept" and so does F. Max Muller (London: Macmillan, 1907), p. 483. Meiklejohn (London: Bohn, 1855, p. 369, and London: Everyman, 1934, p. 350), gives "conception" as I have suggested. The point, however, has not much to do with the usual

Bergson speaks of "thinking an object" and "thinking it existent."[1] Later he speaks of "the idea of the object existing." I do not want, here, to enter into difficulties which may raise problems about translation. The point is simply that expressions like "conception" and "idea" seem naturally to refer to some special entity either interposed between thought and thing or lying on the side of thought. Either way, they suggest a chasm which has to be crossed by some kind of bridge. To speak of "thinking an object" on the other hand, loads the issue the other way. Whatever his terminology, Kant, in the discussion of the ontological argument *is* quite plainly thinking of a sort of mental map, open to inspection in various ways, but also possibly misleading in some special way which is not made very clear. Bergson, generally, is thinking of direct access to the real — either to the domain of possibilities which he wants to distinguish from the actualities of process — or, through his rather special intuition, to the actuality of process itself.

Up to a point, this makes no difference. For, at the level of referential objects, it does not seem any additional kind of mistake is possible. When we start to distinguish between referential and other objects, however, the issue has to be decided.

It will be convenient, therefore, to distinguish between "concepts" as purely logical entities, and "conceptions" or "ideas" as psychological entities. When the two are identical, we can talk as Bergson does — at least at the level of referential objects — of "thinking the object"; and when they diverge, we can talk of thinking about an "idea." When we don't know whether they diverge or not — when, that is, we want to conduct just Kant's inquiry into a possible divergence — we can talk of "conceptions." We can thus admit that we have "ideas" of dragons, though the concept of dragon is one which, very likely, cannot be formulated. We might talk of our "conception" of the Absolute since we do not know, at this stage of our inquiry, if there is a "concept" of the Absolute or not.

The question about other modes of "being real" can then be put: "Are there concepts which purport to be concepts of something more than referential objects when, in fact, they are not?"

Now, notice, some concepts would not generally be taken to be concepts of anything other than the concept of a referential object. Our concept of the number two is, exactly, the concept of something whose nature is exhausted by the logical and mathematical operations which result from our

German-English equivalents — either "concept" or "conception" will do if we are given the word in isolation. The point is that Kant has clearly in mind a psychological entity rather than a logical one and "conception" more naturally fills that function. If one makes the distinctions that I am suggesting here, at any rate, it seems clear that "conception" is what Kant understands. Indeed, he speaks of "my conception" (*meinen Begriff*) and so on whereas a "concept" — as I have defined it — is not anyone's.

[1] One of the passages (*op. cit.*, Felix Alcan edition, p. 309) reads: "Penser l'objet *A* inexistant, c'est penser l'objet d'abord, et par conséquent le penser existant."

being able to refer to it at all. Our knowledge of it is, itself, logical — meaning that the epistemological route to it is through logic and not, apparently, through sensory experience or some other mode. Its place in the scheme of things is discovered by such devices as Peano's axioms of the number system. There might be some dispute as to whether it belongs to a part of mathematics somehow "given" in a very special kind of intuition or whether it is constructible by some logical operation, but, even so, it does not seem to *need* any status beyond that of referential object. Generally speaking, such entities might well be described as "logical." (If we cling to the point that to be is to be an actual or possible object of knowledge then it will be as well to classify modes of being by reference to the epistemological routes to them, though this will not be the only classification possible).

For non-logical entities, however, it appears that there can be concepts which are misleading in respect of ontological status. If I can form a concept of the "present king of France" it appears very likely that I could confuse a referential object with something which is more than that.

But can I form a concept of "the present king of France"? It is here that the issue seems to become confusing. If I think of the present king of France in the terms appropriate to determinate being, the answer is "yes." But the requirements for membership are purely logical. So are the requirements for membership in the domain of systematic unity. Similarly, a proposition asserting the "reality" of the "present king of France" will succeed in referring to pure being or pure disjunction — but only for the logical reason that all bonafide assertions do that. It is when we start to think of the "present king of France" as somebody who is busy in the world of processes and things actually doing things and "making a difference" to the world that the issue becomes pressing.

Pointing this out, however, makes it reasonably clear that, if we are to think of the property of having an ontological status as being related in the way that I argued it was to the property of being an actual or possible object of knowledge, then we shall have to think of a series of levels and domains in each of which the ontological references will be differently construed. For the kind of knowledge we can be said to have is directly related to the logical construction we put on the assertion.

At *this* new level, it is difficult to believe that we can form a concept of "the present king of France." For "present" now has a clear meaning and "France" does as well. If "France" is regarded as designating a complex of geography and social, economic, and political processes in a unique way and "present" as designating a restricted phase of it, then it will be hard to find a sense for "king" which will fit into this pattern. The kinds of goings-on which are constituent of present-day France are simply the kinds of goings-on which preclude there being a king. When we come to the domains presided over by the process categories, we do not seem likely to be able to form a "concept" of *this* entity. At this point, the "idea" becomes incoherent.

Imagination and reality may diverge. Thought and reality do not seem to.

But this is not the only kind of mistake we could make. The kind of distinction involved can also go wrong through twisting experience into an inadequate or wrongly contrived logical mould. The college freshman looking through his microscope in the biology laboratory may draw all sorts of queer things which the instructor and the demonstrator, alas, do not see. Subsequently, after acquiring the necessary conceptual structure from the text book or from his lectures or just through trial and error he will probably come to see "what is there." Did he originally have a "concept" of a "referential object" which he wrongly thought to be more than that? Did he subsequently get the "right" view of reality? Presumably, some referential object was involved: the student and his instructor certainly can and possibly will discuss a "conception" which the student had originally and agree on a "conception" which both had subsequently. The case here is unlike that of the present king of France. At least the last held "conception" offered by the student — the one from the textbook — seems to accord with all the requirements which thought, for the present, can impose on it. It is, therefore, apt to be taken as a genuine and logically viable concept. But given what is probably the present state of the science, it would be wise to take it as a "conception" — as a candidate for acceptance as a concept and not as a mere idea. Having moulded our experience by putting on a certain kind of conceptual spectacles, however, we may think that we are apt to be taken in indefinitely — that we have lost, perhaps, the ability to bring thought and reality into harmony at all.

This seems to be a mistake which I will call "the fallacy of the univocal world." It involves the assumption not merely that there is only "one world" (which in some sense must be true) but the assumption that that one world is susceptible of only one interpretation. If the second assumption were true, then it would follow that it would be possible to be trapped in this way. For we have already seen that it is possible to "mould" experience in a variety of ways and that it is, indeed, plastic in the hands of logical schemes. Thus it might turn out that the original "conception" of the student was correct and the text-book wrong and that, if everyone were educated as the student, no one would ever "see" what there was to be seen in the microscope. But the fact of the matter is that there are many things to be seen though very few of the conceptual schemes which might come to mind are capable of standing up to the rigours of expansion so as to take account of the whole range of things which the multitude of human observers is likely to see in biology laboratories, and the instructor was probably quite right to "improve" the student's conceptual apparatus.

The point of this seems to be that, if one can form a coherent conceptual structure which *is* adequate to the rigours imposed upon it by any serious intellectual endeavour which takes account of the whole range of logical and observational activities open to enquirers there is good reason to think that one has hit upon one of the ways of conceptualizing the world and that one has passed probably from "conception" to "concept." In most scientific enquiries of course there are still tests to be passed or tests that will be conceived in the future and few people would willingly maintain that they have passed beyond "reasonable conceptions." But this is not to say that they are imprisoned in a special logical cage. Where thought leads, there is reality. The fact that thought may lead to a variety of focusses or interpretations seems to bring us more naturally to the view that reality is multifocussed, as well, than to the view that all but one of the conceptual systems is necessarily an error. One can only get to the view that thought and reality separate at this point in our analysis of what it is to have one ontological status or another by insisting on the univocal view.

The alternative, of course, is necesarily to develop a conceptual scheme in which it is possible to envisage a variety of interpretations in conflict with each other but leading naturally so as to form a coherent whole from a larger perspective. And this is what a dialectical logic is.

So much, then, for the general enquiry. The details of the problem naturally fall within the analyses of the various categories we are trying to develop. And the trick, of course, is to show that the problems can be solved on each level as they actually arise. This brings us to the problem as it appears in the context of the category of "pure process."

The problem, here, is that we have two kinds of referential object: ordinary logical possibilities in which reference is enough to establish membership, and "becoming" or "process" itself about which we may be misled.

This "becoming" or "process-in-itself" I earlier described as "existent" in contrast to the merely "real" background of possibilities. It stands out from them and it also — as Bergson was constantly insisting — transcends them. It differs from the merely referential objects we have been dealing with in the past in additional ways as well. Most importantly, of course, it is an imperfect referential object. No act of reference can wholly encompass it. Thus it has, at any rate, the appearance of going its own way towards ends not merely undreamed of in philosophies which glorify the static state but toward ends which, literally, could not be dreamed of in such philosophies, by such philosophers or by anyone else. For, to transcend referability, *is* to transcend the limits of static possibility — to transcend everything which is available to us now.

Such a notion, all too obviously, presses hard at the heels of the notion I was just advancing: the notion that to be is to be an actual or possible object of knowledge. But it does not actually bite for, as we have seen, something is known of becoming or process itself. It is merely an imperfect object of rather special kind of knowledge. It is this fact which will lead me — though it did not lead Bergson — to the notion that we will have to press on to still further categories.

Meanwhile, the question is: Can we show, just here, that thought and

146

reality *still* do not diverge? The question is — in the terms that I have laid down — to be translated as: "Is it now the case that we may be able to develop thought forms which we may take to be concepts of process but which, nevertheless, are concepts of nothing more than referential objects?"

The answer, I think, is a quite categorical no. There is only one such "becoming" or "process" so there is no question of literal misidentification. Furthermore, to do its work, it must have many of the characteristics (in the special way of having characteristics which I outlined) which Bergson thinks it does. If mistakes are made in assigning these, thought and intuition are capable of correcting them. Thought still will not lead us astray unless we make the kinds of mistakes which Bergson himself charts in *Creative Evolution*.

X

I think, in fact, that the whole trend of the earlier argument is decisive on this point. Still, there is another kind of mistake which I think Bergson made and which he, presumably, would still think he did not make. Bergson thought that the most complete and successful way of viewing the world was the one which he laid down in his major works, and that there were no "higher categories." Thus he thought that process was not merely the actual and existent as contrasted with the "merely possible" world of static possibility, but that the subject "becoming," which his propositional reform made basic to the structure of thought, was the final or ultimate real. I mean, here, by "ultimately real" whatever it is (if anything) which is finally real in the sense of providing a description of the world which falsifies less than any other description and on which every other mode of description depends in some logical way. Bergson, that is, wants to assign to becoming or process an ontological status which I want to withold from it. Indeed, I shall eventually argue that *nothing* has quite this status — that it is a status which cannot be assigned. But that will depend upon a special account of the last category in this system.[1] Meanwhile, we must enquire as to what prevents us from bestowing such a status here and now.

The obvious answer is that "pure process" collapses under analysis because it demands of us logical feats which, within the category, cannot be performed. Somehow the domain of possibilities and the becoming or process itself must be united in order that, even by negative reference and intuition, we can grasp the nature of the process. But the union, though demanded, is consistently resisted by the logical structure, or lack of structure, of the concept of process itself.

---

[1] The argument is that all the categories are necessary, that the last category exhibits the necessity for a system of categories, and that though, ultimately, the world is a set of "dialectical individuals" it must also be conceivable — for just that reason — in other ways as well.

It was natural for Bergson to emphasize "creativity" and to insist that this way of viewing the world — as something which transcends the tawdry constrictions of mere logical possibility — opens to us a vista of freedom denied us by other conceptual schemes. On this ground, essentially, he insists on sticking by the intuitions which are formulable and comprehensible by the exclusion of the domain of static possibility. He resists, stoutly, the temptation to follow on to the "higher" categories contrived by post-Kantian philosophers. Since, in fact, Hegel did not develop (at least in any straightforward way) a category of "pure process" or one embodying its functions (his earlier accounts of process are deliberately "mechanical" and his "life process" is highly conceptualized) Bergson was entitled to suppose that he had discovered something of importance which had been missed in the Hegelean synthesis. Obviously, too, he was not faced with a specific set of arguments for transcending what I have called "pure process."

Furthermore, he *was* right in supposing that one of the major difficulties which had prevented philosophers (Western philosophers, anyway) from grasping the notion of freedom was that they insisted on conceptualizing the world in a basically static way — as a set of possibilities out of which, somehow, events decended in a law-like way. By insisting on the unity of process and the transcendence of discrete states, he was able to overcome questions about how one can get out of the world what was not in its earlier states. For it follows from this analysis that there is always more to be produced by process than can ever be exhausted by *any* analysis of "states" and that genuine novelty is in no way inconsistent with the initial postulates or later constructions of his system. Indeed, all attempts to find out "what" is latent in the earlier phases of process miss the point if process simply is not analysable into a set of discrete states.

XI

Yet I think he did not see the consequences of taking this analysis to be ultimate as well as legitimate. It seems to lead, for one thing, to a confusion between freedom, and mere randomness, capriciousness, or basic disorder. From the point of view of our knowledge, the world, on his view, will seem to be full of surprises. But this is not what constitutes freedom either for Bergson's "life force" or for us. Neither does it actually seem to lead to an intelligible view of randomness, chance, chaos, or basic disorder. Rather, it seems to me to hang perilously between rival conceptualizations, demanding a kind of determinateness which simply cannot be provided for it.

Let me try to explain: The "creativity" of *Creative Evolution* cannot, in the ordinary sense, be a kind of "freedom." For to be free is not merely or primarily to be relieved of restrictions, in the way that process as such is free from the binding influence of static states. It is to be able to do something. I am free to raise my arm, if you like, because when I decide to raise

148

my arm, my arm goes up. I do not find myself jumping out the cabin window or throwing my typewriter at my wife. I just find my arm up. If "surprises" were the result, I would not say that I was free but that I was the victim of malign circumstances.

It is true, I think, that the understanding of this kind of "freedom" does require a reversal of the usual order of explanation. I do not require an explanation for the fact that, when I will to raise my arm, my arm goes up. I require an explanation when that doesn't happen. If you habitually find that your limbs do not respond to your will, you go to a doctor and expect (rightly, most of the time) that he will provide you with a reasonable explanation: Your nerves have decayed or your muscles atrophied or, perhaps, there is something wrong with your mind. If you went to the doctor and demanded to know why your arm went up when you willed it, he would look blank or perhaps send for a psychiatrist. But this is not the reversal which the category of pure process offers or which Bergson's philosophical programme (which I am taking, of course, as being imaginable as a description of the world as viewed under this category) offers us. Instead, we are offered a world of surprises. Indeed, the reversal I am suggesting for understanding freedom is part of the later phases of our story here. But it is useful to see what would be required for such a reversal, and what it seems to me to require is a basic notion of what it is to be an individual exhibiting itself through a process. It is part of what it is to understand me as an individual to know that, when I will to raise my arm, it either goes up or there is something radically wrong. It follows from my nature that I am not a set or compound of static states but something which shows itself in time. The fact that I can be identified at all implies that there are occurrences natural to my unfolding and others which would be quite uncharacteristic. It is true that if I belonged merely to Bergson's world of possibilities or to the domain of possibilities which is part of the larger domain organized by the category of pure process, one could not understand how I could be free. But it is equally true that even given the "deeper self" of Bergson's *Time and Free Will* we still cannot, really, understand what it is all about.

For we still have no notion of individuality. Neither the possibilities on one side nor the "becoming" or process on the other are individuals. Possibilities are general characteristics or blank subjects. "Redness" as a possibility can be attached to any subject not already restricted by some other characteristic. Subjects are — considered just by themselves — possible bearers of all characteristics. Together they make a hybrid which is not the notion of individuality. Nor does talking of them in different terms — as Whitehead's eternal objects and actual occasions, for instance — change the position significantly. Eternal objects also have about them a generality — the capability of entering into any actual occasion, restricted only by the relations which they have to each other and to Whitehead's somewhat mysterious original "conceptual valuation." Actual occasions, equally, are blank until they are characterized by the ingression of some eternal object. But "pure process" is also not an individual, for what it rejects, precisely, is detailed individuation.

So it is not, really, freedom that we have in this category. But it is not sheer randomness either. The earlier argument showed that Bergson had some ground for a partial characterization of the basic becoming or process as having unity and direction at least. But this is where the real difficulty seems to come. Pure process requires characterization but resists it. It is intelligible through a negative reference to what it excludes. The conceptualization of this negative reference does focus experience so that it can be grasped intuitively. But it must have a positive side, too, if it really has this negative reference. Can it have this positive side if it eludes all the possible modes of conceptualization — if it is not a mechanical development, not a teleologically oriented development, not an exhibition of freedom and not an eruption of randomness? Is it characterizable at all if it is none of these?

Notice that it would be all right (by some imaginable criteria at least) to talk of a basic reality which eluded all these characterizations if we did not have to claim that it had some characteristics which we *did* understand. This would be a way of saying "Well, the world is just mysterious at the bottom and when the falsifications of the intellect have been stripped away we are left with the mystery." We would then have to say that the position finally did undermine all rational thought and discourse but if the position was, strictly, that the intellect always falsifies and simply falsifies that would not be a strange conclusion. This does not seem to be the case however, either in the category of "pure process" as I have developed it or in Bergson's metaphysical system. The intellect does and can do much more than that in such structures. It is the partial intelligibility which sets up a marked conceptual clash and drives us on to see whether the position cannot be improved by looking at the other side of the dialectical coin.

In point of fact, it seems to be just the notion of individuality which is demanded by and implied in the category of pure process — but cannot be fully or properly developed within those confines. It is because process seems, as Bergson's system implies, to be something, to be going somewhere, and to be doing things that we are tempted to treat it as a genuine individual. But it resists this along with all other conceptualizations.

XII

It is not unreasonable, I suppose, in this context to talk of the core concept in question "turning into" its dialectical opposite, though the metaphor is more than usually misleading. What it does is to force us to consider its dialectical opposite, to demand for its *complete* intelligibility crucial features of its dialectical opposite and, therefore, to provide the materials from which its dialectical opposite itself becomes intelligible.

150

The usual cautions are, however, required: the dialectical "opposite" of any one of the core concepts is, in the terms that I have established for *this* system, simply whatever it is which focusses a given level of concreteness in terms of the notions excluded by the first core concept on that level. There is nothing very mysterious about this but it is important to remind ourselves of the procedures involved. For any one of the core concepts to have any meaning, it must focus reality at some specific level of abstractness.

Within that level, it will either exhaust the ways of effectively conceptualizing reality or it will exclude something. The way of bringing this out is to discover whether the original concept is complete in itself or demands further extension for which it cannot provide. If the latter, we may expect that what it requires is to be found in what it excludes. The more precisely formulated the original concept has been and the more we know, in a general way, about the level the more likely we are to be able to identify the dialectical opposition. In fact, in this case, the original discussion of the level concerned itself suggested that there were two basic ways of conceptualizing it: One concentrating on the unity of process itself and the other focussing on individuals in process. The original suspicion that the first both required but excluded the second has turned out to be justified by the argument as it developed. There is, I suppose, a strict sense in which one cannot prove that a concept and any particular way of delineating its dialectical opposite actually exhausts the level of abstractness in question. The most that one can do is what I tried to do at the beginning of this chapter: to produce an analysis of the concepts specifying the given level of abstractness and to try to get a reasonable idea of what would constitute a likely set of subconcepts. The satisfactoriness of the result depends pretty much on the soundness of this original operation. That it is open to debate and reconstruction is all to the good. For we do not really know what to make of any proposals for conceptual construction and reform unless we know how to conduct debates about them and about subsequent reconstructions. It would be dangerous and even disastrous if we did not have any idea about how to manage such debates — about what kinds of consideration count, and so on. But then the whole discussion has been intended to suggest just what does and does not count and I should not expect critics with philosophical skill to be in much doubt about how to set about calling the relevant issues into question.

XIII

It seems reasonable, then, to get on with it and to try to develop the notion which I called "determinate process." The best way to do this, again, is with examples.

Let us go back to our earlier example about the lepidoptera. Suppose we reject the discrete phase analysis *and* the undifferentiated continuous phase analysis — the former because it fails, ultimately, to account for the continuity involved and the latter because it fails, ultimately, to provide for kinds of distinctness which make for individuality. Our "intuitions," if you like, are better than the first analysis allows and our knowledge is greater than the second analysis allows. We will, of course, allow that the first analysis gives us a projection of lepidoptera appropriate to determinate being. The second allows us to graft what we have learned from our investigations into systematic unity on to our concept of process and to see how both are related to determinate being. It does, anyhow, call to our attention vital facts about the ultimate interrelatedness of things and about the essential openness of the universe. But it still fails to come to grips with what our logical system demands and, as well, with some aspects of what everyone who has watched the development of moths knows: that they have a kind of individuality about them.

What is left after this rejection is to see that we can regard the moth as an individual which unfolds itself through a succession of stages: that it cannot be understood in any one of them, or as the collection of them, but as the development of them. You do not know that you have a specimen of lepidoptera on your hands until you have seen its development into a moth *and* until you have transcended that experience and seen the development of the creature as a whole. Similarly, you do not grasp a symphony by Elgar until you have heard the last note. But this is not all; you have to be able to grasp the last note in its context.

What we have to realize in order to grasp the notion of "determinate process" is that the concept of a moth is naturally the idea of a process but also the idea of a process seen from a vantage point which includes but transcends the time span involved. The unity and transcendence are properties of the concept exhibited in the thing as a process. And this can only be understood if we are able to form a satisfactory account of the relation between the concept and the thing so that they do not appear as two distinct entities but as a naturally related whole.

Notice, here, that we are not talking about "ideas" in the sense of mental pictures or maps, or of "conceptions" in the sense of entities which may or may not cross the line between those mental entities which we take to represent things and the things themselves. Our ability to imagine moths is not in question though, for all it matters for the moment, it might be very badly developed. Neither is it in question that we sometimes "represent" things in one way or another or form "conceptions" which may or may not have properties in common with certain features of the world. Rather, in talking about "concepts" we are talking about logical entities which we can imagine as being immanent in things and as being exhibited in the processes of their development. For what we need is a way of characterizing the domain of possibilities which will not lead to a destructive clash with the

152

notion of process itself. If we are to do this we need to rid ourselves of important preconceptions.

Most recently, our examination of ideas, conceptions, and concepts was in terms of devices which themselves marked out members of a domain of possibilities but which could be used to mark out phases or aspects of a process, much as a net can be used to catch fish. Once in the net, the phases or aspects were clearly quite unlike the processes from which they were abstracted, and it required a kind of negative reference to grasp "intuitively" the process itself. Earlier, we used concepts as actual structural features of the domains of determinate being and systematic unity — indistinguishable in thought and practice from the referential objects themselves, though given a certain additional "objectivity" on occasion by the experience which they moulded.

But it is clear that not all concepts are either like the static referential objects we first introduced or like the devices we used as instruments for abstraction. Nor are they all like their close relatives the "conceptions" and "ideas" which we employ as mental maps (however *these* are finally to be described and catalogued).

The concept of a moth actually exhibits itself through and as an activity, if we are careful to distinguish it from the concept of the "moth stages" and the rather ill-structured concept of the undifferentiated process within which moth-hood can be discerned. We are conscious of the moth as an individual.

It is only by a different process of intellection that we relate it to the concepts of its properties or come to think of it as being represented by a logical subject to which we can attach a selection of predicates, and by a special intuition that we come to think of it as a manifestation of "pure process." The chances are, in fact, that, when someone asks you to think of a moth, you will think of the moth as an individual — as something which appears to you discrete, standing out from the rest of the world with a focus of its own, undergoing a variety of continuous processes and yet retaining its individuality.

Generally, of course, this is how we think of ourselves. No one sees himself in his normal affairs as one of the late-order manifestations of the *élan vital*. Nor does anyone, usually, think of himself as a collection of manifestations of the reflections of Plato's forms, as the actualization of a set of possibilities, or as a collection of atoms and molecules grinding away as a chemical machine. All these vistas, of course, have their place in the order of things and of thought, and I am not *now* arguing a kind of general superiority for the concept of individual. Much less am I claiming a kind of superiority for some notion of "common sense." I am merely claiming that the notion of an individual as something with a clear identity revealed in and through a process is not particularly surprising.

For various reasons, it seems not to have received very much attention from philosophers (though I think that some such notion was part of what both Alexander and Whitehead may have wanted and this will figure, briefly, in some of the subsequent discussion). The most significant reason is that unless it is given its place in a dialectical system rather like the present one, I don't think it can be made to do much work.

Let us, however, go on with its exploration. When one looks at things from this point of view, the processes which they exhibit — and which exhibit *them* — must be seen as following "naturally" from their nature. When we look at the moth this way, it is natural and necessary to it that it should develop through its four stages, that in the end it should fly, and so on. Otherwise it wouldn't be a moth. From this point of view, we demand to know why the moth can't fly if we see it lying helpless on the ground. It is inconsistent with its being the individual which its concept demands that it should not be able to perform all or any of its natural functions. Similarly, with ourselves, we demand to know — when we are thinking of ourselves this way — why it is, if we will to lift our arms, that the thing doesn't come off. If we can't memorize the twelve-times table, we seek professional help. We don't, in our ordinary affairs, demand to know why we *can* memorize the twelve-times table. More than this, since we know ourselves and other people in some detail, we take some things as following from our natures (and natural to ourselves or others) and others as demanding special accounts. If Smith is a lawyer, we need an explanation if it turns out that he gets up in court and has forgotten the legal definition of larceny or the rule about onus of proof in automobile obstruction cases. If he is a brain-surgeon, we don't demand to know how it comes about that, once he has taken the top off Jones' head, he knows exactly how to behave. But if he turns to the nurse and says, "My God, what shall I do now?" we think that there is something very strange about the inside of the head just opened or else that Smith has taken leave of himself.

It follows, in other words, from the fact that one is the individual one is that certain things can be taken for granted and others will have to be explained. I have emphasized these examples, because they all have to do with activities, with doing things, thinking things, or performing in certain ways. They seem to show that the concept of an individual involves the idea of process and is not separable from it. Individuals are not revealed in a flash. All that could be revealed in a flash is a general rather abstract character. (When empiricists, striving to isolate the flash of the moment, sought for examples of assertions which could be confirmed in a moment and not over a span of time, it is interesting to notice that their choice settled on such exclamations as "Red! here! now!" The cry "Smith! here! now!" would seem quite inane and would not serve the purpose. This is not just because Smith-hood is a compound property which could not be confirmed in a single act because of its complexity but also because it requires a span of time to see that Smith is the individual one intends.)

154

These concepts of individuality which seem to me characteristic of determinate process stand in a dialectical relation themselves to the processes which they illumine and tie down: They are intelligible in and through a process and the process is intelligible in and through them.

There is a certain tendency to circularity in such notions which needs to be weeded out. In a way, to talk like this, sounds almost like saying that opium makes us sleepy because it has a dormative property. What we mean by opium, after all, is, I suppose, partly that, in certain doses and circumstances, it puts people to sleep. If it didn't it would be something else. But to say "The reason that opium puts people to sleep is that it has a dormative property," is clearly to say that sleepy making stuff is sleepy making stuff. Similarly, if we say, "Well, the reason that Smith is a good brain surgeon is that, if you watch him, you'll see that it is just in his nature to make a clean cut in the top of people's heads" is not saying anything helpful. But the point I was making is that the concept of an individual has the logical function of establishing a certain order of explanation or onus of proof. We come to know what and who Smith is because we see what he does — the concept of Smith develops as a device for organizing these notions. Smith's concept of Smith, though, seems to develop more naturally from noticing what happens naturally (because it's *him*) and what needs to be explained. Either way, once the concept is established, it becomes sensible to demand certain explanations and foolish to demand others. Once we know that the stuff in the bottle *is* penicillin, then panic breaks out and explanations are demanded if we give it to Robinson and his pneumonia goes on getting worse.

The idea of a *determinate* process, in other words, is the idea of a continuity of explanation with reference to an individual over a span of time appropriate to the concept. It is thus unified — we do not use one phase of the process to explain the next or one property to explain another — and it has a basic direction which determines the form of the explanations we demand.

XIV

It is at this level, as I suggested earlier, that the concept of freedom comes into play. This is worth exploring a little more not only because it is intrinsically interesting but because it will enable us to throw more light on the process categories as such and to pin down additional significant features of "determinate process."

One's ability to talk about freedom depends significantly, as the earlier discussion was intended to show, on one's choice of locations for the burden of explanation. If you think that every act of every individual — human or otherwise — demands an explanation, then it follows that there is no freedom and no caprice: determinism (given a strict account of explanation) is, on these terms a heuristic necessity. For the absence of an explanation would produce not freedom but caprice. Events would appear to occur at random, things to spring into existence *ex-nihilo*. If one were to take this randomness and appearance *ex-nihilo* to represent not a limitation on our knowledge or a special feature of some conceptual scheme (such as that attendant upon pure process), but as actually definitive of the situation, all explanation would eventually break down. For once it is admitted that events do sometimes have no necessary antecedents, it becomes actually impossible to distinguish those which seem to be capricious and those which seem to fall into law-like patterns. Capricious events are always just as likely as not and just as unlikely as likely. They do not have an antecedent probability of one-half; they have no antecedent probability or improbability. Under these conditions, how can we tell the event which seems to be caused but actually is the product of caprice from the event which seems to be caused and *is* caused? The logical framework for distinguishing them has broken down. The only rational alternative, then, is to hold that determinism is true and that, therefore, all events are caused however odd they may seem and however much they may remain opaque to our knowledge. In short determinism becomes something we assume against the odds because otherwise all our explanations will break down.

What we are apt to forget, however, is the manner in which our logical devices distribute the burden of explanation. Up to now, we have been able to ignore this problem because in the earlier categories the burden was distributed in ways which seemed natural. It was only in the category of pure process that the problem began to look threatening — when we opened up the prospect of a universe genuinely open to novelty and hence, in some special way, closed to explanation. And now, with determinate process, we begin to see it thrown queerly. Clearly this has much to do with some problem in inference (which ought to be a logician's concern) and suggests that determinate process may produce problems whose strangeness is equal to their difficulty.

XV

It is wise, therefore, to look at this problem from the beginning. The explanation of the unity which was described as pure being took place straightforwardly enough: the argument was that we had demonstrated a commonality of reference for all assertions of whatever kind in whatever kind of system (logical or otherwise) that we cared to imagine, and that this unity necessarily transcended all distinctions. For, otherwise, rational discourse would be impossible. If there were not some unifying feature, we would be lost in a destructive pluralism. If there were nothing to make distinctions in, distinctions would become meaningless. If any system belonged outside *that* unity, it lost its reference point from which its difference might be established and so on. What was assumed, in other words, was rational discourse (or certain features of it). What had to be explained was "pure being," the concept that we planned to introduce. Rational discourse, itself, could be assumed on the ground that we could not imagine ourselves to have established a problem to work on without imagining that the minimal conditions for rational discourse were sound enough. All that we were "assuming" in fact was that we knew what we were doing in putting some concept — any concept — up for argument. So that, really, there was a kind of merging of the issues about the concept itself and the issues about the place it held in any system. They were (I hope) shown to be inextricably bound up with each other. Similar remarks can be made about pure disjunction.

When we introduced determinate being, there appeared a distinction between the concept or category itself and the domain of things which could be subsumed under it. Again, for each of these, the burden of proof for the belief that they had places in the domain was clear enough: candidates were to be examined to see if they met certain logical tests. If they did, they were in, if not, not. Proving their status as "parts of the real" amounted only to that.

What is not quite so clear is what happens if we project a human being, say, or a moth, into the domain of determinate being and then ask for justification of the statements which form the counterparts of statements about their "acts." A man, on this view, is a collection of particles meeting the atomic requirements of the domain. Whether they are thought of as "material" particles, or as those particles which entered into Hume's "bundle theory" of the mind, or both, or neither, is not much in point. They will stretch out over a four-dimensional logical space and the "acts" of a man will be seen as a succession of these particles spread out in the appropriate dimensions. We should therefore require an argument to show that all these particles belonged identifiably to one entity. Once given that — whatever it might amount to, it would have something to do with the exhibition of a common property running through the appropriate region of the logical space — it would be natural to ask for some account of the linking *explanation* of the particles. Given that they all represent "events" (there is still a sense of event even if time has been spatialized to fit the dimensional mould of the appropriate logical space) in the "life" of the man referred to, why should these events and not some others fill his life?

Now it is notorious that no answer can be given in these terms. Hume scored a great "victory" over Berkeley on just this issue. Berkeley had thought that some of these events were part of the life of a man, let us call him Philonous for the occasion, because he, Philonous, had willed them. Generally, Berkeley's answer about the rest of the events was that God had willed them either directly or indirectly — directly, I suppose, if they were special events having to do with divine grace or wrath (though Berkeley was not keen on such events if they seemed to run counter to the course of nature), or indirectly if they were by-products of natural laws which God had willed to hold. Hume made fairly short work of Berkeley's notion of will. Put crudely, his argument was that, if one inspected one's own inner goings on, what one found was a succession of impressions between which there was no necessary connection. I note to myself my desire to raise my arm and then I see and feel a succession of events. What connection there is between them neither Hume nor I suppose, on Hume's view, God, knows so long as Hume and God stick to the conceptual scheme involved. For the events in question are, after all, atomic — precisely determined, and therefore, quite separate from each other.

Berkeley had argued, of course, that our notions of cause were derived from our experience of situations of willing. But Hume was able to analyze our notion of cause out into subcomponents having to do with constant conjunction and necessary connection, to argue that no one had any *experience* of necessary connection, and to shatter Berkeley's implied account of the experience involved by the means I suggested in the last paragraph. But is all this what Berkeley had in mind?

I don't really know, but I doubt very much if Berkeley thought our experience of willing consisted mainly or wholly of what Hume would have called an "impression." (I see in any case more connection than most people do between Berkeley's early work and his later, stranger neo-Platonic views of the *Siris*). I suspect that what Berkeley had in mind was that we are aware of ourselves in action in such a way that we don't need an explanation for the occasions when our will is followed by appropriate action, but only for those occasions when we will to do something and it doesn't happen. For *that* he provides the will of God.

The point here is that, within the determinate being scheme, every event is as surprising as every other and therefore every pattern of whatever kind demands an explanation. But none can ever be provided. In determinate being, Hume is king. One reason that none can ever be provided is that, since the events concerned are atomic, every pattern of events *is* as surprising as every other. You could only explain if that were not so. The best we can do, with *anything* in this domain, as I suggested earlier, is to set up standard patterns with entities which are organized into mathematical sequences and talk about probabilities in terms of deviations from those. No explanation is called for when roughly half the tosses of a coin turn out heads. But if three-quarters of a million out of a million turn out tails, you may think that somebody is up to something — though you still can't *prove* that anything is wrong. There is no reason why the tosses shouldn't turn out that way.

But didn't Berkeley have a concept which Hume couldn't accommodate to his domain at all? Perhaps Berkeley was thinking about the things that I have been calling individuals and about determinate process.

When we get to systematic unity, by turning over the dialectical coin, we find a sharp reversal. Now, to talk about Philonous and his life is to talk about a pattern which runs through the whole of the designatable reality and which has just the form that it has because it is that and no other concept. The life of Philonous is wedded firmly to the rest of the universe as a special, timeless, pattern. It has to be just the way it is or else it is another pattern. Thus, thrown against this backdrop (the kind of eternal God's eye view which sees the universe whole and sees it steadily), the life of Philonous is a single, seamless, necessary truth. But it is not, of course, really the life of Philonous: it has only the relative identity which we get by throwing Philonous up against the whole universe and it breaks down as a way of analyzing Philonous and the world. It is a possible view, but it excludes too much. Notice, however, that, here, the burden of proof is different. The struggle (and hence the explanation) is to isolate Philonous from what constantly threatens to turn him into the featureless unity of pure being. Whereas what was hard to show in determinate being was any connection between the components of Philonous or anything else, what is hard to show in systematic unity is the distinctness of anything. In one case, atomicity is taken for granted (and Berkeley is ruined when his philosophy is mapped in this way). In the other case, unity is taken for granted and the possibility of distinction is what has to be shown. In neither case is the "showing" very successful. In the case of the "acts" of Philonous, they turn out to be inexplicable in one domain and necessary in the other.

One may be skeptical about some of the details of the preceding argument and think that Berkeley and Hume are not being given a totally fair hearing. But the fact remains that it shows pretty clearly that the logical mould one chooses makes a vast and vital difference to the location of the burden of explanation. And that is one of our most pressing intellectual concerns.

It will become even clearer, I hope, when we pursue the matter into the process categories. In pure process, it is not merely connections between some of the components which elude explanation. Process itself, considered as pure process, is not susceptible of explanation. But the reason for this is that we are forced to take for granted, once we accept this conceptual scheme, that pure process just is what it is. The burden of forming an adequate notion of it falls on our intuition. That we can see the necessity for this intuition relieves it of the curse of a merely arbitrary postulate. It is not a choice we have made, it is a fact presented to us by the way we have squeezed our experience and our logic. But we become suspicious of it as an ultimate characterization when we see that it demands a kind of conceptualization which cannot be given to it.

When we shift to determinate process, what we have to take for granted is that there are specific entities which form structured processes of their own. We can, then, explain deviations from them, but the natural course of events becomes something given. This, however, seems to be a new kind of notion. Heretofore we have had situations where things are explained in fairly straightforward ways or cannot be explained at all. In determinate being, the "reality" of members of the domain can be explained on logical grounds; the connections between them cannot be explained at all. In systematic unity, the patterns of things are necessary or simply not there. What *is* is the unity of the world. In pure process, the domain of possibilities is given in the same way that it is in determinate being. The pattern of "becoming" can be partly explained by demanding a combination of coherence of assigned properties and an adherence to the evidently minimal requirements of the concept of process. But the explanations are not complete and process itself is unexplained. Now we are faced with a choice: we can explain some things at the cost of taking others for granted. The novelty is relative, however: all along what we have taken for granted has influenced what we could explain.

Indeed, proof and explanation are probably always like this: in law, you must choose between assuming a man's innocence and trying to prove him guilty, or assuming his guilt and trying to prove his innocence. You cannot have it both ways and you cannot sit neutrally and have it neither way. For what counts as evidence, what is acceptable as argument, and what makes for a sound inference all depend on which you choose. If he has to prove his innocence, he must be able to show where he was at all material times, or that he was physically incapable of lifting the blacksmith's hammer, or that by nature, conviction, and upbringing he would have been psychologically incapable of the deed. If the prosecution must prove his guilt, then they must show that he was in the right place, that he could have done the deed, and finally, somehow, that he did it. These are two different undertakings. To try to combine them would leave open a vast ground within which no decision could be reached. To adopt neither stance would be to fail to establish any acceptable canons of relevance. But the same thing is true with certain kinds of statistical arguments. You can assume random distributions of events (if you can define that notion) and seek an explanation for deviations or you can assume some specific order and try to explain deviations from that. But you cannot do both and you cannot escape by doing neither. For then you will have no argument.

This does not, of course, show that the two phases of the activity are necessarily separated by the fact that one of them is impervious to reason. But the reasons will be of different kinds and operate on different levels. If you think that the normal result when people try to guess cards is just the "chance" result, you will start with that and try to explain the deviations by reference to telepathy or cheating. You will have a reason for the original choice and a reason for the subsequent explanation. What you cannot do is to use the kinds of reasons which you adopt to explain the deviations as devices for explaining the "standard" cases. (It is no good saying "Well, Smith guessed in the way that 'chance' would lead us to expect just because, though he was telepathic, and knew which card was which he chose to tell lies so as to confuse the investigator." For then you must produce some evidence *other* than the actual results of the guessing.)

Similarly, in our determinate process schemes, we do have reasons for thinking of ourselves and of moths as individuals in the required sense. For such notions "make sense" of our daily goings-on and of the development of moths. It is just that, when we have made the decision to regard ourselves this way, we cannot ask: "Why on earth is it that, when I will to raise my arm, my arm goes up?" "No one knows" is *not* the answer. But the answer also is not "Well, it's because you have this funny thing called the will and that turns on the switches which operate the machinery which raises your arm." The answer here is "Because that is part of the kind of thing which follows from being a human individual."

If you become dehumanized in some special way, we won't talk about you this way at all. If you lose your personality in the dark wastelands of a schizoid state, we may come to think that hardly anything "goes naturally" with you any longer and seek the explanation for all your acts in some different scheme. Importantly, you will be thought not to be quite in the full sense an individual any longer.

So long as you are an individual, we can think of you as being free in the sense that what you will to happen is just what happens. No one, of course (unless Berkeley's God is a special component of the world and is somehow freed of the burden of his own past) is a perfectly free individual. Everyone is a victim, in part, of his physiology, his personal history, his social and physical environment and so on. In these respects, of course, he is not, really an individual at all but a manifestation of something else — of the human condition, the march of history, or whatever. Similarly, with the moth. It is not *just* an exhibition of moth-hood but it is not a perfectly free individual either. Its conditions set the limits within which its developmental processes can exhibit themselves. Generally, in saying what individuals are in this respect, we are just establishing the limits of their individuality, the terrain within which they are free. We grasp the concepts of individuals largely by attending to these limitations; but we do not usually confuse them with the individual itself.

XVI

This kind of question, however, breeds the next obvious one: The presumption on which we were working was that all the core concepts are ways of conceptualizing the whole of reality. Can we really imagine the whole world as being made up of individuals in this sense?

It is obvious that some of the things we talk about are not individuals at all. To have individuality in this sense is to have a rather private kind of unity and to be separate, in some way, from other things. We cannot think of hydrogen atoms in this way. How does one differ from another? In what does its private freedom consist? And are we any better off with respect to lumps of granite? Surely, just as bits of granite or arsenic or potassium phosphate, they are all alike. They are individuated only by reference to the spatio-temporal grids in which they are given location.

One answer would be to maintain that, after all, there are degrees of individuality. Whitehead would have maintained, for example, that something of the notion of freedom applies everywhere. What he called the "mental pole" of an actual occasion is to be found in some degree everywhere and every actual occasion has its own subjective aim. His notions are difficult to work with because there are difficulties about the "ingression" of eternal objects into actual occasions and because, considered just as actual occasions, the structures of his event-particles are difficult to pin down. But what he has in mind is that everywhere one finds that actual events do have elements which go beyond the confines and structures of mere possibility and have, therefore, to a degree, a life of their own: if they did not our world would collapse back into static states. Thus when we talk about hydrogen atoms, bits of granite and so on our references are really to the formal possibilities which they embody. As actual processes, it may be that there is more to them than that and that our references to the inanimate world are over-simplified by the pragmatic demands of our specialized scientific knowledge. Individuality may be a more pervasive feature of the world than we think; but there is some danger here of being trapped into a kind of pan-psychism which may be difficult (as Whitehead found) to make entirely clear.

Another answer would be that there are large-scale individuals whose activities are manifested in these small-scale phenomena which do not seem to be individuals in their own right. Because they are large-scale phenomena their activities do not usually impinge on our scientific knowledge which is geared to much smaller spans of space and time. In these regions we mostly, in any case, treat things under their aspects as members of the domain of determinate being where such problems do not arise.

Such speculations sound very fanciful and more properly the domain of spinners of romance than of philosophers. But again, it may be only our place in the scale of things which makes them seem fanciful — or rather the place which we assign ourselves by choosing to view ourselves primarily *as* embodied organims of certain sorts when, perhaps, we might view ourselves as users of bodies.

It will prove useful, in any case, to press this issue a little because it will turn out that the demarcation and inter-relation of organisms provides the rock on which this particular conceptual ship eventually founders. If we look closely at Alexander's *Space, Time and Deity*, it begins to seem as though what Alexander is putting forward is the notion that the "space-time" matrix out of which his world develops is, itself, a large-scale individual: It is natural to it, that is, to develop as it does from the discrete states of

162

material universe to the complex organic states which arise with life, to the still more closely integrated affairs of mental life and so on. Thus his, at first sight, curious remark that "Time is the mind of space" — not meaning that there is a kind of all-embracing pan-psychism to be justified by reference to the world, but that what we call the physical world develops as an individual does. Its nature is to be seen only through its development over a long span (as the nature of what I have called an individual is not to be seen in a moment or a flash). Nor is all its future to be explained in terms of its past. It develops "emergent" qualities in passing from inanimate matter to life and to mind and this is intelligible if it is a unity of the kind which an individual is.

It may be difficult to deal with the interrelations involved but it is imaginable that individuals of a smaller scale — such as human beings and moths — may develop within the confines of larger scale individuals such as Alexander's Space-Time.

So, perhaps, we can formulate a total view of the world in terms of the category of determinate process with its primacy of individual reference. If the whole background matrix of space-time systems can be thought of this way there would seem no reason to suppose that anything which thought or experience can turn to will ultimately prove intractable.

XVII

The difficulties which do seem likely to cause genuine trouble are those which arise over the delineation of individuals. There are two of these which seem important to me: One of them concerns the explanatory relations which hold *between* individuals. The other is the latest chapter in the saga of our friend the dialectician's dilemma — surely here, if anywhere, thought and reality can part company. It seems that thought can "construct" individuals where there really are none and that there is no guarantee, here, that thought is, however far and well pressed, self-correcting. This issue can only be dealt with, however, when we have clarified the problem about individuals and I will take them in that order.

The first difficulty amounts to this: Given conceptual devices of the sort which make determinate process intelligible, we can explain the workings of individuals and something of their relations to crucial parts of the rest of the "world." But we face difficulties when we have to decide how, for any given occasion, we should determine which "individual" is at work and how we should deal with problems relating to the inter-action of individuals. For example, it may be hard to tell whether "Smith" is doing the thing in question or whether it is really the work of something like Alexander's all-encompassing Space-Time matrix or something in between, like "the state" or "General Motors."

We can deal with human beings by making use of a conceptual structure such as the one which I used in *The Rational and the Real*. There, I suggested that we could regard the human mind as a tendency to have experiences, and regard it as working against a background of permanent possibilities, actualizing, in an experiential process, related sets of possibilities. Thus an individual human being becomes equatable with a given tendency-pattern which can be traced against the background of possibilities which enter into his life. From the perspective of rational agents, this is a reasonable scheme which enables us to interpret freedom as the opening and closing of possibilities and the restraints on us as arising from the ways in which possibilities are related to each other. But, inevitably, we do not want to regard all restraints on human action as arising out of the interrelations of the possibilities themselves: Individuals influence each other and, furthermore, there are various kinds of individuals between which it becomes necessary to choose.

We may not have much commerce, in our ordinary thinking, with very large scale individuals such as those envisaged in my extrapolation from Alexander, or very small scale individuals such as those envisaged, apparently, by Whitehead in his talk about the fundamental event-particles which he calls actual occasions. But we do have a good deal of traffic with medium-scale individuals (or pseudo-individuals depending upon one's theory) such as social and political institutions, historical tendencies, and ecological structures. If the world consisted mainly of individual organisms like men, birds, mice, plants, and bacteria which could be considered, together with their experiences, and the possibilities which make those experiences intelligible, the problem would not be so acute. But though there is a common presumption that this level has a degree of primacy, it is not easy to see on what basis this presumption is to be defended. A colony of ants or a hive of bees — or even a herd of cattle — has some claim to be regarded as a single entity within which the degree of individuality belonging to the component creatures is a matter of dispute.

In human affairs, such questions are notoriously subject to dispute. There are many reasons for this: the whole of "human nature" is not exhibited in any one individual. "Individuation" takes place, usually, by a procedure which involves contrasting oneself with other people. People change rather drastically if they are made justices of the Supreme Court of the United States, members of the working class, or officials of the Mormon Church — becoming, to some degree, manifestations of the institutional tradition or social milieu in which they find themselves. Powerful biological forces — which may seem to be or are products of the activities of a larger scale individual — have their way with us.

XVIII

Hence such questions as "What actually constitutes an individual?" and "How do individuals affect one another?" are crucial for a whole variety of

164

judgements and yet seem to bring few, if any, intelligible answers. There are, I think, two quite different ways of going about answering such questions.

One of them is to seek, as common sense does, or as Whitehead did, for a "basic" level of individuation and then to regard all the other complexes essentially as "societies" or complexes of these basic individuals, and to think of the societies as dependent on the basic individuals and created by their interaction. The other is to seek the answer in an investigation of the relation between individuals and "universals" and to try to show that there is a kind of inter-dependence between them.

The first solution does not seem to me to work either in a common sense way or in Whitehead's more sophisticated way. In common sense terms one says "Well, of course, there would be and could be no states, classes, religious institutions or whatever without the individuals who compose them. Clearly, they come first and invent the other institutions in which they take part. Furthermore, individuals persist in much the same way through long spans of time though institutions come and go. Men are much what they were under the ancient Sumerians though nearly all their institutions have undergone violent changes." Alas, unless we make a number of special assumptions, this seems to be quite clearly false. If you regard men mainly as biological organisms and all their other functions as by-products of their biological activity, it seems more or less true. But is to be "human" just to be a certain biological structure? Or does "being human" involve such social activities as having a language, certain characteristic mental capacities (like the ability to reason), and certain social proclivities? If the latter, then aren't "men" very much made by their institutions?

If one attempts — as Whitehead did — a much more sophisticated scheme, the difficulties seem to be just as serious. In his earlier writings, Whitehead had talked about "events" as the basic stuff of the world. But "event" is such an elastic notion that it slips away from us when we try to grasp it. Is an event something like Smith's firing a gun at Jones, or Smith's pulling the trigger, or the flick of an eyelid? Or can it be something like the collapse of the middle ages, or the Second World War? Understandably, then, Whitehead substituted "actual occasions" for "events." Actual occasions were to be the basic components of the real, all of the same duration, all having common structural properties, and all equally "fundamental." The trouble is that this becomes highly artificial and incapable of substantiation. Some rather long "events" in fact seem incapable of any fragmentation at all: The examples I used earlier about listening to music seem to substantiate this. It is true that you can listen to an Elgar symphony and then go back and consider your experience note by note or in any fragmentary way you wish. But the moment you do that, it is something else that you are thinking about. The symphony itself is a unity or it is nothing. In any case, if we fragment time, as I argued at the beginning of this chapter, time becomes unintelligible. The success, in part, of the determinate process scheme lies

165

in its ability to enable us to regard the affairs of an individual as continuous. There seem not to be basic units smaller than the units which exactly fit the individuals one wants to talk about. If one cannot settle the question about how one is to determine what counts as an individual, one cannot, obviously, settle questions about basic units, either.

The real reason, I think, that one cannot settle the question by establishing the existence of a set of "basic units" is that there is not a hard line to be drawn between what have been traditionally called "particulars" and what have traditionally been called "universals" and that the notion of individual cuts across the traditional lines.

XIX

In the next chapter I shall try to face the "universals" problem head on. But it is important to introduce certain rudiments of it here because what causes the "process" categories to break down is precisely that no place can be found within them for an adequate notion of universality. Determinate process hangs, uneasily, in a kind of special limbo.

To begin with, then, part, at least, of what I have called the traditional notion of the universal is that it is the sort of thing which can be exemplified in a number of particulars and part of the traditional notion of the "particular," conversely, is that its specificity is complete. "Redness," for example, would usually be taken as the name of a universal. It can be found in many things and no one of them or collection of them "exhausts it." "This red thing," on the other hand, would usually be taken to denote a particular: nothing else can be "this red thing." One thing and only one thing exhausts it. It is very hard to devise a way of speaking which does not prejudice the issue. I do not mean, by this way of speaking, to pronounce upon the ontological status of universals or of particulars. The way of speaking is supposed to be consistent with all the possible interpretations — to permit one to go on to say that universals are things in their own right whose copies or shadows appear "in" particulars, or that universals are simply "in" the things which exemplify them, or even that universals are mere "words" or even noises.

Anyhow, it appears that what I have called an "individual" crosses just this line: It is "exemplified" in the successive (though continuous) ordering which is a process. In that respect, it is like a universal. But it is uniquely what it is and exhausted by the single instance of itself. In that respect, it is like a particular.

There is always a problem about universals with respect to their relations to the particulars which are imagined to instantiate them in that the given particular can be taken as an "instance" of any one or several of a class of universals. A given thing may be red. But what shade of red? Is the redness of the red soil of Herefordshire a special combination of universals or do

166

we regard Hereford-red-soilness as a single universal, complex but subtly integrated? These questions persist in some way, whatever view we take of universals. Aristotle complained of the difficulties posed by what he took to be Plato's theory about this relation because, for one thing, it posits a further relation between the universal and the particular and the status of this relation is itself doubtful and, perhaps, involves us in indefinitely many additional relations before we can fix on the universal we want to talk about. But the Platonic theory that there are independently "real" universals only forces the problem in a special direction. The Aristotelean view that universals are "in" things also forces us to ask about the relation between the universal and its bearer or exemplifier and it is still no clearer how we decide *what* universal we are dealing with and how many of them there are with respect to any given particular. An extreme nominalism does achieve some simplification by the very act of de-reifying universals, but it (rather startlingly perhaps) merely starts the problem working in reverse: *What* has been de-reified? There is now not redness as such and there is not the Hereford-red-soilness and there are not special relations (universals or particulars?) standing between the universal and the particular. But what is there? Can we say anything about the particular? What remains, exactly, as the kernel which has not been banished from reality?

It is this, in only slightly more subtle form, which lives on to plague us with respect to individuals. A given process-phase can be regarded as a determinate process by integrating it under the rubric of a variety of individuals: If it is a human act, we may think of it as the act of Smith, or the Working Class, or the State or Divine Providence. Or we may subdivide it and think of it as the set of acts which are the acts of Smith-cells or even Smith-molecules or a collection of Whiteheadian actual occasions.

In the ordinary way, we simply *cannot* dissolve this issue by turning to rather traditional universals and particulars. Traditional universals will turn out to be much like logical possibilities or Whiteheadean eternal objects: They are fixed and unchanging and cannot be exhausted in any individual or particular. Traditional particulars, equally, cannot spread through a temporal succession. For then their unity becomes something more like a universal. Traditional universals and particulars are most comprehensible as the properties and property-bearers of determinate being. They do not seem to be assimilable to time.

So there is no use in looking for a set of basic "particulars" and then regarding all the remainder of our material as "universals" relating them. Indeed, within the determinate process scheme, we do not seem to be able to get further with the problem. It demands a solution, but none is forthcoming immediately.

To be sure, we can regard the individual and determinate process as beginning to show the seeds of a quite different way of looking at the problem: The individual here is a kind of microcosm of what might be called the "concrete universal": It is the collective manifestation in actuality of the concept of its own individuality and is, thus, both particular and universal. But to press this so as to solve the problem of the hierarchy of universals is to transform process and time into something else. For the closer we make the unity, the more we lose the individuality which enables us to make distinctions within the rather formless unity of pure process.

The dialectical twist, in other words, is upon us again: If we try to get around the problem of the multiplicity of individuals which poses a problem in "determinate process" we will, if we keep the notion of process, be forced back to the unity which is "pure process." If we try to transcend the notion of process we shall have arrived at another category.

Inevitably, we shall arrive at another category. But it should be noticed that "determinate process" is useful as a countervailing way of looking at the situation which we saw in "pure process." It is a distinct and — as will turn out — uniquely valuable way of focussing the world. But it is not the end of the story.

XX

Before we try to introduce another category, however, it is necessary to see how we have fared with respect to the dialectician's dilemma.

It is true, evidently, that, with respect to the notions appropriate to determinate process, thought can, in some sense, go wrong: Thought is capable of discerning individuals where there may be none and, equally, of failing (however hard we may struggle and however well we may think) to discern individuals where they may actually exist. But it is not the case, all the same, that thought and reality "diverge" at this point. For the point is, exactly, that with the conceptual equipment open to us within such a category, there simply are not final answers to questions such as "Is X a genuine individual?" We are not finally misled because there is not a final answer to be led to. The discernment of determinate process is, by its nature, a provisional and relative undertaking.

Given what we know of ourselves and the ways in which we can organize our own experiences, we are right to consider ourselves as individuals. Wherever, indeed, it makes sense to delineate processes in the relevant way, we are entitled to do so. It is just that, while such delineations do designate appropriate ways of looking at things, they do not, all the same, delineate final ways of looking at things. There are always alternatives.

Thought is not misled so long as it leads us to conceive of individuals in an intelligible way. But the mode of existence of individuals, in this sense, is by its nature provisional and relative to the region of experience being organized.

To some degree our attempts at constructing accounts of individuals are

168

constrained by moral issues.[1] The continuing identity of an individual human being, for instance, is significantly a matter of continuing moral aim and of continuity of moral responsibility. If he is so dominated by external influences as to be incapable of certain kinds of moral activity it is no longer morally proper to regard him as an "individual" and to hold him responsible for what he does and for what happens to him: We blame or praise some individual of larger scale — his society or his class or Divine Providence. If he changes so radically that it no longer makes sense to hold him answerable for his past, we are entitled and, indeed, morally compelled, to ask whether we ought to regard his past self and his present self as distinct individuals. If he manifests a strong continuity of moral aim, it becomes incumbent on us *not* to regard him merely as the byproduct of some individual of larger scale and to consider his interests and rights as standing against those of some more amorphous individual such as the state. How such moral claims are to be adjudicated is, of course, a question mainly beyond the scope of this discussion though it will be influenced, perhaps, by parts of what comes later in this book. We are not, it should be remembered, trying to discover the whole truth about the world but only categories under which the truth is to be understood and shaped, and the logical structures within which it can be calculated. It is significant to notice, however, that, here, the scope for moral discourse comes to be of considerable importance.

But is not this kind of provisionality logically difficult or even disastrous? It is, after all, quite open. It is not, again, that experience might aid us where reason fails. For experience is moulded by the structure of the category and gives us no more final answers than reason does with respect to the ultimate delineation of individuals. It does provide us with something on which the concepts we are able to form can bite, but it is equally susceptible of organization in any of the ways which are open to us.

XXI

Thus we come once again to situations in which "both and neither" appear as dark alternatives to "either, or" when we come to try to assign predicates designating individuality. As such, this issue was dealt with at the end of Chapter 3 but one of the things which become obvious is that the more traditional propositional forms seem inadequate to the task which is set by the category of determinate process. It is not the case that we establish some subject and proceed to attach predicates to it in a way which could be expressed by forms like "There is an x such that x is S and x is P." For what we want to say is "individuality (of X kind) is exhibited through A, B, C, D ... from time T^1 to time T^n." Here, "individuality (of kind X)" is not

---

[1] There is, I think, a very good reason for this. See Chapter 6.

the name of a subject to which predicates are attached as was "x" in the original formulation. We cannot substitute for it "There is an x such that x is an individual and x exhibits A, B, C, D, from time T^1 to time T^n" or any reasonable substitute of the same general form. For then we imply that there "is an x" which is a subject of some sort and that the other characteristics are properties of it. Individuality is not, on this view, a property of anything but a special kind of quasi-universal whose nature is exhibited through a process. Just as in the pure process forms "becoming" was intended to assert a special kind of relation which was quite different from the "is" of predication, so, here, "exhibited through" or its substitutes "is manifested by" and so on are intended, in a serious way, to exhibit another form. By reason of it, the properties are no longer separate identities capable of functioning as independent values of logical variables. Within the system determined by the concept of the individual, the rules of logical inference work in special ways as the discussion of freedom showed. And any attempt to translate back into the more standard forms of proposition will result in fatal distortion — a reflection back into the timelessness and discreteness of determinate being. But this, though perhaps difficult to deal with in a formal way, can be handled in practice as the earlier discussion showed.

If more formality is required, it can, no doubt, be provided though the special inferences involved will always depend on just what individual is being referred to and how the concept of that individual is to be constructed. The generalities permitted the logician in determinate being are not available here. But then we would expect this if we intended seriously to come to grips with the problem of individuals in any case.

With this, we are in a position, I think, to proceed to the next categories and to tackle seriously the problem of universals. From this point on, the discussion will be dominated by successive formulations of the concept of individuality.

Chapter 5

Further development — unity and individuality — ideal universality and objective universality

I

The further we extend the chain of core concepts, the more subtle the issues become: Pure being and pure disjunction were evidently inadequate and the grounds of their inadequacy were not hard to find. Determinate being and systematic unity might represent characterizations of the whole of the universe of discourse which one could imagine as adequate — if, for instance, one were prepared to deny the reality of time and wanted to insist that the special clarity available to logic at this level represented an optimum which one abandoned at one's peril. Even so, the potential sources of their inadequacy were plain enough and the formation of the requisite arguments was not very difficult even though the estimation of them must necessarily remain controversial. Now, we have a still richer structure which, in the nature of the situation, ought to be more adequate to the needs of discourse and the cracks are not only harder to discern; it is also harder to be confident that one has hit upon a correct diagnosis.

What is lacking in the preceding core concepts seems to me, however, to be, quite simply, the concept of a certain kind of unity. Pure process offered a realm of logical possibilities against the background of which process appeared as Bergson's pure flow. The unity of process was conceptualizable, at that level, at the cost of effective individuation so that even process itself could not be construed as a functioning individual. Determinate process offered a notion of individuality against the same logical background, but still excluded an effective notion of unity so that it became difficult and finally impossible to specify effectively the interrelations between individuals. The concept of process provides the link between the two categories; the specific exclusion reference is the notion of unity in diversity — the notion of a linkage between things which will not break down either in a hopeless atomicity or a faceless unity.

The delineation of this specific exclusion reference will form the main task of this chapter. Once that is done, it will turn out, I think, that it is fairly clear that the normal pattern of dialectical interrelations between the pairs of core concepts will develop quite naturally and we will get a pair of concepts which, though by no means identical, bear some resemblance to Hegel's subjective and objective notion — though the differences are important and I shall use different names for the categories. Obviously, the doctrine which I shall develop bears important likenesses to what has come to be called the "concrete universal," but that expression has come to denote a variety of doctrines which are not easy to understand and I am hesitant about the terminology. The reader can compare what I have to say to what is said in the literature on these topics and form his own conclusion. He will realize that my debt to that literature is large. The issues are complex enough in their own right, however, and I do not propose to introduce additional complexities by trying to undertake a historical review in depth or detail.

Evidently, the problem of unity in diversity *is* the problem of universals in its ontological guise. In its epistemological guise, the problem of universals is the problem of classification and of its objective justification. That, in turn, is the problem about how we are able to structure our universe of discourse so as to be able to get into it something more than logically proper names and still maintain that we are talking, directly and effectively, about the world. Since what we need to know is how to structure our special requirement for a specific exclusion reference which will exactly focus what was deficient in the preceding categories and then how to relate this reference to the rest of the system, it will be a good plan to undertake, in the relevant respects, a brief review of the problem of universals.

II

Perhaps an additional word of explanation about the present point in the development of the system is in order before such a review is attempted. For it would seem natural to think of "universals" as belonging to a very distant level of abstraction. Even those who are "realists" in the strongest sense would, I suspect, be inclined to think that the level at which we finally separate universals and particulars in our discussions of "the world" represents a stage at which we have departed a great distance from the concrete and earthy objects of everyday life.

It seems to me — and it seems to follow from the whole line of the preceding discussion — that we meet with the universals "problem" exactly when we come to look at things in the full richness of their inter-relations to each other. So long as we are content to atomize the world — as in determinate being — or to concentrate on the overwhelming unity of things — as in systematic unity — the problem is not very intrusive. Universals have a perfectly natural place, apart from particulars, in the carefully compartmentalized world of determinate being. And everything is a special kind of universal in systematic unity. Even in pure process, the distant domain of formal possibilities is adequate to lock universals away from the seamless unity of process and our attempts to characterize process take on some of the characteristics of attempts to describe Plato's shadow world. It is when individuality comes clearly to the fore in a concrete way in determinate process that the problem becomes pressing. Unity in diversity does seem to imply yet a stage further in the descent from the perfect generality of pure being. Thus, while such expressions as "abstract" and "concrete" are slippery and apt to confuse more than they clarify if they are not handled with care, it is not really so difficult to maintain that we are moving, still, from the abstract to the concrete. It will turn out, I think, that it is quite natural to maintain that we are moving from categories which emphasize the most general features of things to categories which emphasize the effective individuality and interrelatedness of things.

III

If, however, what we need in order to provide the required specific exclusion reference is a functioning notion of unity in diversity, it appears that we shall be forced to face up to all the conundrums which have traditionally beset philosophers in search of a general solution to the problem of universals.

Roughly, those problems arise and beset a variety of philosophical enterprises because, quite apart from the special considerations which concern us here, intelligibility and objectivity require that references to universals should be possible and not merely arbitrary. But the notion of a "real" universal creates metaphysical and epistemological difficulties which seem incapable of rational solution. To say anything about a component of the world requires, if one is to go beyond merely naming it, that one should ascribe to it some property which will serve to identify it and to establish some relation between it and other things. This, in turn, involves a measure of classification, and reference to properties which are not merely in the particular things but exemplified elsewhere as well. Thus to say that something is red is to establish a relation between the thing and other coloured and non-coloured things, and to make reference to a classification which must, somehow, be intelligible independently of the particular things referred to.

If nominalism were true, such references would not, objectively, extend beyond the mere word or name used for classification and the assertion "P is red" would convey only information about our determination to use the word "red" in a certain way. Realists, on the other hand, maintain that "redness" is the name of a property which has its own being and provides the standard "redness" to be used in determining both what "P is red" means and on what occasions we are entitled to say "P is red."

If the issue is pressed, however, it seems to be not merely objectivity but

173

also intelligibility which is at stake. For no world would be intelligible in which properties did not carry over from one thing and situation to another. Physics is possible, for example, partly because the property of being a physical body is specifiable and partly because it is found to run through a great many entities. There is thus a clear connection between a certain minimal view of what it is to be a universal and what it is to be a natural law. If, in some sense, there were no universals, there could be no physical laws either. A world of wholly unrelated "particulars" which have no common features is not a world which can be talked about let alone one which can be theorized about in the ways which we usually suppose lead to "knowledge."

The traditional debate, though, is about what it is to "be" a universal, whether any rationale can be provided for any particular account of "being" a universal, and whether various principles of parsimony can be squared with the consequences of such accounts.

It is useful, as a preliminary, to state as simply as possible the doctrine which may be called "realism" and to look at some of the consequences of it. A realist, let us suppose, is simply someone who thinks that universals have an ontological status which entitles us to list them in our catalogues of the furniture of the world along with whatever we take to be particulars or individuals. His nominalist opponent, of course, does not think that "There are no universals" in the sense that there are no words which function as universals and no referring activities which count as "referring to universals," but rather that such expressions and activities can, ideally, be analyzed out in such a way that the referential objects will, ultimately, turn out to be particulars. Thus universals, for him, function only at the level of verbal and logical entities while, for the realist, they function beyond this as actual features of the world.

It is not that the realist says "There really is redness" while the nominalist says "There are only red things." For the realist may be one of those who thinks that universals are located in the things which they unite and thus may agree that (in one sense) "There are only red things." It is that the realist insists that "What are properly called red things really instantiate redness," while the nominalist insists that "redness" is only a word or a name which we use for the purpose of bundling certain things together. The nominalist also asserts that things are just what they are however they may be bundled. The universal, as whatever it is that may be in many things at many times and many places, but is always, somehow, the same, simply is not a feature of the world.

It is often thought important to make a distinction between the "extreme realism" usually ascribed to Platonists and the "moderate realism" which derives from Aristotle, on the ground that the former involves the specially vexatious doctrine that universals inhabit a special eternal realm of their own while the latter confines itself to the more pedestrian doctrine that universals are to be found in just the things which are said to instantiate them. But I think this rather odd problem — which might be called the problem about "where" universals have their being — is really relatively minor. For, in neither case, will universals be literally "exhausted" by their instances of the moment and, in either case, there will be the traditionally burdensome problem about just how they are related to the particulars in which they are instantiated. If there "are" universals, the problem about "where" they are will not worry us if we can get them adequately located in relation to the particulars which have to be related to them.

But it is at just this point that the problem begins to get interesting and troublesome. For it is here that one has to try to make explicit the distinction between universals and particulars and to do so in a way which will keep them related without confusing them. Evidently, this is more difficult than one might expect. Suppose there is — in whatever sense of "is" one chooses — redness in the world. Then is not redness some particular thing in itself? One can ask, for instance, if it is red itself, or some other colour, or no colour at all. If it *is* red, it seems to be just one more red thing. If it is not, then will it not, anyhow, have just the sorts of relations to red things that other non-red things have or fail to have. (In this canvass of minor absurdities we can, perhaps, excuse ourselves from considering the possibility that redness is really some other colour and merely suppose that it is either red or else it is not the kind of thing that could be coloured.) The main difficulty is, of course, that if one reifies universals and puts them amongst the things in the world, they seem in turn to function very much like the things they were supposed to unite and not much like universals.

One can, of course, try to back off and contrive more subtle ways of looking at the issues. One of them is to say that redness is not another and special kind of thing but a kind of standard by which one identifies the red things of the world. There is a special sense in which the standard metre in Paris is not one metre long in the same way that other things are. It makes no sense to try to measure it if it really *is* the measure. If, by some unlucky chance, it should be run over by a large truck, we should not, if we really meant it as the standard, say that it had become elongated in the squashing process but rather that everything else had become shorter. We would not actually do that, I suppose, partly because we have by now more sophisticated measures and the standard metre has symbolic rather than literal force, and partly because our commitment to it is hedged by other commitments to other standards. But a real universal which was the standard for the attribute which it marked out would literally function in this way. Thus, one would say that it was not red in the usual sense, but the measure of redness.

Perhaps that solves one problem — though it will make the nominalist even more suspicious since he will maintain that what we are really referring to by redness is just some particular entity, like our standard metre which we have decided to take as a standard. But it still does not explain how the universal can maintain its reified independence and still be whatever it is that unites all the things of its kind. The more independent it is, the more it is one thing amongst others. Even the Aristotelean universal which has, perhaps, the happy knack of only appearing in the midst of the things which instantiate it, only disguises its awkwardness by this tactic.

Another move, of course, is to make more precise the realist commitment to various kinds of things, all of which one might, at first glance, think of as universals. Quine, for instance, is prepared to be committed to classes but not to universals.[1] There is some initial advantage here since classes, if reified, are not so easily confused with particulars. The class of all red things is, at any rate, not another red thing though it is, perhaps, what "redness" refers to.

The trouble, here, is that there is, at least, a confusion between reference and referability. It may be — though this is still doubtful — that "redness" refers, if to anything, to "the class of all red things" but such a class, if it exists objectively, surely does so just because there is an objective "attribute" which is the defining property of the class. As Ewing puts it "Membership of a class depends on qualities and relational properties" and "Extension, after all, seems dependent on intension."[2] If one is a logical pragmatist, as Quine is, then the possibility of objective reference and the dependence relation involved here will not matter or at least not so much. But I have already argued against that position.

Still, both these points are useful if only because they call our attention to the fact that we are not necessarily very clear about what it is that we mean to designate by the expression "universal" and because they make clear that not everything which appears to be a universal may be of the same kind. The assumption that there is a general problem which must have a uniform solution is one that needs to be watched.

What all this suggests, however, is that the realist-nominalist controversy may be predicated on a misunderstanding and, until we are clearer about the distinction between universals and particulars, we cannot expect much enlightenment. At any rate, neither traditional realism nor any of its obvious variants seems capable of providing just the notion of unity in diversity that we require at this point in our discussion. The course of wisdom, therefore, seems to be to examine the basis of the distinction and the sources of unity and disunity which seem to give rise to the bifurcation of the world and/or the components of our discourse into two distinct and basic types.

IV

Part of the confusion, perhaps, results from failing to see the problem

[1] Quine makes the point repeatedly but references are richest in *From a Logical Point of View* and *Word and Object*.
[2] *Non-Linguistic Philosophy* (London: George Allen and Unwin, 1969), p. 114.

against the background of clear examples. When we talk about red things and redness, intelligent men and intelligence, or even bears and bearishness, there is an apparent convergence and divergence of reference which may be misleading: The classification and the thing classified are portrayed as coinciding but the distinction between them is demanded both by our choice of words and by the very way that we state the issue.

Suppose, instead, that we consider the following situation: Imagine that we have at our disposal a great library so arranged that, somewhere amongst the books, everything in the world is perfectly described. By some miracle it is also the case that our collection includes no books containing false statements. If there is, then, a correct classification for the books, there will be a correct classification for the things in the world.

We therefore have at our disposal a world, a set of books reflecting that world as perfectly as can be imagined and, hopefully, a set of classifications which will render the books, and so the world, accessible to an orderly and intelligent investigator. We could, also, of course, have descriptions of the books, the world, and the classifications; but the books, by hypothesis, already describe the world. In effect then — though not every *kind* of description of the books will be a description of the world — we need only the books themselves, descriptions of those features of them which are not descriptions of the world, and descriptions of the classifications.

As a beginning, we might think of the descriptions of the books as being about "particulars" and descriptions of the classifications as being about "universals." But it is obvious that the soundness of this distinction will depend upon our point of view. The book, thought of as a physical object, may be imagined as a particular; but as a *book* it is very like a universal: There are (or may be) numerous instances of it in a variety of places and times; it is related in the same way to all its instances and not dependent for its "existence" on any one of them. It is arguable (as it usually is about universals) whether it depends for its existence on all of them or on the last surviving one. (If all the copies of Plato's *Republic* are destroyed, is it gone or does it still "exist" as one of the possibilities of the human mind? It is, after all, in some interesting sense, a collection of ideas. It is often said that ideas cannot be destroyed by burning books. So long as there are — or might be — human minds, the ideas remain latent in the scheme of things.)

If it is not so clear that the books are particulars, is it so clear that the classifications of books are universals? Surely not. For though they can be thought of that way, they can also be thought of as concrete collections of actual books in our library. If they are genuine classifications (and not, I fear, like the ones which we find in the libraries whose existences lie outside this example) they will define actually related sequences of books which have whatever kind of unity the classification demands. These actual unities may well overlap — if every reasonable classification is employed they will, in fact, overlap — but each of them, taken singly, will, nonetheless, constitute a concrete unity. Given the terms of the example, each such unity will, by its nature, include everything which could be included in the entity whose unity it exhibits.

It will, of course, be argued that the actual particulars being referred to are the objects in the world itself (including the books considered as physical objects) and that the things which the library example brings out are all, in their various ways, *abstracta* of one kind or another which can be construed as pseudo-universals and pseudo-particulars. It will also be argued that I have been greatly muddling the issues by confusing books themselves, statements in the books, and classifications of books with the various referents of these entities.

But we need to know whether the things in the books and in our systems of description are very different from the things in the world or not and, if so, how. The books, indeed, consist of words and sentences from one point of view and black marks and white paper from another. The "classifications" from one point of view consist of concepts variously expressed in some notation, and from another of collections of actual books.

Furthermore, our descriptive system is not, admittedly, complete, for though it is imagined that everything can be described (for purposes of the example) and that we have or could obtain not only the books but also descriptions of them, it is not to be supposed that we can obtain descriptions of those descriptions of those descriptions and so on *ad infinitum*. But we can imagine, if we like, that we can see, on some principle, a law of diminishing returns here. Just as the books describe the world and we do not need descriptions of *both* in the relevant respects, so descriptions of the descriptions will only be required to the extent that the form and not the content of the description needs to be included in our account of the matter. The divergence of form from one level to another can be predicted and dealt with in an appropriate theoretical way so as to allow us, very nearly, to believe that we have the whole "system" within our grasp.

The issues, then, about the divergence between our library system and the world its contents describe come down to these: There is an ambiguity about the library and its contents which, supposedly, there is not in the world outside: Each entity in the library has two aspects and, by passing from one to another, we seem to be able to shift from universal to particular and back again as we please. Furthermore, the library system has about it a certain openness and incompleteness which, perhaps, the world outside does not have: the mirror never quite reflects itself in a perfectly adequate way even though we mirror it in another mirror.

But perhaps the same ambiguities apply, in any case, to the outside world. A red patch is, from one perspective, a particular thing and, from another, an instance of redness, and from a third, a member of the class of all red things. A man may be imagined as the sum of the events of his life or his life may be regarded as a series of instantiations of him. (Surely none

178

of us is really *exhausted* by the events which actually compose his life; he *could* have done many other things and still have been himself. It is a fact that he is instantiated in just the things he does, but it is only from one special perspective that they *are* him. Again, each of us, surely, is an instance of humanity and humanity, again, can be regarded from either perspective.)

Just as the book, somehow, needs its instances but is not exhausted by them and perhaps not, finally, in some more remote sense, dependent on them, so a man must do something in order to show himself but is not exhausted by what he does and even a red patch is both itself and its universal.

Nor is the outside world really more "complete" than the system of library descriptions. For the universals which are instanced or are their instances, are related to each other in one dimension just as are the descriptions and the descriptions of the descriptions. Only by a final kind of self-reflection which I shall describe later, can the system be imagined as "complete", and that self-reflection would have its counterpart in our wholly imaginary library too.

All this, however, needs to be pinned down and made into clearer sense.

V

I think the issues can be clarified if we look at them in the following way: If we start from the standpoint of words and meaning, it seems to be a necessary though not sufficient condition of meaningfulness that each term or expression which makes reference to the world must be related to some other term or expression which will give us information about the *kind* of property which is intended. Thus for words like "red," "green," and "blue" we need to know that we are dealing with ways of being coloured. For such words as "monkey," "horse," and "giraffe," we need to know that we are naming or marking out kinds of animals. It is not enough to say that we can define "red" by pointing at a red thing. For we need to know that it is the colour and not the shape that is being attended to. (Logically, any number of coloured patches pointed at will have something in common by way of shape — all the shapes will fall within *some* geometrically definable class so that we cannot imagine that we learn the "meaning" solely by some kind of "association," nor that we can build up the meaning by logical construction from a set of ostensive referents.) Similar points can be made for other classes of expressions. Equally, words like "red," "green" and "blue" will need to be related to other expressions which will specify the sorts of things which can be instances of them. Meaningful discourse thus requires a number of levels.

We can express the way these levels are related to each other by adapting terminology used by both Hegel and W. E. Johnson and speaking of determinable and determinate.[1] Thus determinate forms of the determinable colour are expressed by particular colour words like red and green. But, in respect of specific forms of them, red and green are determinables under which various (and various *kinds* of determinate) forms can be found. Equally, being coloured is a determinate of such determinables as the property of being the occupant of a spatial surface. When we talk about "universals" we are, I think, talking about expressions in their determinable function. When we talk about "particulars," we are talking about expressions in their determinate function. Generally, any expression can be made to function either way, given an appropriate context and given that it has, on that occasion, a logical function such that its place in the meaning structure being invoked is appropriate to the function being assigned.

If we adopt this framework, we can pose, again, the terms of the realist-nominalist dispute and see what answers we get.

If "nominalism" were true, there would be a set of lowest order determinates which could never function as determinables and, furthermore, these would have some special kind of logical primacy. If "realism" were true, there would have to be at least one determinable which could not function as a determinate and it would have to have some status which was not derived from reference to a set of determinates.

Neither of these contentions is, I think, true, at least from the standpoint of language and logic. (I will, in due course, endeavour to examine the issues, equally, from the standpoint of whatever it is that is imagined to be unlike logic and language.)

One might think, indeed, that "pure particulars" or "lowest order determinates" are to be found in the expressions which we used to designate simple sensory expressions and that these do play a primary role in the construction of our knowledge and of our discourse. It is true, however, as Johnson remarks, that "The fact that we can and do attend to impressions of one order in disregard of concurrent impressions of other orders, explains how our primitive perceptual judgements, from the first, assume a logically universal form."[2] It is because we can distinguish colours *as* colours that we do not confuse them with sounds. But this suggests, of course, that we impose a universal form on them and that the content of our awareness consists, perhaps, of particulars. Still the particulars, as particulars, then would not be intelligible. For it would not be them that we were identifying and distinguishing but a more general characteristic

---

[1] The terminology really derives from W. E. Johnson, *Logic* (Cambridge: Cambridge University Press, 1921, 1922 and 1924; and New York: Dover, 1964). But there is *part* of the same suggestion in Hegel's *Science of Logic*, e.g. the three "forms" of the "notion" are called "the three determinate notions." (Johnston and Struthers, Vol. II, p. 247; Miller, p. 612; Felix Meiner, Vol. II, p. 253.) Hegel, by the way, goes on to tell us that counting the determinates is unwise — but that is another story.
[2] *Op. cit.*, Vol. II, p. 191.

which they happened to share. Genuinely pure particulars, of course, can only be identified by proper names. But to know that this "name" is the "agreed name" or the "name we have undertaken to assign" or whatever to a given thing is to be able to identify several different instances of it or the same instance on several different occasions — it is to be able to suggest, and then to find, in other words, a set of actual or possible determinates for which it can function as the appropriate determinable. Pure proper names have only a provisional function. With them we metaphorically hang labels on things but finding the labels again and using them is a different matter. Everything we can *say* about the particular red patch we want to deal with consists in locating it, appropriately, in the determinable-determinate hierarchy.

In any case, however, if the determinable-determinate structure is essential for meaning, nominalism cannot be true. For meaning depends not upon construction from particulars but upon the location of determinates vis-a-vis appropriate determinables and vice versa. Every intelligible expression of a genuinely referring kind must be located somewhere in the appropriate scheme and there can be no obvious primacy for anything one would wish to call "particulars."

The "realist" may seem to be in a stronger position in such a scheme because it must, surely, be the case that there is a highest order determinable and such a determinable must hold a special logical position — apparently such a position as to make the "realist" right about at least one universal (which is enough, after all, to make his technical point.) The exploration of this issue is somewhat complex, but it will be important for our general investigation here and not merely as part of an attempt to short-circuit aspects of the traditional universals controversy.

First of all, one might offer two different sorts of reasons for the view that there is *not* and need not be a highest order determinable at all. The doctrine that there must be determinable-determinate relations was offered, essentially, as a condition of meaningfulness. To know what "red" and "green" *are*, one must form some notion of what it is to be coloured. To know what "being coloured" is, one must form some notion of such things as "occupying a spatial surface," "being an interceptor of light rays," "being an object of perception" or whatever it *is* that is appropriate for what one has in mind. ("*P* is coloured," like nearly all expressions, does not, as such, have a unique meaning and its various meanings may be related to one another in any of a number of ways.)

Now all this may suggest, first of all, that enough is enough, and, secondly, that there need not be a unique highest order determinable which unites everything. The first point is valid enough for practical purposes. When we want to teach someone to use colour words, it is usually enough to make clear to him, somehow, that being coloured is a way of occupying a spatial surface and also a way of being an object of perception. He need not have *much* information about what it is to be either a coloured surface or an object of perception. But, if we really want to have knowledge in the sense of knowing what it is that we are talking about (that is, of being able to distinguish it from anything else which may accidentally come our way), we have to be able to go on fitting in the pieces of the determinable-determinate hierarchy as far up the line as may be necessary to take care of any mistakes we can envisage. In principle (though not, to be sure, in practice) that means going on until we find something which is logically certifiable as the highest order determinable. But why, to take up the second point, should we imagine that the branches must all belong to the same family tree? The lines, do, as we saw with "being coloured," usually run off in all directions.

In some sense, of course, everything must be a form of something. The argument for the unity of knowledge was either made (or not) in the first chapter and I cannot add anything important to it here except to point out, in *this* context, that the whole structure of meaning and knowledge is always as shaky as that of the least well-defined determinable which enters into the region of discourse under consideration. That is not equally true of the least well-defined determinate under discussion. For the lowest order determinates in any region will function merely as provisional proper names. (For instance, one may deal with redness in terms of being coloured, for its relation to a determinable and by marking off things which one simply names Joe, Harry, and Fred as its determinates. Once one's interest switches from "redness" to "Fredness," the matter becomes different, of course.) One can, therefore, argue the need for a highest order determinable, without insisting that there should be lowest order determinates.

Thus the first "kind" of reason does not carry much weight — at least if I have made any progress toward carrying the general point of this book. But the second kind of reason is weightier: Surely, if there were a highest order determinable, it would, by its nature, violate the very condition which led us to start talking about determinable-determinate hierarchies in the first place. Unless, indeed, the highest-order determinable is of a special kind, the thesis that there *is* such a determinable may well turn out to be self-contradictory.

The most obvious way to solve the problem would be to look for the most general of all possible properties and then to argue that such a property was immune from the requirement that it be exhibited as a determinate of a further determinable on the ground that, by definition, there could be no higher order determinable. It might then be alleged that it took its meaning from references to lower order determinables which functioned as its determinates.

There are, however, several things wrong with this "solution." One of them is that generality is not the only requirement. Obviously determinables are more general than their associated determinates just because they do

182

serve to unify a more divergent sub-set. But being more general is not a sufficient condition of such unities. The highest-order determinable must actually be capable of structuring what it associates. The most general of all imaginable properties, "being," is one which we have already investigated. Its emptiness as well as its own kind of fruitfulness should, by now, be obvious. Everything is a kind of "being," but being, by itself, provides only the kind of starting point which got this enquiry going. It does not, by itself, structure anything. It merely, as it were, runs through everything. "Pure being" does, indeed, verge upon meaninglessness, though it is not quite empty. We need, therefore, a term which will combine this scope with more structure. Such a term, to avoid the meaning problem, must take its meaning from its ability to reflect back upon the structure which it unites and thus to unify in a way which will make it clear that there can be no further determinables and that its own position is unique without being unrelated to the rest of the structure (as, by being abstract, "pure being" is.)

There is, so far as I can see, only one property which provides this special dialectical relationship and that is the property of being an actual or possible object of knowledge. If anything has that property then it also has some other property in virtue of which it may be said that it can be known. The property of being an object of knowledge, therefore, extends in a parallel way through the domain and the term naming it takes its meaning from that domain. Furthermore, nothing can be *said* to be a property of anything or a feature of the world unless it can be known and therefore be a possible object of knowledge. To designate a property *is* to claim to be able to separate it from other properties and thus to have knowledge of it. If anything did exist and was not a possible object of knowledge, it could not be said to be distinguishable from other things. And this would be a special kind of nonsense.

Thus there is a strong case for thinking that we have identified the highest-order determinable, but this also disposes of the case of the "realist." For the most general and pivotal of universals turns out to depend for its special place on the rest of the system which it unites.

Is it now, however, true that a parallel case can be made if we start not from language and logic but from "the things of the world"? If it is we shall surely have identified our specific exclusion reference — the meaning of unity in diversity. If not, we shall have to admit that, finally, we have fallen victim of the dialectician's dilemma: For thought and the world will finally turn out to be separated if the specific exclusion reference at this point in the dialectic turns out to have two separate references.

VI

In fact, however, this task is not so formidable as one might think. The remarks at the end of Section IV of this chapter apply, in general, to the more sophisticated version of the situation developed in the last section.

It is not just that there must be properties associated with the *terms* which we use to talk about things so as to provide the determinable-determinate hierarchies which make discourse intelligible. The same properties must run through the *things* referred to if such modes of talking actually succeed in their purpose.

We can consider the question which this poses under two different guises: First of all, what would be the position, if it turned out that discourse was structured this way while "the world" was structured differently? And, secondly, what do we know about the "things" in the world which would lead us to question the "existence" of such a structure?

In general of course, the answer to the first question is that we would know that there was a world which had a certain negative property (the property of not being able to "mesh" with discourse which is structured in a certain way) while we also knew that, in a certain sense, we could not talk about such a world.

This situation is not unfamiliar in the history of philosophy: It is like the situation posed by Kant's distinction between the phenomenal and the noumenal world, and lesser philosophers (presumably Herbert Spencer for one) have found themselves in analogous situations. One general objection is that such a situation is untenable for it really amounts to saying that we know that "*X*-ness" is a property of things while denying that we know what "*X*-ness" is and, if this proposal is pushed, it will surely turn out to entail the assertion that we both know and don't know something about the world.

This general objection, however, is too gross. For we know — if the argument of this book is correct, for instance — that we can say a good deal about the world before we get to this particular divide. Kant knew, too, that there was much that he could say but, also (on account, generally, of the limits which he thought he had discovered to the scope of pure reason) much that he could not say. His account of the noumenal world is, as he suggests after all, a kind of negative knowledge. If we found, at this point, that we could not go further and impose the next category of the dialectic on the world, we would simply have to conclude that the dialectic had broken down, that we had, as Kant thought *he* had, reached the limits of reason.

The difficulty is that this would, in a way, invalidate the earlier stages of the dialectic. For it would end in unfinished business. We would then have to say that we had discovered a sequence of ways of categorizing the world but that we had had to stop short of discovering the "underlying nature" of the world. We would then be, as Kant thought he was, simply trapped by the limits of the human mind. But one *would* know that the "world" somehow transcended these limitations. We could then admit the general point that we were trapped in a special kind of contradiction but allege that this stage marked the limits of human enquiry.

What is *finally* wrong with such an admission is simply that it seems that it ought to issue in a demand for a reworking of the whole scheme. For we started, somehow, in touch with reality. If we lost our way, why not retrace our steps? But that is to imagine that there is an error locatable somewhere and anyone who could find such an error would not have left the earlier parts of the system to stand, anyhow.

One need not worry about such a predicament, however, unless there is reason to think that a split does develop at this point. The revised theory of universals which I have been trying to develop does not seem to lead to the difficulties involved in the traditional theories. Universals and particulars, now, are simply to be understood as determinables and determinates. Any referential term can be either, depending upon the aspect of it demanded by the context in which we find it.

This would be difficult to maintain if there was reason to think that "real" things were simply not "open-textured" in the way described. But it seems more likely that they are.

I do not know of any object — from men to red patches — which does not seem to have just the property of being a particular from one standpoint and a universal from another as the examples I used in Section IV seemed to indicate. The reader who is not satisfied will, however, find more detailed examples as we go along.

If we can accept the negative point — the point that there is no obvious reason for thinking that there is a split between thought and reality just here, something follows from it: For, if we started the system in contact with "the real" and, if we have not faltered, we should have carried this contact with us all the way. Thus we are not forced to offer a special proof of continued contact.

It does not follow, of course, that this notion of the world as a determinable-determinate hierarchy is complete in itself. What it is supposed to be is simply the specific exclusion reference from the last category. Combined with the unifying factor from that category — the idea of process — it will form the next category. Thus the point is not that the world is, somehow, a frozen and complete system. The notion of universals and particulars I have developed applies within a context of continuing process in such a way as to provide an additional category.

We must now look at this new synthesis.

VII

Strictly speaking, indeed, the world could not be construed as a kind of *static* system exhibited as a determinable-determinate hierarchy. For each level of determinables would then be simply the class of the determinates subsumed under it. The description of each determinable could be exchanged without loss for the set of descriptions of the appropriate determinates. The *world* would "dissolve" into a cluster of particulars.[1] In a literally static world — one in which nothing ever had happened, was happening, or would happen — redness would be exhausted by the set of actually red things. Then redness would have no referential meaning except that class of entities, and our entitlement to talk about it, apart from the red things, would rest on very shaky ground.

Such a world would exhibit a primacy of particulars, and actual links between things would be lacking so that the possibility of using universals as explanatory devices and as devices for providing intelligibility would dissolve. To talk about universals in such a situation would, in any case, be to court the classical dilemma of the one and the many. If what we mean by referring to the man, Smith, is simply a set of currently existing occasions, we have both a unity and a plurality and the link between them is obscure. Perhaps the whole notion would turn out to be contradictory.

If we combine the notion of a determinable-determinate hierarchy with the notion of process, however, the whole issue becomes more manageable.

It is then the case that there is something, redness, which is instantiated through a series of occasions. It is intelligible to refer to it just because it is not exhausted by the instances it happens to have and, therefore, transcends those instances. The unity of process becomes intelligible, equally, because it is possible to construe the unity as the unity of a single universal and the successive instances of it as manifestations of that unity. Similarly, what we then mean by "Smith" is whatever it is that is manifested through a series of occasions. "Smithness," in turn, can be regarded as one of the determinate forms of the universal "humanity" or whatever turns out to be appropriate given the theories we can formulate in such a domain.

It is, perhaps, worthwhile to pursue this kind of example in some detail in order to see the directions in which such a doctrine will push us.

At any given moment it is, of course, possible to take as the referent of "Smith" a set of actually existing determinate states. To describe him by saying that he is five feet eleven inches tall, weighs 160 pounds, has an I.Q. of 135, is married, breeds race horses, and worries about the ontological argument is to say that he is determinate with respect to the determinables height, weight, intelligence, occupation and philosophical interest. But to say of him, "Smith may be the man who finally shows the unsoundness of the ontological argument" is to allege that, with respect to such determinables as intelligence and philosophical capacity, he is not, after all, wholly

---

[1] We could — and would, I suppose — retain our "universals" as pieces of epistemological apparatus. But they would not correspond to anything in the world since the world would consist of just those determinate forms of the determinables which happened to exist and there would have been no possibility of others in the past and would be no possibility of more in the future. It seems possible, in other words, that a case can be made for nominalism (of some sort) if the world is static. I don't think it is and this book is intended, amongst other things, to prove that it couldn't be.

186

determinate. In that case, there is more to come. Indeed, to say that someone is "intelligent" is, generally, if it does not report some specific performance such as a score on an intelligence test, to suggest that the determinable intelligence is part of what goes into his makeup and that it may issue in a variety of determinate forms over a period of time. The commonest current philosophical custom is to refer to such properties as "dispositional" but this is obscure and tends to obfuscate the issues.

When we say that someone is intelligent we do not mean, of course, that such a person is constantly thinking profound and important thoughts (his mind may be often or usually empty) but to say that, given certain circumstances, certain outcomes are likely. But why? Do we really mean that there is always a certain determinate set of particulars which compose the man and that they can be "stirred up" by the circumstances we have in mind? These particular states of affairs are either identical in description with the results which we expect to be stirred up or they are something else. If the former we should have to think that Smith had stored up within him a mass of detail about the ontological argument just waiting to be poured out when someone opened the mental sluice gates. But this is surely nonsense. If the latter, the particular states of affairs won't actually explain the results. The most that we shall be able to find is some regular conjunction of events such as that people with high I.Qs tend, after suitable teaching, to respond in one way or another to certain standard examination questions about the ontological argument. And that, though useful, is not an explanation. If, however, what we mean is that part of what goes into Smith is a certain determinable property which is capable of issuing in a range of determinate forms and which tends to do this when something else does not get in its way, we are on the way to something more like an explanation. When we form a theory about physical objects generally, we actually get information not about this and that particular physical object but about physical objecthood in general. Given that, we can specify the range of determinate forms which physical objects can take and put ourselves in a position both to "predict" and "understand." If our information were just about a heterogenous cluster of particular determinate forms, our intellectual powers would never run beyond that cluster.

It is true, of course, that with respect to determinables like intelligence, our information is very limited and, with respect to such notions as physical object our information is incomplete so that we generally use (quite properly) more restricted notions. But that we have to make use of some such notions in order to understand a world in process is surely not much open to question.

The usual objection to such ways of talking is epistemological: We have information only about particulars and our talk about universal properties — even in the elaborate form in which it appears as talk about scientific natural laws — depends finally on inductive generalization from particular instances. That all such inductive generalizations are shaky is usually admitted.

But such a position depends, of course, on a basic nominalist position about universals. If, however, our knowledge actually consists, insofar as we have any, equally of particulars and universals and if we construct our knowledge of universals by formulating our information into intelligible accounts of determinable-determinate hierarchies, much of this difficulty disappears. Beyond our knowledge of particulars, in that case, lies a kind of rationalist grid of intelligible interrelations. In practice, we construct such grids without too much difficulty just because, even in our direct acquaintance, there is a natural fusion of universal and particular.

We develop the notion of "redness" in part by attending to red things but, in part, we are able to identify red things because we have a notion of redness. These develop together out of a dialectical interrelation which is a common enough part of everyday life.

The history of science is also full of them: Out of rather basic notions (including general notions about space, time, and causal interaction) Rutherford and Soddy were able to develop a "particle" account which led to the early formulations of atomic theory. Such a theory gave rise to a search for determinate forms of these very general determinables. The location of some of them, in turn, led to refinements of the general notions out of which the theory was compounded. The tendency to give special prominence either to the most general "rationalist" notions out of which the beginnings of theories can be constructed or to the observations of specific determinates can distort the process so that one finds oneself frozen either in a sterile rationalism or a sterile empiricism. But the gathering of knowledge seems to work much more nearly in the way that this discussion suggests. And there seem to be reasons for it.

Admittedly, the need for precision and simplicity is apt to lead to scientific theories being projected back so as to make use of the simpler logical and mathematical structures appropriate to determinate being or one of the other early and intermediate categories and there are, as I have already suggested, good reasons for this. But actual *enquiries*, as opposed to detailed and logically precise theoretical structures, are more likely to take place in terms of the categories we are now discussing. And ultimately, no doubt, all knowledge is best displayed in terms of the higher categories.

VIII

Equally, this way of looking at things helps to make the notion of process intelligible: We now have conceptual tools which enable us to grasp the notion of continuity through a series of phases. The determinable is intelligible so long as it *does* issue in a set of determinates. It is not, now, the case that we have a single "thing" contradictorily described as being the same and different through a series of phases. The determinable is not a "thing" at all. It takes its meaning from the determinates in which it issues and they become intelligible through it.

Thus process is rescued from its incipient contradictions and thus, also, the notion of a genuine individual becomes important. For we now have not merely the universal and the particular, but the continuing, specifiable process within which both come to be intelligible.

If we consider Smith, his individuality is not to be found in the determinable properties which characterize him (many people are intelligent, breed race horses, and are given to philosophising), nor in the particulars which are the determinate forms of those determinables. (Events such as scoring "x" on an intelligence test, being the registered breeder of the horse Watering Trough, showing the unsoundness of the ontological argument, *could* be "attached" to anyone's biography.) But the specific unity which is formed through the manifestation of these determinables in these instances actually marks off someone. It is, to use Hegel's language, when we see the universal and particular as "moments" of the "becoming of individuality" that we approach something which we can genuinely take to be an individual.[1]

Thus the notion of individuality, originally posited in the last chapter as one of the grounds for introducing the notion of process itself carries over naturally here. But to introduce it is to lead us to what is, I think, the final dialectical division of the system. For it now appears that there are two different perspectives which force themselves on us. I will call them "ideal universality" and "objective universality."

They have both been latent in the discussion of the last few pages and that discussion has become, as perhaps the reader will have noticed, uneasily ambivalent: From one perspective we can look at the world as a system of "ideas" which forms a single unity and which serves as the "explanation" of whatever there is. From the other perspective it appears as a sequence within whose affairs we can discern the unities which give rise to our notions of system. Neither seems to be primary and yet there is an important clash between them.

IX

We can begin, perhaps, to bring out the issues with some examples: Suppose we consider Hegel's account of the history of the West.[2] Crudely, but importantly, he sees it as "nothing but the development of the Idea of Freedom" — "the glory of the Idea mirroring itself in the History of the World." Thus, we can, if we choose that perspective, see the "idea of freedom" developing from the oriental despotisms of the near east in which freedom takes root as

[1] *Science of Logic*, Johnston and Struthers, Vol. II, p. 253; Miller, p. 619; Felix Meiner, Vol. II, p. 260.
[2] *Philosophy of History*, translated by J. Sibree (New York: Dover, 1954), p. 456.

the absolute freedom of the despot at the expense of his subjects, through the recognition of individuality in Greece with its power struggles and the disorders which Plato so disliked, and on to the notion of law in Rome and (perhaps) the notion of a freedom which is not attained by some at the expense of others. From this perspective, once the world makes an opening for the idea of freedom (as, for example, when tribal societies become open to new options and cease to be governed by convention and custom), freedom becomes actually operative in the world and comes to determine the forms, structure, and development of society. In the process, it will determine the form and content of the sub-individuals who compose a given society. (One might argue, for instance, that Caesar was made what he was by the opportunities for military ambition, the need for money, and openings created by the Roman law in the way characteristic of Roman society of the period.)

But equally, one might argue that the idea of freedom itself develops out of social conditions such as those created by oriental despots who, unwittingly, created a visible contrast between their own behaviour and powers and those of the populations they controlled and oppressed — that individuals make the ideas which come to control and dominate societies, that it is not ideas which make individuals but individuals which make ideas.

Or consider this kind of contrast: Suppose we ask *why* Smith is able to propound a clever argument showing the unsoundness of the ontological argument. One obvious answer is: "Because he is intelligent." Intelligence is "in" him and, other things being equal, will have its way just as the kernel of the idea of freedom was, perhaps, in the oriental despotisms and, other things being equal, was bound to have its way. But, then, we can give a different kind of answer about Smith just as we can about the idea of freedom. We can trace, instead, the slow growth of "intelligence" from simple physical and chemical states of the world, through more complex organic states, to states of complexity sufficiently rich to permit a range of actions and reactions out of which it becomes feasible to develop a place for the concept of "intelligence." Smith, perhaps, is made what he is, in part, by his intelligence. But intelligence is developed out of the growing possibilities for complexity, the growing capacity of organisms for action and — perhaps above all — the genuine discreteness which comes into the world as it becomes increasingly a system of individuals and not merely an aggregate of particulars. (A world of material particles would be more readily conceived as an aggregate of particulars than a world whose components were mainly organisms. It is not just that one hydrogen atom must be like the next. It is much more that a single instance does succeed, significantly, in being an exhaustive instance of the universal property involved, while a connected process running through a sequence of phases is necessary to instantiate the property of being an insect or a cabbage. A momentary slice of the universe would yield much — though not all — of the information

190

required for physics. A moment in the life of the hydrogen atom, at any rate, is much more revealing than a moment in the life of a man.)

The tension, here, is not the tension between universal and particular, for that has been dissolved, hopefully, by adopting a certain way of looking at the universal-particular relation. It is the tension between the individual, conceived as a process which increasingly defines a unity of idea, and the idea conceived as expressing itself through the instantiations which provide the unity of the individual.

If ideas are related to one another through a relation which is comprehensible as the determinable-determinate hierarchy, there will be ultimately, not a single dominating idea, but a single unified structure of ideas so related as to form a unity of explanation. For any particular case, the tension can be dissolved by pointing out that there is a dialectical relation between idea and individual and that they reflect back into one another. But when we try to generalize so as to form a unified theory, we find that the two ways of looking at things, though ultimately inseparable are also, on this level, ultimately incompatible.

X

At this stage of the dialectic, however, the interrelation of the pair of concepts is so close that it is virtually impossible to consider them separately. I shall try, as best I can, to preserve some measure of independence for purposes of discussion. But I think it will be obvious that ideal universality and objective universality tend, constantly, to collapse into one another.

The man who sets out to theorize about history in terms, say, of Hegel's idea of freedom, will constantly find that individuals keep intruding, the more so, perhaps, as the scheme advances. Anthropologists can sometimes describe the workings of tribal societies with little or no reference to specific individuals within the tribe. As soon, however, as government makes room for freedom — even the special freedom of a single despot with absolute powers — the very social framework which makes the idea possible also begins to lay increasing stress on the individuals it creates. It now makes an important difference whether the monarch is greedy, lustful, and cruel; generous, impotent and kind; or generous, lustful and kind. The succeeding phases of the history of Greece are full of colourful personalities. Without reference to them neither history nor momentary description will make any sense.

Equally, however, the man who focusses on individuals will find himself forced beyond them at every move. It was not just that Caesar was a large figure on the Roman scene. It was also that the political, social, and legal facilities of the time made it possible for a man with ambition and connections to make up for his initial lack of money by a cunning combination of military activity and political manipulation. The ideas which dominated

Rome cried out for large and swashbuckling figures and got them just as the intricacies of American politics in the period of Lyndon Johnson cried out for intriguers, "fixers," and professional compromisers.

The force of the division between the two views lies, however, partly on the emphasis and twist which is given to the notion of freedom and this does produce, in the end, a kind of contradiction which requires a new dialectical solution. From the standpoint of ideal universality, the world is determined by a set of ideas, and individuals exhibit, as Hegel sometimes seems to have thought, the destiny of those ideas. From the standpoint of objective universality, the ideas grow out of the development of the individuals and the destiny of ideas is worked out by individuals.

Thus Hegel sees — though one must not exaggerate this tendency beyond reason — the idea of freedom having its way with the world. Individuals at any point in history are the creations of those ideas and have not only the opportunities but also the formal limitations of those ideas. Their affairs are not completely determined, of course, because they have just the kinds of freedom which the current instantiations of the idea of freedom permit. But they also cannot transcend those kinds of freedom just because their very individuality depends on the social structure which is offered at that moment.

At a simpler level, if one thinks of the hydrogen atom as the instantiation of a given idea, it is determined to be what it is by that idea, but that idea may, of course, have in it an element of indeterminacy. It is open to some possibilities and closed to others at any rate just because, from this perspective, it is the instantiation of a given idea. In the one case individuality depends on a certain structure involving such diversities as space and time, biological organization, and social structure. In the other, a simpler structure of spatio-temporal orientation and physical conformation makes it possible to locate and speak about a particular hydrogen atom.

Thus, while Hegel need not be (and presumably was not) a "determinist" in one of the more usual senses of the word, the twist and nuance given to freedom in such a view is important. The contrast with the alternative view is considerable.

For, on the alternative view, ideas develop out of individuality. The world, on this view is essentially a sequence of objects each of which gives rise to a set of ideas which, though they determine further objects, are themselves replaced as new entities come into being in a process of development. The individuals will still be bound, in some way, by their origin but in the case of high-level individuals of relatively great complexity, internal coherence and self-sufficiency, such as human beings, there will be a stronger bias toward freedom on this view than on the other.

Even more seriously, from the standpoint of ideal universality there apparently needs to be a kind of overall general plan for the universe and the temporal workings out of this plan will seem to be successive phases in

192

its instantiation. From the standpoint of objective universality there will not be a plan in the same sense. This, too, will have a bearing on the "bias toward freedom" which derives from one scheme or the other. There will also be logical consequences: Viewed under the category of ideal universality, it would seem that there would be difficulties about "atomizing" our discourse into independent propositions while, viewed under the category of objective universality, there will be a logical plurality.

In neither case shall we have propositions which we can symbolize as "There is an x such that ..." where, after "such that" we can expect forms such as "x is A and x is B," and we shall also not get propositions of the form "For any x ..." For, in the one case, we have ideas of determinables forming the referential subjects of our propositions and, in the other, we have individuals conceived of as unities of particulars. Both these notions are open and not capable of specification by reference to determinates and something will have to be substituted for the logical copula. There seems no difficulty about doing this, in either case, but we shall have to remember that the forms will be different for the two cases and that we cannot expect translations back into symbolic forms appropriate for other categories.

There is a case, then, for constructing specific accounts of the two categories, at least briefly.

XI

It may help to do this and also avoid some confusions if I contrast, here, the account I have been giving and shall develop with the accounts of the Hegelean categories which occupy an analogous position. Hegel calls his categories the "Subjective Notion" and the "Objective Notion."

Hegel arrived at this point — the point in the dialectic at which the universals problem is dominant — by a different route, but the problem retains a demonstrable similarity and there are major features of similarity in the gross outline map of the route as well.

From the categories of "being," which are dominated by the structural features of attempts to focus the whole of discourse and of the world as a series of unified systems in which individuality appears as a series of perplexities, Hegel passes to the "doctrine of essence" in which emphasis is on things and their relations. In the "essence" trilogy we pass from essences, to appearances, to actualities and, with actualities, back to the complex interrelations of things. The chain of "essence" categories ends with determination as "reciprocity," and has affinities to the category of determinate process with which I ended the last chapter. The "process categories" which form the middle part of the chain of core concepts and categories perform something of the same function as Hegel's "essence" categories — for here, too, the emphasis is on problems posed by individuality, modes of determinacy in actuality, and ways of escaping the conundrums which stem, in part, from the abstractness of the "being" categories.

Just as in this system, however, genuine individuality seemed to elude us in the process categories, so Hegel finds that the relations of reciprocity — the dependence of everything on everything else — with which he ends his account of the "doctrine of essence" fail to provide the right notion of unity in diversity.

He thus begins to search the notion of universality for the solution. The notion of reciprocity did provide him, as McTaggart remarks, with the germ of a link that he needed.[1] The notion that Hegel is looking for is a linkage of similarities which can still admit of difference. Though reciprocal determination is not a linkage of similarities, nevertheless things whose natures are determined by relations of reciprocal dependence are determined by those relations to be similar to one another.

Now the "subjective notion" is first of all this similarity conceived in the context which has been carried over from the doctrine of essence. It is also to be considered, given Hegel's mode of relating the categories to one another, as the first move in the synthesis of the major categories of "being" and "essence." Thus it must be a synthesis, as well, which will carry over the finished notion of "being in general" and the finished notion of "being in essence and actuality."

But the first move is essentially the development of the "subjective notion" in the traditional terms of universal and particular and thence to the notion of individual. It is called "subjective" because it represents the nature of things, as opposed to their relations to other things and because it represents things from the standpoint of the dominant ideas which are essential to their natures, and not from the standpoint of their status as objects.[2]

---

[1] *A Commentary on Hegel's Logic* (Cambridge: Cambridge University Press, 1910), p. 194.
[2] The distinction between things, as such, and relations between them is perilous and in any case only provisional. McTaggart denies categorically that "Subjectivity means inner as opposed to outer." (*op. cit.*, p. 242.) But he refers the reader back to an earlier discussion in which he is concerned to refute the possible but gross misunderstanding that what Hegel is concerned with in the category of "subjective notion" is "the workings of our minds." He then asserts that the "subjective" in Hegel "is the particular, contingent, and capricious, as opposed to the universal, necessary and reasonable." Stace casts some doubt on McTaggart's view (*The Philosophy of Hegel* [New York: Dover, 1955], p. 263). But he is not very clear. The point, I think, is this: The "subjective notion" involves a viewpoint from which we look at the universal-particular-individual relationship independently of the relations which hold between entities of different kinds. The relations involved in "subjectivity" are "contingent and capricious" just because no given particular or individual, *as such* is necessarily related to any given universal. It is when the overtly causal categories — mechanism and teleology — are introduced that "capriciousness" is apparently overcome. But those categories do have to do with the "external" relations which hold between one "object" and another and not with the "inner" relations of the particular and individual to the universal idea which shapes them. Hegel, indeed, says (Johnston and Struthers, Vol. II, p. 348; Miller, p. 710; Felix Meiner, Vol. II, p. 359) "First, then, Objectivity in its immediacy is *mechanism*. In this immediacy its moments

194

Hegel's progression is not altogether clear, but, if we follow McTaggart[1] (who seems sensible and right) it appears that Hegel proceeds from the "universal subjective notion" to the "particular subjective notion" by considering the fact that, in different kinds of classification, particulars and universals may be interchanged. (Thus, to use McTaggart's example, if we classify paintings in a gallery by reference to their painters, we may distinguish them, for instance, by their frames. In that case "painted by X" will be the universal property shared by the pictures while "having such and such a frame" will refer to a particular. But we *could* classify pictures by their frames so that "having a frame of such and such a kind" would refer to a universal property and "painted by X" to a particular.)[2] Hegel, more impressively says "Thus the particular not only contains the universal, but also exhibits it through its determinateness; and in so far the universal constitutes a sphere which the particular must exhaust."[3] He says (on the same page) "The particular is the universal itself, but it is its difference or relation to an Other, its *showing outwards.*"

The individual, at *this* point then, is the determinate state of affairs which shows the particular in the universal and the universal in the particular. But we are still in the realm of the "subjective notion" since we are still considering the thing from the standpoint of its determining ideas.

Hegel goes on to a discussion of ideas from the vista of formal logical concepts — the judgement and the syllogism — to indicate that the standpoint from which he is talking is the standpoint of abstract ideality.

But this structure, he thinks, requires something to supplement it just because the whole system, from this point of view, is still capricious and contingent. We can interchange universals and particulars and shuffle the concepts of individuality as we please from the standpoint of "subjectivity" — forgetting that genuine determinateness requires reference to other

persist external and independently to one another, as Objects, by reason of the totality of all the moments; in their relation they have the subjective unity of the notion only as inner or as outer." The long discussion about the ontological argument with which Hegel prefaces this introduction to the straightforward business of the "objective notion" is, I think, intended to make clear that it is when we come, in the Objective Notion, to posit relations between entities that we face the problem of the relation between idea and existence. His general answer to it is that what existence demands is an effective system of ideas which, *as a system*, cannot fail to be instantiated.

[1] *Op. cit.*, p. 197. The example referred to below is on the same page.

[2] It should be noticed that this is *not* the kind of interchangeability of universals and particulars to which I was referring in earlier sections of this chapter. I was suggesting a determinable-determinate hierarchy in which both terms and things have about them a dual *nature*. The suggestion is, here, that we can arbitrarily assign to terms a dual *function*. But Hegel and McTaggart are talking about the rather abstract Subjective Notion.

[3] Johnston and Struthers, Vol. II, p. 240; Miller, p. 606; Felix Meiner, Vol. II, p. 246. The quotation does lead one to *expect* a richer account of universal and particular and so of individuality. But it is not, really, forthcoming *here* for Hegel remains emphatic about the distinction between the subjective and the objective notion.

things and that there are relations of determinateness, which he goes on to expound in the category of the "objective notion" as mechanisms and teleology. Individuals, in other words, must stand in some relation to one another and are fixed, partly, by relations which are external in the sense of being their relations to each other as opposed to the inner relations they have to their own defining ideas.

Somehow, however, there has to be a resolution of this tension between "inner" and "outer" determination. To concentrate on the "subjective notion" is to picture a world which is formally unstable in the sense that its concepts do not determine a fixed individuality. To concentrate on "outer" determinations — such as mechanism and teleology — is to get a system which, in the end, has nothing to grip.

Hegel's solution is to try to show that one can regard the system of ideas in the "subjective notion" as a teleologically effective causal structure. Thus the last category in the "objective notion" is "teleology" and the first category in the next subsystem (the category of "the idea") is "life", and "life" is exhibited as the first approximation to a teleologically oriented system of ideas developing "objectively" through a temporal process.

Ultimately Hegel generalizes this doctrine into the doctrine of the Absolute — the idea of that which is, on the one hand, a complete system of ideas, and, on the other, a teleologically effective system of causal relations. His final view, most nearly, is that the Absolute is whatever it is that actualizes itself through the successive developments of such a structure. It does not, by itself, "exist" — any more than the "subjective notion" exists in things apart from the "objective notion" — but it is the efficacious driving force behind the world.

I shall have more to say about this in due course, but the point at present is to distinguish this way of looking at the situation from the way in which I seemed to be driven by the line of argument in the earlier parts of this system. Hegel does come down on the side of those who would hold that the position of the universal is dominant, and against those who would hold individuals dominant, and this is consistent with the position I suggested that he held in my summary example drawn from his account of history.

Where he goes wrong, I think, is in not realizing that the issue is not between those who think that things are determined by ideas in the sense of his "subjective notion" and those who think that the world is dominated by "things" in the sense which might seem to be covered by his "objective notion." If that *were* the position, his synthesis would, most likely, be the right one and the problem would be solved.

It is worth pointing out, however, that, within the terms that both he and I would (I think) accept for the discussion of dialectical systems, neither the "subjective" nor the "objective notion" seems to represent a genuine category. A genuine category should, on his view and mine, actually be capable of encompassing the whole of reality. But the relations which Hegel concentrates on in the "objective notion" cannot be encompassed (i.e., have no counterparts) in the "subjective notion" and vice-versa.[1] The distinction of "inner" and "outer," or determining ideas and determining things, allows no room for this. Thus, in fact, the synthesis of the two is the first genuine category we are offered. And, from that standpoint, there *is* another category as I have already suggested. Hegel's "Absolute" thus appears to be at least one level below the logical "peak" of the system. The reason for this seems to have been that Hegel's notion of the individual is inadequate. The "individual" which is dealt with as a component of the "subjective notion" lacks, as Hegel is clearly aware, adequate determinateness. But the components of the "objective notion" are no better. External causal systems serve to render individuality relative and shifting and, in any case, appear, if they really are external, to be rather arbitrary devices, almost literally gods from machines.

(The problem of causal connections has, after all, been befuddled and confounded throughout a variety of philosophical traditions exactly because causes cannot be discerned within individuals. This is surely one of the bases of Hume's contention that, since we are only directly aware of particulars, we do not actually have a concept of cause which can be adequately related to experience and one of the bases of Kant's contention that causality is a concept which belongs [so far as we have knowledge of it] to our modes of organizing experience and cannot be carried over legitimately to an account of things-in-themselves. That neither position can be easily sustained in the system in which it arises — Hume is in trouble over the buried causal notions involved in his account of the relation between impressions and ideas, and Kant must face difficulties about the relation between the noumenal and the phenomenal world — is perhaps obvious. But the problem nonetheless remains and it is a dubious tactic for Hegel to deploy causal facets of the "objective notion" to make good the deficiencies in the concept of individual he employs in the "subjective notion.")

The upshot of all this, then, is that Hegel's final synthesis is, so far as I can tell, somewhat shaky and it seems to lead, in various departments of his philosophy, to an excessive emphasis on something very like what I have called the category of ideal universality.

---

[1] Hegel does not structure his system so as to make the distinction between categories and other features of what I have called the chain of core concepts. Thus he does not develop such notions as "unifying property" and "specific exclusion reference." The concept of universality as such — which figures heavily in his "subjective notion" — is one which I have treated as the specific exclusion reference of the preceding process categories. It would, similarly, be the specific exclusion reference of Hegel's "essence" categories though it would, perhaps, appear somewhat differently in Hegel's system. Had he used such a structure, he would not have been tempted to create a concept which would not quite fulfil the function of a category.

We can, however, develop the concept of ideal universality and also add to the discussion of the last section by saying something about Hegel's categories which form the two sides of the "divide" between the more embracing categories called the "objective notion" and "the idea." The account of the "objective notion" ends with the category of "teleology" while the account of "the idea" — the synthesis of the "subjective" and "objective notions" — begins with the category of "life."

Teleology still belongs, in Hegel's view, to the "objective notion" on the ground that it is "still affected by externality as such":[1] In considering the world as a teleological system, that is, we think of something whose nature is determined by an "end" which, to some extent, is external to it, at least in that, considered as something actual, it is as yet unrealized.

Hegel's own discussion is extremely complex and also, as it happens, interwoven with a long historical discussion culminating in a fairly detailed account of Kant's views. To follow it would take us further from our current concerns than seems to be justified. I can, however, put the matter in my own way: Though teleological systems relate cause and effect in such a way as to separate the two clearly and so posit a kind of relation which does not merely stem from the inner nature of the individuals related, they are not related to each other in the way that they are when we consider the world as a mechanical system. For, if teleological relations hold at all, there is a certain necessity about the connection between purpose or end on the one side and act or event on the other.

If it is, genuinely, my "purpose" to write a book on dialectical logic, then I will actually do certain things and refrain from others. If I spend my time making minute revisions to the details of the text of *Principia Mathematica*, it cannot actually be said that my serious "purpose" is the writing of a book on dialectical logic. Nor can it be said that that is my purpose unless I actually spend some time considering such notions as "category," "dialectical opposite" and so on. There are, that is, minimal outcomes to having such a purpose and, outside a certain rather large range of activities, anything that I do will actually count as conclusive evidence that that is not my purpose. In teleological cases the dominating idea — whether it is a purpose in the case of an act, or an end in the case of events which we would not classify ordinarily as "acts" — is closely bound up with certain outcomes in the sense of setting up a range of restrictions which are actually necessary to the situation.

Thus at this point in the discussion of the "objective idea," Hegel inevitably reaches the point at which the "internal" and "external" distinction

---

[1] *Science of Logic*, Johnston and Struthers, Vol. II., p. 380; Miller, p. 739; Felix Meiner, Vol. II, p. 390.

begins to break down. The dominating ideas in a teleological system do not merely specify external connections between individuals. They determine, in part, the inner nature of those individuals.

It becomes essential to consider — if one has followed Hegel's procedure — a synthesis of the "subjective" and "objective notions." Life offers a case of a concrete unity which does seem to transcend the distinction at issue. A living thing has a set of parts each of which is what it is by reason of its relation to the whole organism and, equally, the whole organism is what it is by reason of its parts. We can no longer make a sharp distinction between the parts themselves and the external ordering in which they find themselves.

(A brain cell is one sort of thing when it is playing an active part in the life of a functioning man who is thinking about the ontological argument and quite another when it is abstracted and considered in and of itself. In the first case, it is necessary if the activity is to go on in just the way that we know it. *If* teleological explanations hold good, its place in the thinking structure at the moment of its functioning is fixed and determined by just the end in view. Abstracted, it is merely a rather simple electro-chemical device, having to do with the input and output of electrical impulses. One cannot translate statements about such electrical impulses into statements about thoughts about the ontological argument but, in the context of a complex teleological structure, statements about such thoughts do become intelligible. Essentially, the point is that we cannot put together an account of thinking about the ontological argument from a lot of bits and pieces of statements about brain cells, nerve cells, motor activities and so on on the one side, and minds, words, and logical processes on the other. If, however, we think of the whole activity as an organic unity dominated by a motivating idea, it becomes intelligible in its own — admittedly disputatious — way: One can argue that rational thought requires stability of reference, effective information storage, a variety of routes to and from the information stored, procedures for representation and so on. If thinking is an activity which is efficacious in the universe, the concrete actuality of thought will establish and control the appropriate environment. But we shall have to think of this process as an effective organic unity: We cannot think realistically about our own thinking processes without thinking of the special environment which it requires, and we also cannot grasp that environment without thinking of the ends required. The brain cell (on this view) is what it is because it is part of a thinking organism and the thinking organism is what it is because such things as brain cells are possible. Each has a place in a structure which is intelligible as a unity. Similarly a heart cannot, in one sense, be *understood* except in relation to its functions. It is one thing considered merely as an interesting collection of cells and quite another considered as something whose activities are necessary to and dominated by the unified idea of the organism of which it is a part. Like the brain cell, it is determined in its structure — still, of course, on the teleological hypothesis — by the unified idea of the organism. But the unified organism can only be what it is so long as the heart continues to function.)

At any rate, the notions of teleological order and organic unity do, if they are put together, establish a special kind of interrelatedness which is of significance here.

There is, of course, something somewhat odd about Hegel's categories and much that is very odd about the concatenation of notions so ordered: Once again it is not immediately obvious that the concept of teleological system can be generalized so as to form a way of viewing the whole of reality. Much less does it seem likely that the Hegelean category of "life" can be so generalized. (The same complaint might well have been made of Hegel's earlier category of "mechanism.") But the complaint here is not the one which I made against the more embracing categories of "subjective" and "objective notion" as such. There the difficulty was that the entities subsumed in one of the domains could not have counterparts in the other. Here the difficulty is not that. For what, from one perspective, can be looked at as a teleological system (e.g., the human brain) can certainly be viewed, from another, as a mechanical system. The difficulty is, simply, that it seems that some entities which we do find in the world (and would expect to as a result of the earlier categories) do not seem, easily, to fit the required mould at all. A system of molecules so structured as to form a gas is an example of a system which it is somewhat difficult to envisage as a teleological system. What "purpose" will explain the Brownean movement of the molecules unless we include, by definition, the movement in the purpose itself? And what kind of mechanical explanation will suffice to deal with certain social phenomena such as trials at law? (The last case is, perhaps, instructive: If a mechanical explanation were forthcoming the event would cease, on any reasonable account of the matter, to be a "trial" at all. The effect of the introduction of such an explanation will be, in the end, to mount a serious complaint against the concept of "trial" as such. But, equally, perhaps the example about gases is one in which the introduction of teleological notions would seriously undermine the concepts which are used to mount the example in the first place.) Even more obviously, any attempt to regard the whole of reality as "alive" will meet with difficulties. Can we regard systems of stars, or gaseous clusters in deep space under the category of "life"?

These complaints are not foolish, but they do exhibit a subtle and important difference of perspective which is, hopefully, illuminating at just this point in our investigation. For what Hegel has in mind in these categories, obviously, is that, though they are all-pervasive, the entities which one would subsume under them exhibit various degrees of fidelity to the appropriate structure. Not everything is alive but, in a sense, since the category of "life" is to be found in the development of the logic, there is a perspective on the world which is that of life. When we find living things, we find that they are dependent on the totality of their environments in a variety of ways. The relation of a living thing to the rest of the universe is, perhaps, not unlike the relation which holds between a man's mind and his body. The state of his mind at any given moment is apt to depend fairly heavily on the state of his brain. It depends less on the state of his toenails. Indeed, he might survive very well without toenails at all. But the organic relation which holds between his toenails and the rest of his body is very likely such that one tampers with it at one's peril. (A drug which made your toenails stop growing would have various effects on your body and it would, at any rate, make it a subtly different organism and that *might*, in the end, have an effect on your mind as well. Similarly, the state of distant gaseous structures in space is not such as to form an important part of the structure of any known living thing. But cabbages, for instance, as we know them, do require a three-dimensional space exhibiting certain properties of continuity over time, and such spaces cannot literally be filled with "nothing" or literally "come to an end." Hence the region occupied by the gas has to be there and have something in it [even if it is only a dispositional something like a path for a potential light ray]. If it had something else in it the prospects of the cabbage would be either dramatically [if the space were a path for death dealing rays] or subtly different.)

I think, therefore, that the point Hegel wants to make by the introduction of categories of this kind is that the idea of teleological system and the idea of life introduce a pattern of ideas which, however subtly, does structure the whole of reality.

This suggests, however, that the categories in question are importantly misleading in another way: The entities which we call living organisms, systems of molecules arranged to make a gaseous structure, human brains, and so on are all conceivable, in various forms, throughout the whole system of categories. In the system developed in this book, a brain can figure as an object of thought in all categories.[1] It may be that its inner nature is revealed more fully in the process categories than in determinate being but even that is a matter of the potency of various theories about brains. It is also true, perhaps, that there are things to be said about it which are of considerable importance and which are best said with the conceptual equipment for what I have called "ideal universality" at hand so that one would expect theories about organisms to make use of this structure, whereas one might not expect such activities as the chemistry of gases to be carried on in these terms very often. But even that will depend on what we

---

[1] Indeed, everything must be able to figure in some way in all the categories. But there is an important distinction to be made here. The example I used earlier about trials at law brings this out. The *features* of the trial have their counterparts in determinate being, for instance, but, cast in that way, they lose just the features which are interesting to us. Thus, though the trial components can figure in every category, the trial-as-such cannot, for the features that are important require the specific structure provided by the later categories.

want to do. If we are trying to get neurology and certain departments of physics into line, we may well want to make use of the notions appropriate to determinate being. And when we are talking about the relations between theories and data, we may want to make use of the notions endemic to ideal universality in order to make clear examples about the chemistry of gases.

The Hegelean categories, then, seem to be somewhat misconceived. But what they *do* serve to do is to call our attention to certain structures which serve as excellent examples of the way in which the category of ideal universality can be formulated.

We do not, in other words, need to become embroiled in disputes about whether life is really teleological any more than certain chemical structures are. All we want is a way of making clear how a certain way of viewing the world can be rendered intelligible.

We can see that the combination of teleological orientation and organic unity, which quite common *features* of life forms call to our attention, does suggest what is involved in the notion of ideal universality. The bits and pieces which go to make up the body and the mind of a man or the structure of a cabbage — whether they are conceived of as the structural features of the momentary states of such an organism, or as the set of events spread out over time which go to make up the "life" of such a thing — suggest at once the notion of a unified idea which gets its concrete expression through these structures and events.

These features can be imagined as going to make up a world. Everything which can be said about such a world will form part of an ideational unity of the sort which I called a determinable-determinate hierarchy. But this hierarchy, in its turn, will depend for its intelligibility on the actual bits and pieces which we can identify in various concrete ways.

The result will not be merely a teleological system unified by the same overall purpose — the actualization, say, of the detailed structure specified by the terms of the hierarchy. It will also be an organic unity of the kind Hegel finds actualized in living things. For the hierarchy will depend for its specification on the parts just as much as the parts will depend for their identification on the unified structure itself.

In practice perhaps (as, again, one of McTaggart's examples suggests) we may be more familiar with systems of this kind in the creative arts. The significance of the parts of a painting depends on the unifying idea which, if you like, is "behind" the painting. The words in a poem, similarly, take their significance from the unifying idea to which they are intended to give expression. But the unifying idea, in its turn, is not in any real sense intelligible without just those components.

This two-dimensional determination is not (or at least is not intended to be) an expression of a paradoxical circularity: The idea determines the appropriateness of the parts, but the parts give the idea the degree of determinateness which is required for its identity. There is a dominating idea running through Milton's *Paradise Lost*. But it is subtly and importantly different from innumerable similar ideas expressed through a different set of parts. Milton's Satan comes to life and establishes something rather unlike the vague and pious orthodoxies which would constitute the expression of the idea independently of the details Milton had to provide to give it life.

Indeed, this seems to be just the point which is vexing here. As we pass from the abstract notion of universality, which formed the specific exclusion reference of our last categories, to the union of this and the concept of process which provides the basic focus of the category of ideal universality, we pass to a situation in which the individual comes to have increasing prominence. As we read *Paradise Lost*, we rather quickly lose interest in the pious orthodoxies which form the original idea of the poem and begin to become interested in the characters, especially Satan, in their own right. The individual Milton has created comes to dominate the idea he is trying to express and it takes its shape from him.

The same thing happens when we look at the entities which form the examples from which Hegel begins to draw his categories as he nears the "Absolute." Consider forms of life: You may well go out to look for a dog which is an ideal specimen of its breed, the perfect instantiation of an idea which has motivated generations of breeders. But, if it is any sort of dog at all, and not merely a fop bred for shows, your interest in it is soon centred on its individuality and, more subtly, you begin to think of the idea in terms of the individual.

Hegel deals with "life" surprisingly in terms of the "life process," "the living individual" and "the kind" and then goes on to "cognition" (which is dealt with asymmetrically and does not actually parallel his treatment of "life") as the "antithesis." The new and final synthesis is the "Absolute." But his treatment of life seems to draw a strange conclusion from the examples he uses — for the "kind" is surely more abstract and further from the richness of actuality than the "living individual."

Even in "cognition" the examples we can find seem to lead from the domination of the idea to the domination of the individual specimen. It may have been the idea of a dialectical logic which has led us thus far through this ominously difficult enquiry. But surely our interest and our concerns come to be dominated increasingly by the individual specimen of it as we come to work out the details, and that specimen — whether Hegel's or the one which forms this book — comes to shape our notion of what a dialectical logic is. The specimen may prove utterly deficient but even so it will be its deficiencies which give meaning and body to the new attempt we make to formulate the general idea.

It is the nature of this kind of unity, in other words, that it shows itself in individuals and that these, in their turn, lead us on to new general ideas.

Thus we are forced from the notion of ideal universality to what I have called the idea of objective universality — the universal exhibited as a set of full-blooded concrete individuals.

The dialectical operation works both ways, however. The point that the individual is to be understood as a set of events or structures linked by a unifying idea still remains. But what happens, of course, is that the individual tends to produce a new set of dominating ideas.

To revert to our examples: Milton's Satan gives a whole new tone to the theological idea which *Paradise Lost* was intended to convey. The dog which you actually raise gives a new sense to the idea of the breed which you set out to represent. The dialectical logic which you actually build restructures the notion of a dialectical logic.

So, presumably, with the larger structures which go to make up a world or which go into the segment of it that you want to investigate. It is not just that what the Romans did by way of inventing a legal structure instantiated a new phase in what Hegel would have called the life of freedom. It also made possible new ideas of freedom. Here, again, there is a subtle distinction between the two views. You can think of the idea of freedom slowly being actualized or you can think this *and* that the evolutionary process of history also creates wholly new dimensions to the ideas because the individuals who instantiate the ideas are more than just instantiations. They also have detailed features of their own.

Logically, indeed, that must be so. The particular, viewed just as a particular, may be a copy of the universal stored up in some Platonic heaven (assuming for a moment that we waive all the difficulties inherent in that view), but the individual cannot be. For the individual is a unity of particulars spread out through a process. Two things follow from this. At any given moment it cannot be a complete instantiation of the universal. For then the universal in question could not be what unifies it but only what identified one of its moments. More than this, however, the universal which is, itself, in a special way timeless (*it* is not the process) is unlike the individual just by reason of this fact. Every concrete individual, therefore, is something more than the unifying idea which it instantiates. It, therefore, creates the possibility of another unifying idea.

The truth about the matter, then, is that ideal universality leads to objective universality and objective universality leads back to ideal universality. We have, therefore, two categories which represent, in a very clear way, the standard dialectical relation: Between them they exhaust the region mapped out by the unifying concept and the specific exclusion reference of the preceding categories. They each represent one facet of this domain and they each lead to one another with a kind of inevitability. They are, it is true, more closely bound with one another than, perhaps, any of the preceding dialectical pairs have seemed to be. But as the relations expressed by the core concepts come to be more complex and (to use what is admittedly a metaphor) organically related, we must expect that this will happen.

Evidently, too, the pair of concepts so delineated needs, once again, to be transcended: Each of them tends to collapse into the other and the relation between them, though it is one that can be worked with, is one of demonstrable instability.

XIV

The difficulties inherent in these notions and the problems they might seem to pose for the overall structure of the system have mostly been dealt with overtly or by implication in passing.

Nothing in the later parts of the chapter would seem to strengthen the doubts which I tried to allay about the possibility that thought and reality might, in this region, part company. It seems that what must be said of one must, *mutatis mutandis*, be said of the other.

It may be, however, that the relations between thought and experience do or should give rise to doubts at this stage of the argument: Ideal universality gives rise to the notion of a complete and integrated system which, after all, experience might well not confirm. Furthermore, the construction of an effective determinate-determinable hierarchy might very well lead to the introduction of concepts which, if they are to make sense at all, will have to serve, in some cases, to pattern our experience in an intelligible way. Might not this lead to a head-on collision between thought and experience and might not the dialectician have to jettison experience wherever it failed to conform?

The answer, here, seems to be negative, for the reason that the concept of individual intrudes into the rationalist dream in a rather important way. One cannot, literally, by a straightforward technique, infer the description of the individual, just because the individual, for the reasons given in the last section, is, ultimately, a unique instantiation. One must "look for" individuals in just the ways that the particular case demands. It took an act of creation for Milton to describe Satan in *Paradise Lost*. It takes acts of invention to create an individual dialectical logic. It takes acts of perception to grasp individuals whose properties are such as to make them objects of sensory awareness if they exist at all. To get at the individual, the techniques of exploration suggested by the ideas they instantiate are, after all, required.

What the theory requires is not the ratio-mania which might be thought to form one horn of the dialectician's dilemma. All that is required is the belief that individuals can be characterized in ways which will maintain a viable interrelationship of the kind demanded by the notion of ideal universality. And how, indeed, could they fail to be so characterized unless they turned out to be not individuals, but bare particulars?

It follows from this, of course, that the inferences possible in these domains will be of a complex kind. We can work our way, with the help of the appropriate techniques, from universal to particular to individual and back again to the new universal. But the arguments will depend heavily on the specific concepts involved. The difficulties in this, however, seem to be the difficulties posed by a world which actually contains individuals and there is nothing very surprising about *that*.

Chapter 6

The completion of the system:
systematic individuality — pure individuality —
pure activity — dialectical individuality —
"the absolute"

I

Evidently, the last categories bring the system near its completion. It began with a concept embodying the utmost generality of reference and each subsequent development of the system of categories involved an additional level of concreteness and specificity. The most recent categories came to be dominated by the concept of individuality.

Moreover, the polar tensions which seem to hold the categories in place involve not only the poles of generality and individuality and the interwoven notions of abstractness and concreteness, but also the poles represented by the concepts of static state and activity. Though activity is represented as dominant in the process categories which mark out the middle regions of the system, it is even more so in the categories of ideal and objective universality. In the process categories it dominates discourse because we have chosen to represent things in a certain way while, in the categories of universality, it dominates because it is seen to be the nature of the things represented. Thus, in both respects, we have moved from one pole to the point at which, at least, the opposite pole is discernible.

II

There remain tensions. The last two categories lead to one another, but collide at least to the extent that, between them, there is an important shift of emphasis and perspective. They are alike in their perspective on universality and individuality. Indeed, their unifying property can reasonably be called systematic individuality.

Inevitably, the unifying factor which binds any two categories together will be a development of the specific exclusion reference of the preceding categories. Thus universality or identity-in-difference was the specific exclusion reference of the process categories. Its development into categories, by a synthesis with the concept of process, becomes the notion of systematic individuality. Similarly, the specific exclusion reference of the categories of determinate being and systematic unity was the dialectical opposite of their unifying factor. Thus they were united in the notion of static state and excluded time and change. The development of this notion into categories produced the concepts of pure and determinate process which combined the referential notions of the earlier categories with the requirements of time and change — representing time and change against a background of permanent possibilities. (Evidently, if the specific exclusion reference of one set of categories turned out to be the uniting factor of the next, we would have failed in a synthesis.) After the categories of universality, however, what is excluded? Only, one would think, the polar extremes of the original categories — pure individuality and pure activity.

III

The construction of the next category, then, must, presumably, start from there and we must seek some way of explicating these notions and then seek for some way of dealing with them together. Thereafter, the problem will be to find a synthesis between the combined notion and the notion of systematic individuality.

If, however, the next category is the final one in the system, it will have other features. It must be possible to see that it *is* the last category. If it is, it will either produce no dialectical tensions or it will lead back into the system again.

It has usually been assumed, I think, that the first alternative is the natural one. The "absolute" after all, is supposed to be whatever it is that is not relative to anything else. It should, therefore, be complete and self-contained. It should "lead" nowhere just on the ground that there is nowhere to go. If it represents the "final synthesis" then it sums up the earlier parts of the system and there is no need for reference beyond it.

This line of argument, however, seems to me to vitiate the whole idea of a dialectical system. We started with the thesis that a certain concept was necessary to our discourse and that it represented not merely a possible but a *necessary* perspective on the world. That this perspective, when developed, led to difficulties and could be shown to be inadequate *if taken by itself* was, of course, the reason for going on. But if the line of argument was sound, the same applies to each of the other concepts developed. Each perspective is seen to be a necessary complement of its predecessors. How can it be, then, that the last concept is complete and self-contained? If it were, would the others be necessary?

The reasonable alternative is to hold that if there is a last concept, it will lead naturally back into the system: It will exhibit the necessity for the whole system of concepts and will not, literally, be the summation of them. If we called the last concept "the absolute," it would, if this view were true, be paradoxical in that it turns out to derive its meaning from the other concepts

208

in the "core" of the system though it would be "absolute" in the sense of being just that standpoint from which the necessity of the whole system could be seen. Questions of nomenclature can, however, be settled later. The point here is that we need to develop some view of what the requirements for a last concept really are and then to give careful scrutiny to whatever concept is offered in that place.

IV

It does seem that we have reached the point at which, since we have moved from pole to pole within the domain of the concepts which we have developed, we shall either have to show that what we do have *is* a last concept in the system, or abandon the scheme. For, if we do not have anything which will serve as a last concept and yet we have reached the point at which no further development is possible, we will have proved the inadequacy of the structure.

The latitude open to us is not very great with respect to the initial moves in the development of an additional category. The concepts of individuality and activity produced two ways of looking at things. Together they excluded only what seems the unpromising ground which I called pure individuality and pure activity.[1] (Anything else would either involve the notion of systematisation and so take us back to the categories of universality or the re-introduction of notions of static state and so throw us back in the earlier categories. The choice of exclusion reference is, thus, extremely small.)

The difficulty, here, is to make any sense of these notions at all. It is not, for instance, the notion of particularity which constitutes pure individuality. That has been dealt with and absorbed into the structure already. And it is not the unstructured unity of pure process which is demanded by the notion of pure activity.

What, in fact, is left? And, in particular, is there any way of linking these notions so as to get a coherent specific exclusion reference?

V

It should, at any rate, be possible to construct an exemplary situation from which the relevance of such concepts could be seen by asking ourselves

[1] It will be noticed that we have, apparently, a double "exclusion reference." Both pure individuality and pure activity have to be dealt with. It will turn out that they are linked notions but we are left, initially, with two concepts or subject matters here. The strategy adopted through the development of the categories has been to separate, as much as possible, the lines of argument which go from static states through the forms of process from those which move from the abstract to the concrete, though it has turned out, all along, that they are linked. If it were not the case that activity and individuality turn out to be unintelligible without one another this doubling of exclusion reference would, I think, be evidence of a mistake. The links between them will, however, emerge as the discussion develops.

what, in certain circumstances, we would mean by individuality and by activity. If the dialectic really works as a system for revealing the logical structure of perspectives on the world, it ought to be difficult to go wrong. For all one needs to do is to take *any* example of a genuine object of reference and apply the concepts in question to it. Thus, here, as throughout all the examples I have been trading on, there is a kind of built-in test for components of the system. Concepts which are supposed to apply to everything can always be tested by reference to anything one chooses. In delineating various categories, I have, indeed, explicitly tried to show that this process works for various apparently difficult cases. There is a problem, however, in that many of the concepts we deploy carry specific category commitments with them. This is particularly true, perhaps, of scientific concepts but quite ordinary ones are apt to have category commitments or, at least, inclinations. It is hard to think of a cabbage without becoming involved in notions appropriate to organic processes — though the data organized by the concept are susceptible to other modes of organization. And we usually do not think of a man as the set of discrete states which would be required to exhibit our information about him in the way appropriate to the category of determinate being. These concepts, of course, have to be dismantled before we can use the subject matter in any effective example. In any of the domains ordered by one of the categories, some referential objects drawn from our ordinary life will be prominent and others will appear heavily disguised.

In the present case, the problem is complicated further by the fact that we know that — if the system is reliable — no example will be wholly workable with the concepts drawn merely from a specific exclusion reference. It is only when the missing components required to structure a new category are supplied that the example should really prove workable. Any well-chosen example should, however, show just those deficiencies which point to the necessity of the other elements which will go into the synthesis. Thus, if we find examples for the notions of pure individuality and pure activity, we should also find that we need the elements of the notion of systematic individuality.

The place to start, I think, is with an examination of certain features which are common to our thought and discourse about people and some kinds of animals. Wherever "personality" intrudes, we do seem to find something like pure individuality and pure activity. We find, that is, examples of situations in which the individual transcends the boundaries of whatever system it has a place in, and cases in which what is going on seems to break away from the kind of process which exhibits the individual as part of a larger system.

It is difficult, however, to develop concepts which will structure this situation even though it is a quite ordinary part of our experience and figures

210

in important ways in our everyday commerce with the world. It is, therefore, important to approach it with caution.

Certain features of the situation in which people establish and maintain their identities are potentially helpful. It is, in general, against the background of a complex social process that we get to know who and "what" we are: I know that I am like certain other people and unlike others in that I am male, a professor, given to messing about in boats, fond of cattle and so on. I have, thus, an indefinitely large number of reference points by which I can establish myself. Behind this lie a number of much more general techniques for distinguishing myself from the rest of the world as "subject" from "object" — techniques which make me aware of the intrusion of the world on my volitions, which establish the notion that I can have experiences which other people do not have, and create feelings of continuity which run back through my memories.

Two features stand out as one tries to pursue this rather complex jumble and as one tries to put some precision on the very vague concepts involved. One of them is that I cannot offer an exhaustive description of what I am and of what distinguishes me from other things. If I could, then, in principle, we could find, construct, or create someone who matched the description and who could be substituted for me without anyone noticing. It will turn out that there are important reasons for thinking that this cannot be the case. The other is that a very rich structure of social and psychological orientation is required for the necessary distinctions to be made at all. If there was no such structure, how would I ever identify any of the region which I call "my experience" as belonging to me at all? I might, after all, identify the whole world of thought and experience with myself, regarding its more remote components with the same sense of proprietorship as I regard my big toe. Or, even more strangely, I might regard myself merely as a spectator of my own experiences and think of what I now call "my life" much as a man thinks of the life he sees when he puts a penny in the slot of a seaside machine and sees "what the butler saw."

In a way, these features are related: We can, by pursuing the first of them without careful attention to the logic of the situation create, in quite insoluble form, many of the constituents of the traditional philosophical problem of "other minds." Equally, by allowing ourselves to be incautiously over-impressed by the second, we can elide the notion of person with that of social and physical system in such a way as to effectively destroy the notion of individuality and, perhaps, become locked in a sterile kind of behaviourism or social determinism and persuade ourselves to abandon the notions of privacy and activity which are associated with just the concepts we need to develop at this point in our system.

The solution to the problem of this chapter hinges, precisely, on being able to get the right balance into the relations between the concepts involved and then on being able to generalize the result so as to produce a category which will do just the logical work which is required to sustain the dialectic.

I shall, therefore, look at each side of this in turn and in as much detail as seems necessary for the rather limited purpose at hand. (Obviously, these problems contain, in themselves, sufficient material for several books. But the point here is simply to develop the concepts which are required for the dialectical system. A way of testing the result, of course, would be to conduct a full scale independent inquiry into issues such as these and then to see if the result could be squared with the system of categories which compose this system. But the issue here, is not, in itself, to construct an account of the concept of "person," "personal identity" and so on. For human beings, like everything else, must, if the system works, be conceptualizable under each of the categories in turn. The point is to develop the suggestion that certain *aspects* of the concept of person suggest the development of a category which will fill the role required for a last concept in the dialectic.)

VI

The first issue can be put this way: For some purposes, of course, human beings *can* be substituted for one another. It does not matter to a candidate for a political office whether it is Smith's vote or Jones's vote which gives him his coveted majority of one. It is, indeed, the principle of democratic politics that, as voters, all men are equal and inter-changeable. Equally, it does not matter whether it is Smith or Jones who turns the screw which secures the gear box of a motor car while it is moving down the production line. As workmen, considered in a rather abstract way, most men are inter-changeable if the task is simple enough and the social situation is ignored. But there are other ways in which men are unique. "Doing just as well" and "being just the same" are not the same thing.

Perhaps the most compelling ground for thinking that men *are* unique is that they can do certain things, the most impressive of which is the giving and taking of reasons and, in particular, the kinds of reasons which are generally called justifying their activities. It makes no sense to speak of a stone or a hydrogen atom or even, perhaps, a tiger performing or failing to perform a justifiable act. The stone and the hydrogen atom either do what they do because their nature is the expression of a general governing principle or because they are, by their nature, indeterminate in such a way as to produce random results. To be a stone is, amongst other things, to be the sort of thing to which the law of gravitation applies in the same way that to be a lump of arsenic is to be the sort of thing which, when heated, passes immediately from a solid to a gaseous state. In principle, all the activities exhibited by stones and lumps of arsenic can be expressed in the form of principles of this sort. If they failed to do so it would be because (as may be the case with certain microcosmic entities) they were indeterminate with respect to certain specifiable states and thus exhibited some condition which could be called randomness. Similarly, the tiger does what it does without much recourse beyond the demands of its nature. The tiger does not have open to it the complex kind of conscious choice and reasoning capacity which would make it reasonable to ask whether it was justified in eating other animals.

With respect to men, however, it is sensible to ask whether they ought to eat other animals, or start wars, or undertake revolutions. More seriously, it is sensible and feasible to ask a man, toward the end of his life or even in the middle part of it, whether or not he has any grounds for saying that he has justified his existence. In the main, this is because he is capable of giving and taking reasons. If men lacked this capacity, of course, we would not be able to undertake the kind of investigation in which we are now engaged. For just the kind of investigation which constitutes the subject matter of this book is, after all, an inquiry into the whole of the rational underpinnings — the ultimate presuppositions — of discourse. If the questions can be asked and continue to make sense in the face of the kinds of answers we can get, then we are entitled to presume that the giving and taking of reasons is an activity which runs through all possible discourse including that part of it which is about our own activities.

But this kind of activity cannot be the sort of interchange which would follow if the giving and taking of reasons were the sort of thing the tiger does when it is in search of its prey — if it were, that is, something which simply followed from our "natures." For then it would not be a review of the evidence and a coming to conclusions in the relevant sense. It has turned out in this investigation that a condition of one's being able to undertake such a review is that one should be able to undertake acts of construction as we pass from category to category and that these do not elide into straight-forward formal rules. There is an element of creativity involved. If there were not, we should only be able to report mechanically the demands made upon our reason, and the answers given by our "natures," in the way that the tiger responds to his stomach according to *his* nature. In that case, we would not be reporting the truth about the situation but only how our organisms responded to their environment. Independence of judgement — and consequently objectivity in the sense of considered, as opposed to mechanical, judgement — would be impossible.

The same line of argument suggests that, if we are not like the tiger (in respect of his hunting habits) and the stone (in respect of its predictable response to gravitation) we also cannot be like the hypothetical indeterminate features of the hydrogen atom. For response exhibiting chance is no more considered and independent judgement than is response to the necessity of one's inner nature.

If all this is true (and I have argued similar cases in more detail in other — and, in certain ways, richer — contexts)[1] then it will follow, apparently,

---

[1] *The Rational and the Real* (The Hague: Martinus Nijhoff, 1962), and *The Concept of Truth* (Assen: Van Gorcum, 1969.)

that it is not just that we give the appearance of being able to (and sometimes of labouring under the duty to) reason by way of offering alleged justifications of some of our acts. For if they do not follow from our natures or from chance, then they emerge as potentially justifiable or unjustifiable acts just because they come clothed in the apparatus of reasons. Thus it is not the acts which are done by men in a torrent of emotion, or idly without thought and on whim, or while not in control of themselves on account of insanity, drink, and drugs which present themselves for justification. It is those acts which are done with thought and deliberation — under the guise of reason. (Admittedly, people also require "justification" from the man who lets himself fall prey to his emotions, or drink, or drugs, or some madness of his own design, or even one who fails to check his idle whims. But this is because, I suppose, we imagine him amidst a pool of reasons, choosing or choosing to ignore, before he gets into the appropriate state. From the man who *cannot* control his emotions — and all of us are *sometimes* in that state — or whose madness is not of his making we do not, if we are reasonable, demand any accounting. Even the man whose terrible craving for drink or heroin is quite beyond the limits of normal human control is not susceptible of judgement.)

It is, in short, the close association between reason and free action which makes free action the proper object of morality. If — as some philosophers have sometimes supposed — the two objects of judgement were ultimately separable then we could, of course, question the relation. But given that they are not, we must accept it.

If action, judgement, and reason are bound together in these ways, then it follows that we cannot, in advance, decide upon an important sub-class of moral issues and other issues which belong to the related cluster. When a man does something we are often entitled to ask him how he justifies it. But we cannot predict what justification he will give. If he is free to give reasons, he may give a new and surprising reason and we may have to revise our whole scheme for dealing with such issues in the light of the reasons he gives and even of the criteria which he provides for evaluating those reasons. This will not apply to *all* cases of this kind. (For instance, killing people presumably is not justifiable by any set of reasons. For the justification of murder would depend upon the showing that the right to continued existence of the victim had in some way been forfeited. But that would presume that the existence of the doomed individual was confined to his past — that he was not free to do new and supremely justifiable things and also that he was not free to offer new and surprising justifications for his past actions. In general, no actions which inhibit the giving and taking of reasons could be justified on these grounds. The general upshot is that morality is dependent on the continuing attempt at rational agreement in

214

the same way that the search for truth in general is dependent upon the continuing attempt to search for and evaluate reasons.)[1]

But this leads straightforwardly to the notion of uniqueness. If men are not fixed by nature in this special and relevant respect, then no man can ever actually be replaced by another. For there is never any guarantee that any two men will, in the same situation, produce the same rationale for their actions or the same pattern of rational action.

To a degree, in other words, each human being endowed in this sense with reason represents an independent structure which cannot be elided into any related set of similar structures. Each man is a special perspective on the world and represents, in a degree, the concept of pure individuality.

VII

The notion of the pure individual as independent and self-activating does, however, suggest such notions as the "pure ego" which Broad maintained was "prevalent" and also suggested was "so disreputable that no decent philosopher would allow such a thing in his mind if he could possibly help it."[2] It is somewhat difficult, however, to find literature accounting in detail for its prevalence — if it ever was prevalent — and also to find adequate accounts of its disreputability. Broad discusses two variants of it, neither of which seems to meet the requirements which the argument I have just completed seems to create. On one of them, the "pure ego" is regarded as a temporally extended continuant which runs, like a thread, through the life of the individual. On the other, the pure ego is regarded as a timeless particular which, however, is a constituent in all the events of the individual. It is not clear why either of these views should become prevalent or why it should appear to be disreputable. What the argument here requires, however, is something which cannot be characterized in the ways suggested. It cannot be, as Broad speculates that his "pure ego" might be, an *object* of introspection, for, if it were, it would have, again, a determinate nature. Neither can it be extended through the life of the individual like a thread or a timeless "particular." If it were extended through time, it would become involved in the demands of the concept of process and, again, become determinate in just the wrong ways. If it were a timeless "particular," it would be referentially related, as the last chapter suggested, to an appropriate universal.

What it seems to be, on the other hand, is something which is only intelligible in and through the activities which manifest it but which, in order

---

[1] For more extended accounts of these and related issues see my essays "The Duty to Seek Agreement," *Journal of Philosophy*, December 3, 1959; and "Value Data and Moral Rules, *Philosophical Quarterly*, July, 1962.

[2] *The Mind and Its Place in Nature* (London: Routledge and Kegan Paul, 1925). The first quotation is from p. 278, the second from p. 214.

to explain and sustain those activities, must, itself, transcend them. It is, in a way, a *subject* of cognition and activity which cannot, itself, be turned effectively into an *object* of cognition and activity except insofar as its existence is a presupposition of these occurrences. We will, in other words, find ourselves in Hume's position if we go out to look for it or if we turn inwards on ourselves in search of it. But this is because of its nature. If Hume's "search" had been successful (as, logically, it could not have been if this is the situation) it would have turned up precisely the wrong kind of thing.

If, as I suggested earlier, we miss this point, we can, of course, become embroiled in the whole classical dispute over the "other minds" problem. For we may easily imagine that each of us is, somehow, directly aware of his own "pure ego" — cognizes himself, if you like as a pure individual and sees his own goings on under the aspect of pure activity. If that were the case, then each of us would be in a special position vis-a-vis himself — having privileged access to his own "closed system." But that is just what does not and cannot happen. We are aware of ourselves through the processes of our thought and reason and we can really see that, wherever thought and reason actually occur, there behind it is, at least, the implication of something like the "pure ego."

To say this, however, is to invite further questions: If no one were aware of himself in the way that now seems objected to, what reason would there be, after all, to think that we were not being taken in by the "appearance" of reason in ourselves? Equally, what does "I" mean in this context? If "I" claim to have "identified *myself*" on what *grounds* do I claim identity between identifier and identified? And will this not, still, leave us open to various confounding forms of the "other minds" problem? For however we look at the problem, either "I" am connected with my own reasoning and thinking processes in ways which do not apply to anyone else or I am not. If the former is true, will it not turn out that I am better entitled to claim for myself that I am or possess a "pure ego" or whatever than I am to claim that status for anyone else? But if the latter is true and I am not specially connected to my own thought and reasonings, the doctrine that a pure ego is required as a presupposition of effective reason will not help us to solve any of the problems. In that case, we shall not have found the sought-for example of pure individuality and pure activity but rather have shown that it is very likely that the concepts involved cannot be made to do any work.

I shall try, therefore, to dispose of these difficulties by showing that they rest on a series of misunderstandings. If I can do this, the process should also serve to add some clarity to the notions concerned and to the line of argument I have been employing.

VIII

First of all, we cannot really be "taken in" by the appearances. If we can

216

argue for the position that we are "taken in," then we actually are reasoning. The very basis of the possibility of raising the skeptical position depends on the presupposition being questioned. Suppose we say: "Perhaps, after all, no one ever does give and take reasons. Perhaps everyone is merely misled by the kind of activity which might be expressed by the sayings of a record player or the combination of mechanical and random behaviour which can be programmed into a computer." Then, if the supposition turns out to be true, how are we to understand the position of the skeptic who makes such a case? Surely, he is taken in by his apparent reasonings and so on. Nor will it help at all to seek the "modern" escape by means of the introduction of some doctrine of levels of language or some clever variant of the theory of types. It is not merely that (as we saw in Chapter 3) such schemes involve the arbitrary introduction of devices merely to avoid awkward kinds of self-reference and, thereby, the demand for an objective rational scheme. It is also true that these conceptual devices will not work at all in this context. For if we say our skeptical questioning does not apply to the region of discourse in which the question is formed but only to the region of discourse to which the question refers, the problem merely breaks out anew at the next level. What are we to say about the reasoning powers of the questioner on the level at which his question occurs? If he is taken in *there*, we are in the same position. If he is not, the problem is solved.

This line of reasoning which (again) parallels one which I used in *The Rational and the Real* does not, admittedly *seem* very satisfying. For it makes the situation look as though we have trapped the skeptic by some kind of trick. It is not really a trick because what it is intended to show is just that, if this skeptical position holds, everything falls. Rational discourse is no longer possible. But we know that rational discourse is possible just by the fact that it is eminently sensible to be skeptical about so many things.

For the purpose of this chapter, however, we can, actually take what may be a more modest stand and still succeed in making our example hold. At any rate, we can take a slightly different, though not inconsistent, stand and succeed in making the position slightly clearer.

We can, that is, ask what it would be like to be "taken in" by our own seeming reasonings in the sense of believing that they were reasonings when, in fact, they were something else. I think that the position is often made to seem unusually difficult because we do not ask ourselves this question or we fail to put it very clearly.

If you hear an argument on a record and think you are dealing with a man you will very soon find out that you have made a mistake. This situation actually arises fairly commonly. Anyone who has dialed a telephone number and found himself connected to one of the telephone company's recording machines knows what *that* is like. The reason that one finds out is exactly that the responses of the machine quickly come to an end and it begins to repeat itself insanely. Of course, we can programme a machine to behave much like the telephone recording except that it will go on for a very long time and, perhaps, be very flexible in its responses. But it consists of a lot of stored information and a set of devices for organizing (whether according to a rule or according to some randomizing principle) that information and feeding it out in response to appropriate (but pre-determined) stimuli. In the face of a stimulus for which it is not designed it will turn out like the telephone company's recording. Faced with the kind of situation which seems to be required for reasoning — the kind of situation which this book is designed to explore — it will, surely, break down somewhere. For, however good it is at simulating the known behaviour of its programmers — and machines may eventually be designed which are perfectly adept at that — what it cannot do is to create anything new in any sense except that of random response.[1] Thus, to be "taken in" would be, in principle, at some point in such an investigation to break down in the face of a genuinely adequate chain of reasoning. It should be noticed, of course, that what is required is not that one should be able to *solve* all one's reasoning problems for, so far as we know, that is not given to men, either. The breaking down, indeed, consists either in not being able to solve the problems *or* in giving the sort of idiot response which the telephone recording offers — going on, that is, saying the same old thing or a random variant of it when the situation has changed so as to make that response inappropriate. People sometimes do *that* too, but the point is that they don't *have* to and the machine, after all, has no choice. Men produce, machines reproduce.[2] The test for this, of course, is to try to build a coherent structure of thought and to see what happens. But anyone who can, say, follow the chain of argument in Hegel's logic, has reasonable confirmation. For even to follow such a chain of argument involves more than simulation just for the reason that it does not

[1] Remarks about "machines" are apt to be highly contentious, especially in an age of rapidly developing technology. But the binary computer, for example, works necessarily on a straightforward "two-valued" system. It is a set of devices which depend, in the end, on switches which are either "on" or "off." Numbers can readily be dealt with using the appropriate base and so can "propositions" considered as either "true" or "false." The restriction imposed by such a device is, fundamentally, that it cannot accommodate anything which does not fit this pattern. It cannot, for instance, deal with a "dialectical tension" for that cannot be dealt with in terms of the "on," "off" structure — a structure which seems to fit, exactly, the requirements of the category of determinate being, and no other category. Thus the machine — conceived of this way — cannot do what we know the dialectician can do and will necessarily, however programmed, produce idiot responses at some stage. It is, I think, literally impossible to imagine a machine which does not have some analagous restriction. For this is just the line between a mechanism and a dialectical individual. (See the later discussion of dialectical individuality, Section IXff.) It remains true, however, that everything does have some aspect under which it is viewable as a component of "determinate being" so that the limitations on machines are intensional rather than extensional.

[2] For a useful discussion of this issue, see J. M. Burgers, *Experience and Conceptual Activity* (Cambridge, Mass.: M.I.T. Press, 1965), p. 150ff.

218

follow from a chain of formal mechanical rules or from that combined with some randomizing device. We know, as a matter of fact, that some people can either do that or, alternatively (even if they misunderstand Hegel) create an analagous chain for themselves. And we also know, if the argument of this book holds, that nothing would account as programming a machine to do that. If we had a notion of the scheme and programmed a machine to follow it out, that would be evidence that we had the wrong notion of the scheme.

It is not, to be sure, that there is something special about dialecticians. It is just that, in trying to construct such a logic, one is forced to make the appropriate distinctions between the kinds of thought which require a creative unity and the kinds of thought which, more nearly, can be reduced to formal rules. If one *can* make such distinctions and make them intelligibly, then one is not a kind of machine. For what the machine cannot do is to adopt a standpoint which is impossible to it. (We need to be careful, as well, not to be trapped into thinking that we are talking about something quite different — the real or imaginary distinction between men and their contrivances. We might — though not easily as things stand now — produce a "contrivance" which did dialectical logic. It would not, however, be a machine in the sense of something which obeyed mechanical laws, or a combination of laws and certain random outcomes. It would, in other words, actually be an individual in the special sense of this chapter.)

Most forcefully, the material we can draw from the present book suggests that, if it is possible to have the kinds of thought structures which are produceable by machines, then there must be *other* perspectives on the world, such as those provided by the process categories and the one I am trying to provide in this chapter, from which the world appears quite different. Merely being able to entertain these alternative perspectives surely guarantees just what is at issue. The proof of the reality of the perspective is just, after all, in the awareness of it combined with the effective awareness of the logical links which hold between it and other perspectives.

There is nothing to stop anyone from holding the position that what is not reducible to a formal structure, in the special sense of something which could be fed into a computing machine or something like it, is simply beyond the bounds of rationality. For we could only convince him by getting him to grasp some other perspective. But if anyone has some other perspective and actually understands the logical structure which links it to the rest of a coherent system there is, equally, nothing which could logically count as persuading him that he was being "taken in" except an argument designed to show him that his system did not fit together in the way he imagined. But, if he has one of the perspectives at issue, the new argument can only serve to show him that it does not fit into a viable system in the *way* he supposed. We can imagine, that is, a reconstruction of any given system of categories, but once we have a perspective which is essentially non-mechanical we cannot imagine its complete reduction to a set of mechanical perspectives. We cannot give men back the moral and rational stance of the tiger except by destroying their capacities through physical or psychological conditioning. Being "taken in" in the general way imagined by the skeptic does not, then, seem possible.

We are entitled, if we can accept any of these lines of argument, to think that reasoning of the right sort actually does go on and that it establishes the occurrence of a genuine individuality and an actual creative activity. But how do we pass from this to establishing something like the notion of personal identity? *Have* I identified myself by recourse to this rather specialized if important kind of rational activity?

IX

The clue to the answer to this question lies in the fact that this kind of reasoning activity establishes, as I argued earlier, the conditions for moral responsibility — the conditions under which we can be asked to justify ourselves. For to exhibit rational activity of the kind in question is to fall within the ambit of moral discourse. To do that, in turn, is to exhibit the kind of unity of aim and activity which makes the notion of personal identity possible.

Merely to examine the alternatives makes the reasonableness of this doctrine rather more obvious. It has been suggested that personal identity might consist in continuity of body or in continuity of mind, or in continuity of some *special feature* of continuity of mind (or of mind and body) such as memory.

But none of these proposals seems to stand much examination. People are identified by their bodies for numerous practical purposes: Policemen look for fingerprints, passport authorities have faith in photographs, and friends, naturally enough, look for characteristic appearances when they are waiting at the railway station. But all of this seems to depend on one or other, or both, of two rather fortuitous facts: Usually only one person is associated with a given body over a human lifetime and, less importantly, "identification" sometimes has little or nothing to do with "personality."

Unless it is a *necessary* truth that only one person can be associated with a given body during the lifetime of that body, then it will be merely a stroke of good luck that we can often identify people by their bodies. For we will, in that case, only be identifying a body, and relying on a usual and useful conjunction of body and man to arrive — by some inductive technique — at the conclusion that we have identified a person.

But it is not a necessary truth that there is a one-to-one correspondence between persons and bodies. A man may change so much in outlook, attitude, behaviour, and so on that it would be foolish to go on thinking of him as the "same person" except for some rather peculiar purposes which

I shall consider in a moment. If Smith is arrested in a bar-room brawl, escapes before his trial, and turns up twenty years later as the Archbishop of Canterbury, it will be rather silly to bring him to trial for the original offence. In fact, it can even be the case that more than one person is associated with a given body over a relatively short span of time. Surely not *all* multiple personality cases are pathological though, no doubt, most of them are annoying and confusing to someone.

In any case, having the same body is not, presumably, a sufficient condition for personal identity. If — however oddly — someone were able to prove that his body was composed only of particles which had once been part of Napoleon's body and that they were, furthermore, assembled in the characteristic "Napoleon pattern," would anyone think this adequate to give him moral title to whatever we might still identify as Napoleon's property? But what else does "having a body" mean? (We usually think of a body as a pattern of some kind rather than as an assembly of particles since the particle content of bodies changes a good deal.) Would it help if the man could prove that he had the same genetic structure and what is now called the "genetic code" which had belonged to Napoleon? It seems absurd. Part of the reason that it seems absurd is that we would have accepted Napoleon as Napoleon no matter how much his body had changed during his lifetime. (Anyone who has ever seen pictures of the young McTaggart and the McTaggart of late middle-age will know how much a body can change in a fairly short time. But no one has ever suggested that two philosophers were involved.)

Bodily identification, in other words, is handy but shaky. Logically so, because our concept of a person bears no special connection with the concept of any particular sort of body. (We do not have to raise the question which seems to have concerned some philosophers in recent years: Does one have to have some sort of body in order to be a person? But the answer, actually, seems to be "no." Spiritualist mediums frequently claim to make use of "spirit persons" in the course of their transactions. No such "persons" may exist but they know and we know what they are talking about. Novels are quite often written in the first person portraying an "observer" whose bodily features are never described, but we can identify the "personality" at work. Again, we quite often know very little about the bodies of historical persons, but their personalities come through plainly enough in their writings and deeds for it to be quite sensible for historians to argue at length as to whether a given book should be ascribed to a certain author or a given deed ascribed to a certain politician. For me to identify myself, of course, I would have to have some continuity of reference. It is convenient that most of my experiences include an experience of a body. But not all my experiences are bodily oriented and any number of other continuants might do for the purpose.)

Thus the "body theory" of personal identity surely does not work.

Nor, in the ordinary sense, would a "mind" theory. It is not quite clear what "having a mind" means unless one elaborates a theory, but, presumably, minds would be distinguished from one another by their contents or by their dispositional tendencies.

Two people are often, though, "of the same mind" at least for short periods of time. Two mathematicians thinking of the same equation and of nothing else during a period $T^1 - T^n$ will likely have the same "mental contents" but they will not likely be the same person during that time span. Thus we would have to demand, a long span of time over which to identify persons on a "mind" theory.

Commonly, memory is invoked as providing what we need by way of a criterion of uniqueness and as providing a time span. The trouble is, though, that memory is notoriously fallible. People sometimes forget, and, worse still, remember what did not happen. Thus, though two men's "veridical memories" might, in principle, always be different (each of them would have had a different perspective), their "actual memories" might coincide as a result of mistakes. But that would not make them the same person. Nor would one of them be a different person if his memories were all obliterated by some device and new ones substituted. We could say, of course, that veridical memories are the *real basis* of personal identity even though, since no one has such a memory, no one quite knows for sure "who" he is. But the reason, again, for thinking that no two people could have the same veridical memory seems to depend rather heavily on a disguised introduction of the "body theory." It is true that I think of myself as being always in a place which is not occupied by anyone else and thus, invariably, having a slightly different perspective and of being conditioned by my own peculiar sensations. But both these notions depend on the supposition that there is only one person attached to each body during its lifetime, and that, as we have seen, is not absolutely certain.

Thus we are left, I think, with two theories — the dispositional tendencies theory and the one I want to defend. Let us consider the "dispositional" theory: Smith and Jones are different because each has a characteristic way of responding to events and a characteristic "mental organization." But this only sounds better than the other previously discussed theories because it is vaguer. We do not know very much, of course, about what one might call "casts of mind" but it is not too unlikely that people who have been closely associated with one another for long periods (husbands and wives, for instance) will develop pretty much the same "cast of mind." We might want to think of them as one person but then, again, we might not: It will depend, surely, on whether or not we are prepared to hold them responsible for each other's acts, to accept their justifications as interchangeable and so on.

Indeed, this is surely what we are interested in. If it weren't for the moral issues, would it matter if we sometimes mixed up Smith and Jones? There

222

is not an identity problem about hydrogen atoms despite the grave risk of actually mistaking one for another because no such issues arise. My concern with establishing my continuing identity is, inevitably, deeply inter-twined with moral concerns.

And this does seem, in any case, to bring us back to just the position I set out to defend. Surely what matters about personal identity is the problem of moral continuity. The reason I insist on being regarded as a continuing person and not merely as a heterogenous collection of material particles or an assembly of constantly shifting biological "works" is that I sense a continuity of responsibility in myself. If there comes a time when I change my affairs and outlook so drastically as to become a "different person" it will, entail, surely, a change in my situation such that I can, no longer, look on myself as responsible for the actions which compose what I now call "my past." I shall, then, look on them much as one would look on someone else's biography.

The rejoinder to this will include, I suspect, reference to the kinds of identification which have little or nothing to do with personality: The state is concerned, for practical reasons, to make sure that the number of voters does not exceed the number of bodily identifiable individuals. One does not want to multiply the number of voters to meet the number of "personalities" if the latter number is larger than the former. The possibilities for fraud are only too obvious. Equally, if Smith leaves his money to Jones, Robinson will not be able to contest the will on the ground that Jones, though occupying the body probably intended by the testator, is now a different person. Here the issue is just that the money, in any case, has to go to someone and we take a chance on the person likely to be, if not the person intended, at least more like that person than Robinson is. Again, one cannot claim sickness benefits for two persons under a national insurance scheme on the ground that one is a split personality. But here the issue is that the state wants, presumably, to look after bodies no matter how many poverty-stricken "persons" are attached to any given body. All of these cases only tell against the analysis being offered for the extraneous reason that we confuse a number of other kinds of identification with actually identifying persons.

If that point is made, the rejoinder is likely, still, to focus on the notion that the criteria for continuing moral responsibility do not individuate precisely enough so that we can still make the mistake of taking Smith and Jones for the same person. This rejoinder, however, misses what seems to me to be the crucial point already made: We are worried about confusing Smith with Jones because the mistake might well cause us to make wrong moral judgements. If we use moral responsibility as the criterion, however, we cannot, if we make the judgement correctly, make *that* mistake. If Smith and Jones show the same pattern of moral activity in such a way that each can actually be said to be responsible for the doings of the other then, surely, they *are* the same person.

But is this even possible? The situation is, after all, that, in watching myself and others in the process of giving and taking reasons and in establishing a pattern of activity with which moral discourse can come to grips, I come to see who I am. I put myself into my acts and then I reflect on them. I notice that, given the nature of these activities, I cannot be totally identified with them. There is more that I can do and say. I am open, if you like, to other possibilities. I can perform the same analysis on the acts and sayings of other people with just the difference that I cannot act for them. Thus I find myself in my own activities and other people in theirs but short of becoming them, the distinction between us remains.

I know what it is to be someone else — to identify myself with the hero of a play or a novel and, for a time, while living in the world of the novel, to be that hero — but this, though it softens the threatening grip of the "other minds" problem, does not result in a confusion of identities. It is my awareness of what I have called "pure activity" which makes it possible for me to realize that I am somebody at all, but this, again, is only possible by way of making the contrast between orderly and determined activity which constitutes a kind of closed system and the kind of open system which is characteristic of a rational being.

I can see in the case of others that this openness of system must be there. But I can only feel it at work in myself. This "feeling" — the awareness of freedom if you like — is not, of course, divorced or divorceable from the actual pattern of activities which I undertake. I have to look outward to find myself and I am not aware of the "pure ego" in itself but only of the sense of being the active centre of an open system.

Thus I am more directly connected with my own thoughts, feelings, and reasoning processes than with anyone else's but this does not prevent me from seeing that a similar sense of being the centre of an active and open system is entailed by the occurrence of other rational structures whose outward exhibitions are like mine. It may well still be argued that the "other minds" problem arises out of this situation in just the traditional way. I do not know *for certain* that what seem to be the activities of other persons are not really something else which I mistakenly take to be the exhibitions of personality.

This position fails on two grounds if we accept the context of the present discussion. One of them is that it is not merely accidental to the *appearance* of rationality that a genuine individual should be involved in it and that it should exhibit "pure activity." It is a necessary feature of such occasions. Thus I am either mistaken in thinking that rational activity is going on or I am entitled to believe that there are "other minds." But we have already seen what it is to be mistaken about such things and that, though one certainly *could* make a mistake about it, there is no special feature of the situation which makes it intrinsically doubtful.

The other is that if it turns out to be the case that we can generalize this notion so as to provide a category in the dialectical system we are developing then it follows that everything which exists can be viewed from the perspective of that category. Thus, if we develop the notion — let us call it dialectical individuality — there will either be one all-encompassing individual or a plurality of such individuals. But the concept seemingly would not work for the case of a single individual since (for reasons which will emerge shortly) such a being would either have to view the whole of reality as part of "himself" or be like the detached spectator for whom the whole world is a peep show having nothing to do with him. Neither notion will do for the formation of the notion of a genuine individual, however, just because that notion requires an appropriate context in which individuation can take place and neither of these hypotheses seems to provide it. That, however, will emerge more clearly, when we begin to look at the problem from the obviously opposed perspective. Admittedly, this second argument only tells, in any case, against the more extreme kinds of solipsism and not against the more worrying aspects of the "other minds" problem. Even if it turns out to be substantiable that the category is genuine and that it requires a plurality of individuals for its successful functioning, it will not follow that any of the entities we actually take to be persons really are individuals of the designated kind, but only that there are several (two or more) persons in the world if there is anything in the world. Still, if we knew the truth of this last proposition it would seem to be reasonable, knowing what we do, to take the beings we usually identify as persons to be genuine.

This, however, is rushing the argument — a procedure only justified on the ground that the obvious objection was that we seemed very likely to be creating insoluble conceptual difficulties of a rather traditional kind. Our position is just this: We have seen that there is a place for the notion of "pure individuality" and its relative (or correlative) "pure activity." They can be combined into a workable notion of "pure ego" and they serve a function in the context of a human situation which demands a rational morality. Concentration on the "pure ego" leads us outward, however, and into the world — we find it, after all, in manifestations of rationality which, though they may be private, need not be so.

X

If we start from the other side, however, we can see, to begin with, that the distinction between myself and the world is one which cannot be made except in a very complex context. The moral situation on which I have been trading rather heavily is, for instance, only possible in a fairly orderly world. If some events were not usually, or always, followed by others of a standard kind, one could not trace the line of moral responsibility through the world at all. When I pull the trigger on a pistol the result, presumably, is that a bullet is fired and the effects of that bullet are fairly uniform. Suppose that sometimes pulling the trigger resulted in firing a bullet but, sometimes, manna fell from heaven instead and, on still other occasions, the result was an earthquake. Or suppose one never knew whether bullets in the brain would kill the intended victims or render them towering giants of the intellect. It would become difficult to know who was responsible for what. Thus the kind of individuality which makes responsibility possible can only be had against the background of an appropriate world. It cannot exist in a vacuum.

Even more strikingly, it is only because there are other human beings that the notion of an appropriate moral response can really arise. If there were no one else, would it matter whether I could justify my existence or not? We are tempted to answer "yes" because, I think, we imagine ourselves as fully developed individuals in a situation like Robinson Crusoe's. Only we forget that Defoe's hero came fully equipped with a language, a culture, and an elaborate set of perspectives on the world. As I suggested a moment ago, such a person, even supposing that he had acquired, somehow, the ability to talk and think would have a rather peculiar choice. He could regard the most remote features of his world much as I regard my big toe — though, no doubt, with even less sense of affection and sense of belonging. Or he could regard the whole world as neutral to him and see himself as a grand spectator. Alternatively, he could try to draw his boundaries somewhere in between. He might certainly notice that when he stuck a pin into his big toe it hurt, whereas when he stuck it into a tree or a rock, it didn't. But one does not always get sensations from parts of one's body — you may feel nothing if a strand of your hair is cut or even if a toenail is cut. And, anyhow, one can extend and contract the range of one's sensitivities. Most of us feel a stab of pain if we see someone kick a dog or hit a child and we can always disconnect our own sensations by appropriate neurological techniques. Furthermore, all of this is compounded by well-known neurological and psychiatric difficulties about the whole notion of "body image."

How would our strange Crusoe actually make his decision? He might or might not decide to regard himself as roughly co-extensive with his body. But would *any* decision he made make it possible for him to regard himself a genuine individual? It has already turned out in this argument that "body" theories of personal identity are weak in any case and, in this case, they would be weaker still. Most of *us* have our tendency to associate "ourselves" very strongly with our bodies much strengthened by a variety of legal and moral traditions which guarantee the sanctity of our bodies from unwanted outside interference and provide a context in which they become particularly "our" territory. But our Crusoe will have no such surroundings. We all project ourselves, even in our ordinary affairs, into a variety of places and things. Certain places (if we are lucky) are "ours." We are at home there. Certain things take on the flavour of our injected

226

personalities. But we can do this because we can contrast them with other places and things which belong to other people. Our Crusoe will have a much wider latitude, but will it mean anything to him?

Surely, in the end, it is because there is a community of people and an interplay of moral claim and counter-claim that we can make the distinction between what is "us" and what reflects somebody else. And, without that, the notion of what is nobody's — that is, neutral to everyone — seems to make no sense either.

Thus our Crusoe would seem to have the odd choice of taking in everything or nothing, or simply making an arbitrary decision. In the first case, he will not, after all, be individuated. If he opts for the second and decides that he is merely a general spectator of the world, the general spectator will be like the "pure ego" without the underpinnings of genuine connections with the world. It will be quite empty. But an arbitrary choice will also not provide an effective contrast. The concept of "person" only seems to make sense when there are enough "beings" to make a moral community — at least two.

XI

We can also reflect that people *do* find themselves in the outside world, and not — even metaphorically — inside their own heads. The novelist sees himself reflected as the words develop on paper. The painter sees his image — if at all — in his picture. The man of moral sensibility finds out that he is a man of moral sensibility only when the complexities of his life and the lives of his friends and neighbours call for careful reflection and subtle judgement.

We could therefore ask, if there happened to be only one such individual, what he could possibly identify himself *as* and just how. For all the special perspectives which make possible individuation in the ordinary way require appropriate contrasts. We see this easily enough, perhaps, for some cases: To know that one is responsible for and thus is to be found through and in one's own books, one has to have a community in which other men are found in other ways or in other books. Otherwise, the appearance of a "person" through his writings would appear merely fortuitous and no more "me" than the dizzying pattern of clouds driven by a force ten wind. One can easily see, too, that it requires a long tradition and a subtle interplay of persons before a "personality" can appear in a painting or a poem. But, surely, there is some way of individuating oneself which is not so dependent.

Yet this is to suppose that we can readily separate the individuation of persons from the sense of continuity of moral responsibility which I urged, earlier, is ultimately at the bottom of the notion. For otherwise, it will only be when there is a moral community in which we can distinguish each other, and the neutral background of a world which is none of us, that we can really regard ourselves as distinct in any ultimate sense.

XII

We may be led by these considerations, however, to over-emphasize the other side of the picture and to forget that we are only dealing with a kind of dialectical reflection. The more we see that we draw our identities against the background of a community, the more we may be tempted to regard the individual as only a kind of manifestation of the community. Communities, associations, and corporations not only function as "legal persons" — they do, often, have aims, responsibilities, and moral stances which are not easily or simply reducible to those of their constituent individuals.

There are, however, important differences. It is true, as I have suggested, that we cannot find moral individuals — identifiable persons in the terms of the argument — in the absence of communities, just as it is true that we cannot find communities in the absence of moral individuals. Equally, communities have a certain kind of independence from the moral individuals who compose them (though the sense of "compose" here is rather weak) just as moral individuals can be independent of any *particular* community. (Institutions go on though men die and, by setting the framework within which moral activity can take place, they no doubt influence the structure of the moral individuals who compose them.) Yet there is still a kind of primacy which attaches to the individual moral agent. It is he who has the special kind of awareness of freedom and who can be called upon to answer for his institutions. The institution can "answer for itself" only insofar as its justification can be deduced by the analysis of its past and present. It is confined to those terms in the way that the individual is not. The individual can choose to answer for it but he can also choose, when called upon to answer, to abandon the institution. There is no analogue to *that* in the behaviour of the institution. The practical choices open to the individual may be severely limited by the possibilities for thought and action which institutions leave open. But we never know for sure how the individual *will* answer though we can know for sure how, given what it is, the institution *must* answer.

The dialectical reflection, in other words, is imperfect — as it must be in the context of notions which may be imagined to reflect a category which lies near one of the poles of the tension which fixes the dialectical system.

XIII

We may be tempted to over-emphasize the dialectical reflection in a slightly different way and so encourage various kinds of behaviourism. We may, that is, come to confuse the conditions for self-knowledge with the content of that knowledge. It is true that the admittedly polar concepts which I have called "pure individuality" and "pure activity" do not do any work at all unless they are taken to be manifested in activities which can be found in the world (though such activities *need* not be found, for one can keep oneself to oneself). The temptation, therefore, is to think of them as meaningless in that they do not, themselves, mark out anything in the world. Thus one may want to equate the individual with what he does and not with what he is.

But, though it is true that to think about the "pure ego" is to end up thinking about what actually goes on in the world, the dialectical alternative is also true. To start by thinking about what goes on in the world is to end up thinking of the "pure ego" as well. Indeed, the whole line of earlier argument started by noticing certain features of the world which are associated with ordinary human persons and then proceeded to the notion of a "pure ego" by a number of inferences. Activities which require justification lead, inevitably, back in this direction.

XIV

If these reductionist tendencies are to be resisted, we have arrived at something very close to a working concept of dialectical individuality. In the case of human persons, at any rate, we seem to be able to envisage an account like the following:

The essence of such an individual is a pure ego which manifests itself in perfectly free activity. In order to establish itself as an identifiable entity, however, it must act in and on the world. It can only find itself through determinate structures. There will thus be — if there is anything at all — a series of reflections of it in the world.

The dialectical individual will, indeed, tend (however chaotically) to recapitulate something like the structure of the categories. The first condition of his viability will be effective determinateness. But this determinateness must be conceived within a framework which, itself, has to be defined as the process develops. Thus he must be able to see himself as a set of determinate phases within a structure, and the relations between these will be the relations which hold between determinate being, pure being, and pure disjunction — a set of discrete states within a totality as yet undetermined but containing the possibilities for determination. The unity of the individual appears, thus, as a logical tension which holds between his determinate states and the openness of his potential — a kind of alienation, to borrow the language of Hegel and Marx, but one intelligible against the conceptual background of pure being, pure disjunction, and determinate being.

If he overcomes this in an act of self-awareness he will be able to see himself and the world as a unity in much the way that the category of systematic unity prescribes. But this in turn will create a tension between this unity, as a fixed and static representation, and the demands of the activity which lies behind the reflection. Thus he will begin to see the world as a process and himself as a way of reflecting on that process — to see his reflection through the categories of pure and determinate process — a creator and a product of the creative process. These, again, are alienating views which fall short of establishing either effective unity or genuine individuality and he will be driven — if he goes on — to see himself through the universal categories and, finally, to recognize his nature as a dialectical individual.

These are all, I think, phases of human experience in our ordinary interplay with the world though they come, of course, more often, all jumbled up as chaotic vistas which may succeed one another in any order and usually resist any effective logical structure just because we do not, of course, come equipped with a ready-made dialectical logic and because our awareness of ourselves is only partially mediated by rationality and a full consciousness.

Indeed, this representation makes it clear that there must be experience. If the ultimate reality turns out to be a set of dialectical individuals, then they can only exist through their representations and these will be just what we call experience. And this experience will be intelligible only through a structure of categories. If the system of categories I have developed here is correct, then experience combined with reason will tend to show itself through them. If they are not correct, then there will be others. But if individuality is the kind of thing I have been suggesting, then there will be categories. This, then seems to be the point at which the system works back on itself. The individual, thought of in this way, will be like Spinoza's man who is viewable under the attributes of extension and thought and whose components in those dimensions must exactly match one another. For whatever is conceivable in one of the categories must have its counterpart in all the others. If we are careless, of course, we come to identify the individual with one or more of his representations or reflections but the problem of personal identity will force us to the ultimate category if we reflect carefully.

XV

We are now, however, at the point at which a more obvious problem intrudes. Can we, indeed, generalize the notions I have tried to develop by concentrating on certain features of what is, after all, only an example about certain aspects of human persons? Is it feasible to regard the whole world under such a category?

The objections will be like those which I raised in the last chapter about certain Hegelean categories: Much of the world appears to be quite lifeless and mechanical. Indeed, so far as we know, human beings and high order animals occupy only a fraction of the known universe and, even if there are (as seems increasingly likely) other similar fractions occupied by creatures of much the same sort, they will, collectively, not amount to much in proportion to the whole. It therefore seems rather absurd to regard the whole of reality as the byproduct of activities analagous to those by which human beings establish themselves in the world.

Such a doctrine may seem particularly absurd in light of the fact that the kinds of ways in which I suggested that personal identity could be established also seem to provide perfectly good senses for the concepts which we would have to use in order to establish that much of the world that we know about is independent of us. By knowing what we are responsible for and thus who we are we can also tell what it is others are responsible for and, by extension, what no one is responsible for. One very good sense of independence is given by just that phrase — anything is independent of all of us if no one is responsible for it.

This kind of independence is, however, compatible with other kinds of dependence and the question needs to be examined on its merits.

Roughly, what we do know (assuming that the system so far constructed is sound) is that, in any case, there will be a perspective on the world from which everything will be intelligible as an actual or possible object of knowledge — for that property turned out to be the highest order determinable and that, in turn, seemed necessary for the meaningfulness of any set of ways of referring to the world, and part of the required solution to the universals problem. There is, of course, an important loophole in the expression "or possible" — we need not be in the Berkeleyan position of identifying the components of the world with actual objects of knowledge.

On the other side, we know that the logical structure, itself, is independent of anyone. Individuality depends upon the categorical structure and it, therefore, is independent of any knower or set of knowers. We are not, therefore, in a position in which it will be impossible to distinguish what X and Y are responsible for from what no one is responsible for, even if it should turn out that the components of the world are a set of dialectical individuals and their experiences or "reflections" in the world.[1]

XVI

Still, the whole issue requires detailed examination. To begin with it is important to inquire as to just what being "an actual or possible object of knowledge" amounts to. In order to do that it will be as well to see whether there is any justification within the system for it other than the one offered in Chapter 5, if only because such an investigation will likely yield additional ways of discovering what it means.

---

[1] The point at issue here is not about the existence of a special "quasi-Platonic" realm of logical structures. There need not be such a realm — at least so far as the argument goes. Rather, the point is that the conditions for individuation are the same for all knowing subjects and these conditions represent the structure of the categories. Thus there is a common framework which makes communication and objectivity possible. But this framework comes to be reality as, and only as, the process develops.

One way of trying to decide whether an assertion is true is to try to find out what the state of affairs would be if it were false. We know that there are certain conditions such that, if they obtained, they would render anything which met them unamenable to knowledge. The most dramatic class of such conditions are those associated with formal contradiction. If there were married bachelors, square circles, or finite infinities we would not be able to know anything about them just because they surpass the limits which any possible discourse could attain. Their descriptions do not lead, as do those of entities whose descriptions attain a kind of dialectical tension, to a higher synthesis within which they could be grasped. Their descriptions consist, by and large, just of formal assertions combined with formal withdrawals of the occurrence of specified properties. But surely this is just a rather extreme case of the kind of thing one must say, in any event, in order to deny the existence of anything. If one says "There are no unicorns," one is, surely, saying either "Nothing would count as meeting the requirements for being a unicorn" or "If there were any unicorns, they would reveal themselves to our sensory apparatus, but nothing does." In the first case, one is saying that the properties assigned to unicorns cannot be combined so as to instantiate one. The second assertion about unicorns is not, after all, so far different. For the man who utters it categorically no doubt means to imply that all the places where unicorns could be have probably been examined and yet no one has seen one. To say, then, that unicorns exist and are not seen comes close to a contradiction if to be a unicorn is to be, in part, a visibilium. One may imagine, of course, that someone might want to say "Well, perhaps there are things which, were they knowable, would be objects of perception or sensation but are not knowable just because no sensory apparatus exists or could exist which would detect them." Or he might say "For all you know there are things which, were they knowable, would be objects of rational cognition but, in fact, they have no place in any devisable rational system." Both these would seem to be cases of unknowable existence and, if they are, they constitute special objections to the doctrine if, at any rate, it is interpreted to mean that being an actual or possible object of knowledge is a *necessary* condition of existence. Of course if the doctrine expresses what "existence" *means*, it has to be a necessary condition. Yet these are not, apparently, special cases at all. It is, surely, a contradiction to allege that something would be an object of perception or of rational cognition but that no perceiving faculty could be designed or no rational structure constructed for it.

The point here, in other words, is simply another variant of what we have seen many times in the guise of the "dialectician's dilemma": If something existed and yet was not an actual or possible object of knowledge, then thought and reality would have diverged to the point at which the whole system we are dealing with would break down. But the conditions for such a breakdown are just that the system should turn out to require concepts

232

which work if and only if such a separation is supposed. But this only seems possible, in any case, if something like a contradiction were to develop within the system. Thus, in the present case if it turned out to be true that the last concept in the system required us to view everything under the guise of a personal knower but also prevented us from doing so we would be faced both with a divergence of thought and reality and a contradiction in the system. Clearly, it does prevent us from regarding *everything* as a component of a "personal knower" since it does require the possibility, at least, of an impersonal "objective" background to the moral arena in which persons or moral agents are to be found. But, equally, it does not demand that everything should be construable in terms of a personal knower.

For it now seems that the doctrine that everything is an actual or possible object of knowledge only requires (1) that nothing beyond the reach of rational thought should exist and (2) that everything should have in common a certain property construed as being the highest order determinable. Unless (2) should turn out to have some specially difficult additional feature about it, it seems certain that there is no predicament.

Moreover, it was, of course, argued in Chapter 5 that being an actual or possible object of knowledge was not a property which things had in the usual way as something in addition to their other properties. Those other properties are simply reflected as a unity of rational system. It turns out, therefore, that (1) and (2) in the last paragraph are just different aspects of the same truth.

XVII

If we add to this the requirements of what I called pure activity — one of the crucial features of the final category — we get, I think, the following result: We can regard the world as pure activity manifesting itself as the kind of system which is intelligible against the background of the system of categories which our logic brings out. In a way its whole statable content is exhausted by the assertions which can be made within the earlier categories but, in a way, too, each of these categories throws us back on the notion of an underlying undetermined activity. Thus the domain of determinate being, for instance, is occupied by all those entities which can be referred to by assertions which meet certain logical criteria. They are, if you like, perfectly independent of anyone's assertions about them. They are just what they are. But they become actual objects of knowledge and so come to play a part in the scheme of things when someone makes the appropriate assertions. The entities which figure in the domain of the process categories are schematized reflections of an underlying activity which forces us in thought (when they become actual objects of knowledge) to transcend them.

We can, if it turns out to be appropriate, construct a kind of natural history of the world or of the real which will exhibit reality as a special kind of development through the categories. Thus it may begin as a set of material objects whose nature suggests most strongly the early categories such as determinate being. (Imagine, that is, that the world is really to be conceived of, in some ultimate sense, as a set of what I have called dialectical individuals. In the earlier phases of "their" activity, they posit themselves merely as determinate entities. These "positings" can be conceived of under all the categories but if, for instance, they are not yet aware of themselves, the situation will most naturally be described as one in which material objects dominate the situation. For there will not be much that is useful to say about the world under the "higher categories" except by way of ultimate explanation.) If thought and reason run through the real, however, there will be the same logical tensions in the world as there are in the system of categories we have been discussing and the world will begin to develop entities — organisms perhaps — which strongly suggest the process categories and which can be best represented in this way. These in turn — or some of them — will tend to develop into genuine individuals and to create the conditions under which such characteristics as personality begin to be appropriate. At each stage we can invoke all the categories but the entities concerned will tend to reflect some of them more strongly than others. Still, the whole process will reflect the unconditioned dynamism which I have called "pure activity" even though any particular phase of it may suggest, much more strongly, the limited kinds of explanation which are appropriate to specific categories. We can, if we want to, see the development of the world as the reflection through the system of categories of the requirements of the last or highest category.

All this necessarily sounds rather mysterious but the point I want to make is fairly pedestrian: We can look at things either in their guise as objects of knowledge — as parts, that is, of a rational system through which thought and experience run — or we can look at them in their own right. As objects of knowledge they will have about them both a necessary unity and their own kind of independence. If we look at them in their own right, the appearance of the world will include the appearance of the development of knowledge itself. It will appear as if the real is gradually acquiring knowledge of itself. But if the world were regarded as a set of dialectical individuals whose development consisted of putting themselves in the world and then of reflecting on themselves it would, in any case, have just this appearance however the details might turn out. For this kind of self-knowledge is only possible through a kind of recapitulation of the system of these categories, or others which will perform a similar function.

The world as something which comes to know itself is not, after all, an impossible concept. Nor does it obliterate the distinction between what is the responsibility of one individual or another and what is the responsibility of no one. For even if the world is, finally, a collection of dialectical individuals and their histories, the responsibilities they have accrue only from the time that they become clearly aware of themselves, and they never quite absorb the whole of the world into their spheres of responsibility. For there are always those features of the system which require for their intelligibility a primary emphasis on the appropriate "lower" categories.

Again, this is just one more way of looking at the totality of the real. It is a way which forces us back through the categories again and re-enforces the need for a sequence of categories. It does not, of course, contradict anything which we seem to know about the world: A developing process of this kind is consistent enough with our scientific investigations. Nor *could* it, really, contradict our "scientific knowledge." For it merely provides another perspective with which to integrate whatever it is that we do happen to know.

XVIII

It is true that this way of looking at things suggests additional difficulties: If it is necessary to regard the world as a set of dialectical individuals, then there must, it seems, be an explanatory thread running through the whole history of the real and this thread must bind it together as a unity. But there is an important distinction to be made here. The thread, if it exists, is one which binds particular things — in fact the specific histories of dialectical individuals. The categories only guarantee that there are links between the ways of conceptualizing the whole of the real. If there are dialectical individuals and if they have this kind of history, then the thread will have to be possible and this will involve a number of special investigations and demand the ultimate reconciliation of the principle of sufficient reason, the concept of time, and the notion of freedom.

The alternative, from our present point of view, is simply to regard the category of dialectical individuality as providing that perspective from which we see that our knowledge of the world, ultimately, comes home to us — that all that can be known about the world can be seen as the reflection of ourselves in our efforts to establish a framework for postulating our own individuality. It will still have its own independence, for logically it has to be (with respect to its formal structure though not, indeed, its details) just as it is. The possibilities for knowledge and experience, in other words, are logically independent of anyone.

The category of dialectical individuality is neutral to these accounts. All that it requires is that there should be some way of regarding the world as a union of pure activity and pure individuality on the one hand and systematic individuality on the other. In either case we will be able to preserve the notion that everything is an actual or possible object of knowledge, that there is a common "independent" background within which moral individuals can operate, and that everything is intelligible through a sequence of categories.

XIX

There remains a further problem about this which I shall come to shortly, but perhaps this is a useful place in which to emphasize that the truth about the categories is not, in and of itself, "the truth about the world."

It is true that the categories characterize the real and that the properties they spell out are importantly latent in things. But the details of what there is are not, of course, revealed by a study of the categories. Such revelations as there may be about those will be forthcoming only as a result of the appropriate investigations. The features of things which are appropriate to the domain of determinate being yield to certain specific kinds of logical investigation. In the categories of universality complex mixtures of reason and experience and an adequate "scientific method" are obviously required. The category of dialectical individuality suggests specific techniques for moral investigation — and so on. What does seem to be true is that the "real" is comprised only of those things which can be identified, in the appropriate way, in all the categories.

It is also true that the categories do not provide the whole of what can reasonably be called the "logical background" which surrounds and permeates the detailed pattern of identifiable components of the domains they identify. All our inquiries require rational agents to carry them out, and the conditions which must be supposed to hold if rational enquiry is possible can be investigated in themselves as I have tried to do in *The Rational and the Real*. The distinction is that, here, we started with very general organizing concepts and developed their implications from the standpoint of possible systems of rational thought considered independently. In *The Rational and the Real*, I started with the perspective of the inquirer and endeavoured to establish what specific conditions must obtain if his activities — especially the crucial one of "talking sense about the world" — could imaginably be successful. Some of the specific conditions are, of course, more detailed than the scheme of categories here can provide and they also provide direct information about what there is rather than how it is to be organized. But our knowledge of the detailed features of the world has to be seen, again, against the background of these conditions.

Equally, as I suggested a moment ago, one can start from the problem posed by the integration of specific detailed features and ask how they can be — if at all — integrated into a single explanatory unity. This may provide further limiting conditions which could help in deciding on the interpretation appropriate to the category of dialectical individuality. The total field of enquiry, after all, requires investigators, objects of investigation, and schemes for conceptualizing any possible result and each of these enquiries will introduce special limitations on our knowledge. The results must be consistent with each other and also with the requirements for our epistemologies generally — for an account of truth, meaning and knowledge.

236

I have suggested what seems to me the right ordering of our epistemological concepts in *The Concept of Truth* and I have tried to make clear, there, what the function of a "dialectical logic" such as the present one is when seen from that perspective. I think, needless to say, that the scheme described here provides an essential part of the framework of presuppositions which is required to establish the relevance of investigations into the details of the world, and to provide one of the components of a situation in which truth is possible. The reader can decide that question for himself. (As much as possible this book and the other two have been kept self-contained and independent of one another.) But it remains important to see that not everything has to be or can be derived from the scheme of categories though they will influence our understanding of everything.

The interpretation of the category of dialectical individuality will depend, of course, partly on considerations which can be derived from investigations like that undertaken in *The Rational and the Real*, partly by considerations drawn from an exploration of the relations between truth, knowledge and reality, and partly, no doubt, by a specific enquiry into just the explanatory situation which would be posed by adopting one option or the other. I think that the last category is intelligible in the light of what I said in *The Rational and the Real* and *The Concept of Truth*. But I also think the specific enquiry has to be undertaken with as much show of independence as one can muster. I have completed the *draft* of such an enquiry and it does not seem to lead to difficulties which would render the last category impossible. But that is something about which judgement should be suspended here.

XX

Even with these caveats, we are not quite at the end of the development of the last category. For it can still be objected that, on either option, we cannot regard the world, as presently constituted, as a set of dialectical individuals if that means regarding every part of it as, in some aspect, part of a morally responsible individual. We do seem to be involved in that difficulty on either option of interpretation. For ultimate individuality is only possible (on the argument offered) in a context of moral responsibility. Furthermore, the doctrine governing the categories generally is that they should be ways of construing the whole of reality. Now, on one interpretation of the last category, the dialectical individuals are, in part, not yet aware of themselves — they are merely in process of becoming so. On the other interpretation, their knowledge is as yet incomplete and parts of the world are not merely independent in the sense of being logically required for any possible world but also independent of them in the sense of being unknown.

Prospectively, of course, we can regard this situation as being overcome. Either they can develop or their knowledge can expand. In either case, possible objects of knowledge can be converted into actual objects of knowledge.

Actual objects of knowledge are, in an important way, a-temporal and this may help to unwind the difficulty. To know something is to rescue it from the flux of time and, as an object of knowledge, it moves from its immediate place in a temporal scheme to a different status. The facts about ancient Rome which happen to be known by contemporary historians are now freed from time. We have access to them whenever we wish. They are imperfect and incomplete and we cannot move "in the mind" through the world of ancient Rome. But suppose that they were complete and that we knew everything. Complete knowledge, by definition, is surely identical with the thing known except for the fact which makes it knowledge and not the thing — namely that the activity which constituted it is now gone. We can thus imagine ourselves as able to move about in such a world but not able to change it, just as one may live in the world of a novel while absorbed in it, or be "carried away" by a piece of music.

Now if we have shown successfully that thought and reality do not diverge, it is possible to imagine that all that there is to know about the world might become part of the knowledge of a set of dialectical individuals. Such a knowledge would not include the future if by that is meant the domain still open to free activity. For by definition there is nothing to be known about that.

In that case, the past of the world would be detemporalized and the sense of pastness profoundly changed. A detemporalized segment of the world exists as much now as ever for it exists either at all times or at no time. Thus we could, if we wished, regard such a world as immanent in the world which now exists.

We can, as well, imagine further conditions for it. For, though it will be true that there has to be a community of individuals, it will also have to be true that the members of that community form a very closely integrated unity. If they are to have all knowledge between them and yet have it undistorted they will have to share a common perspective. If each distorts knowledge from his own vantage point, the collective distortion will be considerable and that will vitiate the principle. For some things then will not be genuine objects of knowledge. What they know they will have to share. Collectively, too, they will be responsible for the future course of the universe. For all its activity will have become conscious — and perfectly rational. Their responsibility will be conditioned only by the fact that no one is responsible for the logical structure of reality. Thus, though the required notions of contrast will remain, the collective responsibility will be absolute. In that state of affairs, however, having all knowledge they will have to be perfectly rational and so (if the argument holds) perfectly moral. If that state is not merely latent — a possibility envisageable by the logic

238

of the categories — the result will not be far from McTaggart's collection of loving spirits.[1]

But the necessity only guarantees, alas, that there is a perspective from which it is both possible and necessary to view the world in this way. It does not guarantee that it will actually figure in the experience of any of us. Nor, despite the fact that the example about human persons was intended to show that the category of dialectical individuality was a possible way of viewing them, does it follow that any of us is a member of that ultimate collection.

Underpinning this view of the world is still the freedom which I called pure activity. And what it will produce, therefore, no one knows for sure. Certainty does not seem to extend beyond the logic of the categories which tell us, really, what possibilities are latent in it.

The history of any particular entity poses, in any case, the explanatory problem which I suggested. The categories tell us what riches or poverty are available by way of ways of conceiving such an entity, and that the world must contain entities which are *capable* of being viewed that way. How they come to be and develop consistently with being capable of bearing those rational structures is another question. It might turn out that there is a strong tendency for the particular entities in the world to develop so as to actualize in the experience of individuals the community of moral spirits which this category suggests. It does not seem that there could be the guarantee for which McTaggart hoped. But that calls for another investigation.

However much we may find our curiosity titillated or our skepticism aroused, these considerations seem to drive us beyond what we can really expect from a system of categories.

We can, indeed, call the concept of such a community of moral spirits The Absolute.[2] But the last category is only dialectical individuality — a way of looking at the world which provides us with interesting perspectives, invites further enquiry and, in itself, turns us back on the system of categories.

[1] See "The Further Determination of the Absolute," *Philosophical Studies* (London: Edward Arnold, 1935), and the closing sections of *The Nature of Existence* (Cambridge: Cambridge University Press, 1927). We may be skeptical about this but it is, I think, the noblest conception in the history of thought. That is not a reason for thinking that it is not true. Its investigation in detail belongs to another book but it is significant that it is suggested by the logical structure we find here.

[2] More will be said about this in the last chapter. It may be useful, though, to bear in mind a distinction. In one sense the absolute is simply whatever it is that is not relative to anything else. In that sense, the logical structure itself *is* "the absolute". But there is another and deeper sense in which The Absolute is whatever it is that simply *is* in itself, does not require anything outside itself for its intelligibility and, therefore, undergoes no change. If anything meets the conditions for being The Absolute in this sense, it can only be because the development of a universe involves and requires a transformation of time itself. That requires further investigation which cannot be part of *this* book.

Though we cannot tell from these considerations whether there is or ever will be an Absolute, the notion does provide a limit which has to be envisaged if the scheme is correct.

The last category does, evidently, entail the truth of some kind of idealism and it even rules out some specialized forms of that doctrine. Yet it still leaves much unanswered. What remains in this book is to review the structure, explore the possibilities for error, and assess, somewhat further, the prospects for interpretation and development.

Chapter 7

Concluding remarks

I

The argument has come to its conclusion. What remains is merely to focus one's doubts — to see what hard questions seem to demand immediate answers.

The issue which looms up at once is this: The system, essentially, consists of nine categories. Surrounding them are rules for moving in thought from one part of the system to another, for constructing the logical apparatus appropriate to the domains over which the categories preside, and for construing the system itself. But, essentially, the system is a unity and its development is continuous. Why, then, should there be nine categories, rather than any other finite number or, alternatively, either an infinite number or none?

The suggestion in other words is that, since none of the categories is self-sustaining, is it not likely the number selected for presentation is arbitrary? Furthermore, if the system is really continuous, ought we not to find that there are indefinitely many categories?

These issues will have to be unpacked one by one. In the process, we may hope to become a little clearer about the status and nature of the categories as such.

II

To begin with, each category is a way of focussing the totality of the universe of discourse and of things. The first category exhibits the most general feature which must link everything: pure being. The second belongs to the same level of abstractness or generality but exploits just what the first category excludes: disjunction. Everything that there is must have something in common but everything that there is must be different from everything else as well. They are united in their reference to what "is" and differentiated by their references to the polar properties implied by such references. Thus they generate not merely an account of the most distant level of abstraction but also they suggest — as all concepts must — what they exclude. In this case it is the notion of determinateness, the specific combination of identity and difference which makes identification possible.

The conceptual structure suggests that there is a series of levels of density of reference and that all references involve some special combination of reference to a system in which the intended subject matter is located, and also a set of referential objects which give body to that system. At the polar extreme on which pure being and pure disjunction function, the specific referent is lost in the generality of the system and it breaks down just because it is a perfect blank. At the polar extreme of dialectical individuality we find the referent in and by itself but it throws us back on the earlier levels of abstraction because we must provide a system within which it can be rendered intelligible. Without such a structure, pure individuality and pure activity (the final specific exclusion references) are simply empty.

The point, then, is that each category represents one of these levels of reference density — a specific compromise between the demands of system and the demands of individuality. None of them is intelligible by itself since they all take their meanings from references to each other. Meaning lies in the system considered as a whole. Every attempt to freeze discourse to one level results in destructive conceptual tension — the demand for some concept essential for meaningfulness and its denial on the ground that it does not belong to that level.

Thus the system is not continuous in the sense that a mathematically dense set of points is continuous. There is not one category to be found between any two others. The system is continuous in the sense that the categories are unintelligible if separated and they lead necessarily and naturally to each other.

There is thus no reason to think that there should be an infinity of categories. Furthermore, we started with a concept which had a particular structure. What it needed to make good its deficiencies on its own level was determined by that structure and the nature of the next level was inferred by a process which was intelligible even if not foolproof. So the number of categories is not arbitrary, though it is, of course, arguable.

There will be just as many categories as are necessary to provide intelligibility. Given, of course, that the intertwining of thought and experience is complex — that they are not, indeed, as I have argued, separable — the ability of the scheme to provide for the experiences which we actually have will also appear as a consideration in determining the range of categories. If, that is, experience is to be construed as the reflection of the dialectical individual in the world, its actual content will reflect the need for categories in the same way that the pattern of inferences from pure being onwards does. But the two demands should not conflict and there is nothing in this consideration, again, which would make it reasonable to believe that the number of categories is indefinite.

242

This does, however, suggest another kind of consideration. I have argued throughout that the delineation of the scheme of categories is, in part, a creative activity. It does not follow, automatically, by a series of mechanical devices from the original principles. Is it not the case, then, that this creative activity can be undertaken in a number of different ways and that we might well have an indefinite array of categories? It surely does follow that we might construct any number of apparent categories. But it does not follow that they will all meet the requisite tests. For they must produce an intelligible unity, they must lead to a last category which meets the special requirements of the logical structure[1] as a whole, and they must produce accounts of intelligible domains and lead successfully to and from the adjoining categories. And, if the argument in the first chapter is sound, it must turn out that, in the end, we cannot produce two systems which meet all the tests.

It does not follow from that, of course, that the system *I* have constructed will meet all the tests or that I have given an adequate account of all of them. In an enterprise of the scope which this one must have, mistakes are surely more likely than not. But the point is that there is no reason to think that they cannot be found and that the deficiencies of attempts such as this one cannot be made good.

It is, of course, true that, by concentrating our thought on the system as a unified totality, we can de-emphasize the significance of the categories. We can see it, that is, in terms of the tensions which hold the system in place. The demands of unity and generality at one pole and those of specificity and individuality at the other constitute a structure within which the categories necessarily appear as provisional. But provisional structures are necessary and some particular set of them is required to make the scheme intelligible.

Again, we can look at the system from the perspective of the last category. We could say that the world, after all, *is*, if the argument is correct, a set of dialectical individuals. The other categories simply represent ways in which dialectical individuals can construe themselves or be construed. Each provides a partial, incomplete, and defective vision.

---

[1] The argument here, of course, is that the last category is dialectical individuality. Perhaps it is worth noticing that even if I have not specified the last category completely we can infer that *any* last category will have to have a crucial feature in common with the last category I have specified: The last category must mark out whatever it is which is individuated within the framework of the other categories. It will, therefore, have to pivot on a concept which points to something whose determinate features are specified within the other categories.

Equally, however, each has an objective status in its own right. If they, in the end, are only comprehensible by reference to the last category, the last category, equally, is only comprehensible by reference to them. And much can be said about the world without reference to dialectical individuals at all. For we can make indefinitely many provisional arrangements of a logical kind for dealing with discourse within each of the categories. Indeed, most of our discourse is of this kind. If we fail to understand this, we simply emphasize part of a dialectical relationship at the expense of the rest.

v

Perhaps this should be elaborated. Throughout the system there is, of course, an alternating emphasis on unity and plurality. Categories emphasizing unity and categories emphasizing plurality are to be found on each level. Pure being and pure disjunction mark out, after all, unity and plurality as such. Determinate being and systematic unity carry through the distinction just as clearly. Pure process is a unity, determinate process a plurality — though the interpenetration of concepts as the whole unity of the system grows closer is clearly evident by that stage. Ideal universality, again, is dominated by the notion of a unified system while objective universality focusses a plurality. Dialectical individuality, finally, exhibits a last balance of the two — though one intelligible only through the earlier categories. This alternation, of course, stems from nothing more mysterious than the fact that the fundamental division of each level is in terms of systems and their components — a division which derives from the logical situation which makes it possible for there to be levels at all.

Thus any attempt to exploit any of the categories to the exclusion of the others necessarily ends in nonsense.

VI

The special position of the last category derives just from the fact that the *primary* reality must be a set of dialectical individuals. There are other things, too, as the long discussions about "reality" and "existence" suggested. But all of them must be seen as components of or projections of dialectical individuals if our thought about them is pushed to its logical limits. That does not deny them their own status and it does not deny that dialectical individuals are only intelligible through the structure of all the categories. It merely asserts what one expects — that there is a certain primacy to the perspective provided by the last category.

It is in this sense that the argument suggests that idealism, after all, is true. This does not mean in the ordinary way that "There are no material objects" or that the world is, in a simple-minded way, "one great mind."

244

What it does mean is that material objects, for instance, are features or phases of dialectical individuals and that thought and reason run throughout the real.

Equally, however, the primary real is a rational system within which dialectical individuals have their place and within which whatever can be coherently thought in the domains referred to by all the categories has its place. For the dialectical individuals are not separable from the system.

Thus there is a chance that, in the end, we can experience the world as McTaggart's collection of loving spirits. For only this would finally end the tensions between the unity of the world as a dialectical system and its plurality as a set of dialectical individuals intelligible through, and only through, the whole set of categories. But that result is not guaranteed by this investigation. For the tensions and the freedom they provide are equally part of the situation. As McTaggart thought, we are entitled to live in hope.

Index

TITLES

The first reference generally includes bibliographical information. Titles cited are those of the English translations but references include those made to the original works.